LIKE CORDS AROUND MY HEART

Buell Cobb

A SACRED HARP MEMOIR

DENVER, COLORADO

Like Cords Around My Heart:
A Sacred Harp Memoir
All Rights Reserved.
Copyright © 2014 Buell Cobb
v4.0

Cover design by Bren Riddle

Outskirts Press, Inc.
http://www.outskirtspress.com

ISBN: 978-1-4787-0462-1

Outskirts Press and the "OP" logo are trademarks belonging to Outskirts Press, Inc.

PRINTED IN THE UNITED STATES OF AMERICA

Yet when I see that we must part,
You draw like cords around my heart.

— PARTING HAND, page 62
The Sacred Harp

Contents

Introduction..i

    Terms of Use: For the Reader Who May Not Know
    Sacred Harp vi

    And Essay Answers to a Couple of
    Naturally Occurring Questions xii

1   To Start With 1

2   Granny Cobb – and the First Inklings 4

3   A Sustained Bolt of Lightning: the Sacred Harp Recordings .. 19

4   The Ring of Repugnance 25

5   Transitions..29

6   Taking Sacred Harp on Stage..44

7   Miss Ruth 65

8   Dewey Williams...105

9   Roy Avery 123

10   Lawrence and Lula Underwood 138

11   Japheth Jackson and Family..142

12   Buford McGraw 157

13   In Search of the Lost Tribe of Sacred Harp...........................163

14   George M., Remembering and Remembered........................179

15   Ed Thomas and Willie Mae..195

16 Aunt Jewel 201
17 Lonnie Rogers 211
18 An Endearing Prickliness..227
19 Stories from the Civil War...239
20 Cullman and the Courthouse Singings.........................243
21 Amanda 272
22 Singing Days at Antioch..300
23 Tat Bailey..306
24 '. . . and All and Everything . . .'.................................324
25 The Auburn Quartet.. 361

Acknowledgments... 371
Endnotes 377
Index of Names...385

Introduction

As a writing man, or secretary, I have always felt charged with the safekeeping of all unexpected items of worldly or unworldly enchantment, as though I might be held personally responsible if even a small one were to be lost.

— E.B. White
"The Ring of Time"

"It is to me curiously unsatisfying," the letter said, "that one comes away from this fine work without knowing more about who the Sacred Harp singers are."

The writer was a gentleman from Maryland I had met at a singing in northeast Alabama in the summer of 1991. He had bought a copy of my 1978 book, *The Sacred Harp: A Tradition and Its Music*[1] (from this point on, just "my book"), and then had ordered another for a choir director he wanted to introduce to the tradition. He liked the book in general, he had made clear in phone conversations and follow-up letters, but he had found something lacking in it and now wanted to register the point.

"More and fuller biographical sketches" would have been helpful.

And this among other questions: "Are singers usually farmers, lawyers, or cooks?"

Well, all of that and more, I could have answered. My push-back in a letter of response, though, was a bit feeble. I mentioned the portraiture, including occupation, of a few representative figures: "Hugh McGraw as factory manager, Ruth Denson Edwards as a former teacher, Joe S. James as lawyer, E.J. King and family as cotton planters, etc." But I knew he was right, and said so.

In trying to tell the story of a tradition, I had failed to particularize the people, the individuals who carried this tradition on and were themselves carried along by it. Where, I could join my critic friend in asking, were the narratives about individual characters? Where, the dozens of sketches I had framed in my mind over many gatherings over many years?

"Overall, I can't regret having written the book when I did," I replied, "and yet when I look back at it now, I also can't help thinking how much better it might have been if I could have brought to it then what I now am and what I now know. . . . I sometimes toy with the idea of rewriting, or writing anew – so much has changed since the book was first published. . . . In any case, your commentary has given me a focus should I decide to do so."

The seasons passed. But the burden of that correspondence stayed with me and rankled. A life work not yet completed. The unwritten pages called out to me, and called me to account. Though I had shared tales and impressions in conversations with singing friends through the years, the stories of any number of Sacred Harp figures I had closely observed, talked with, sung with, stood at the tables and sipped lemonade with, remained disembodied. The music and the tradition of Sacred Harp had changed my life for sure, but the individuals I had come to know through it had enriched that life beyond the telling.

Something else had been missing in my book – by design, in this case: my own Sacred Harp story. But telling the stories of these memorable characters inevitably meant sharing my own, and setting up the points of intersection between our lives, our communings.

It first became clear that I must undertake the writing of this book when I was asked by John del Re and Kelly Macklin to serve as honorary chair for the 2007 annual June singing in Virginia's northern Shenandoah valley. Traditionally it had been incumbent upon the honoree to "make a few remarks." "A few?" I remember asking John as the date approached. If I knew it was challenging for me on that occasion even to scratch the surface of a near lifetime of Sacred Harp experiences – and felt a little sting of frustration from that – I came to see in the weeks following the event that such a thing was possible only by writing it all out, and that doing so was probably the only way I could find peace from the narratives, restive, unquiet, crammed back into the corners of my brain. (An analogy that should be familiar to Sacred Harp folk came also to mind. Unable to shake a melody running maddeningly through their heads, singers find that the best remedy is to lead the song at the very next opportunity, to "sing it out.")

But how exactly was I to do that? Well, first a few words about memory. It is, surely we come to know, a slippery provider. On some things, I look back to a fairly secure set of images. I have revisited many choice happenings so frequently as to have long ago locked them in. So what I remember well I have reconstructed, sometimes word by word. On other experiences, the loss is now all but complete. On others still, what I have thought I remembered – before a check of the facts – turns out to be off just a bit.

I have, in truth, found my memory mechanism not always as responsive about the verifiable facts of a scene as about its overall color, a distinctively melodied string of words that emerged from it, the poignancy of certain moments or some irresistible twist of humor – even a few throw-away lines I had scooped up at the time and then hoarded for years. My narrative bent is just inclined that way.

For many of the scenes I would have lost entirely or would have been able to remember only sketchily, a fortunate thing had happened. Over a period of years, long before I thought seriously about this book, I contributed to two Sacred Harp newsletters, the National and the Chicago, describing particular singing sessions or sharing details or impressions about notable Sacred Harp figures just passed from our midst. Along the same lines, in the 1990s and early 2000s I contributed a few lengthy posts to an online discussion group created by fellow singer Keith Willard. I sometimes printed out these posts as they appeared, before that discussion train vanished in the ether. That material, along with copies of letters I had written, provided – when I came to the project – a trove of detail, footprints still clearly visible on a path I, in many cases, could otherwise but vaguely recall. With light editing, these reproduced notes, I hope, bring an immediacy to scenes now otherwise faded from view.

A few words about my writing process here: and in trying to describe it, I will lean on a fanciful metaphor left over from my childhood. When I was a boy, the hours of summertime boredom wore on me. (At that stage, I found my brothers – three, six and ten years younger – generally unhelpful playmates.) To contend with the sun's slow-clicking clock, to bridge the interminable time till supper, I plied a desperately motivated and far-ranging imagination. One day, poking around in a rambling field at the edge of our neighborhood, I unearthed a rough but beautifully speckled rock, shaped and sized like a large potato or pine cone. Fool's gold it may have been; it did at least have bits of glittery gold and lustrous pink mixed in with its overall sandy color. I had never seen its like. It took my fancy, and I readily imagined it as magical.

Letting my mind play, I tied a long cord about the rock tightly and, out in open ground, twirling it round and round above my head, would release it extravagantly, with cord billowing behind, to see where it would land and what it would lead me to. Some nifty prize, surely.

And in fact, each time as I investigated the area where the rock had fallen, I found, among the grass blades or partially covered in dirt, a marble, a nickel, a beaten-down penny, a tiny plastic soldier or some other thing of interest or use. Sometimes the search had to be extended beyond the small circle I would first assign it. But that only stretched the truth; it didn't overturn it.

From the start, as I guess children typically do, I approached this exercise on two tracks simultaneously: the fantasy I was playing with and the less exciting reality underlying it. Early on, though, I recognized that it was the search itself that produced and not the special powers of my rock. (Fool's gold indeed.) If I had to sweep wider and wider, something of use or value would always at some point turn up. I didn't, in fact, need the rock or the spin-toss at all. It was the search itself that brought me to the prize.

In little time, I lost or laid aside the rock (I wish I had it still!), but the application of that exercise stayed with me – and reemerges now as symbol for a method that has characterized my writing for this book (and may characterize something essential about me, a prospect I haven't yet plumbed): looking, searching intently for the right thing, the apt word, the better sound.

In taking on my project – so much wide-open ground for trying to create an authentic, telling portrait of Miss Ruth, Ed Thomas, Japheth and Pauline and Ruth Jackson – I have thrown my rock and waited for revelation; peeled back the layers of green blade, finding at last the remembered anecdote, the necessary detail, the hidden coin, the faded remnant of valiant soldier.

So, from memory and from notes or letters written immediately after certain events – and with a halting, hoping, search-and-wait writing method – I have reconstructed many of the high points along my Sacred Harp journey, portraits of people or descriptions of episodes I hope may speak to an audience who never knew or experienced them. If I have met my challenge even halfway, no reader should at last be wondering, "Who are these people, the Sacred Harp singers you're writing about?"

I have said from time to time that there are many thousands of people who love Sacred Harp but who just don't know it yet! My hope is that this book will contribute to the expansive goal implicit in that bold claim.

Terms of Use:
For the Reader Who May Not Know Sacred Harp

For a general reader, opening this book might be a little like walking into a Sacred Harp singing for the first time and finding oneself a bit bewildered. A reader unfamiliar with the tradition will here find depictions of unusual practices ritualistically observed and common terms used in unusual ways. Some explanations, then, would be in order. Here's a brief roundup.

Sacred Harp: Unaccompanied community singing in four-part harmony from one of the editions of the shape-note songbook *The Sacred Harp*: a collection of hymns and religious songs and anthems, along with a few moralistic or patriotic tunes, originally compiled by Benjamin Franklin White and Elisha James King (who died shortly after the initial publication) and first published in Hamilton, Ga., in 1844. With deepest roots in early 18th-century rural England, Sacred Harp music and traditions owe much of their form to the singing schools of Colonial America. (Practitioners of the singing school included some of early America's most notable musical names: William Billings, Daniel Read, Justin Morgan – and, in famous parody, Washington Irving's unfortunate Ichabod Crane.)

Manifestations of Sacred Harp vary from small weekly or monthly informal sessions to annual gatherings that draw participants from wide areas, several states and even (by now) several countries. Overall, the tradition comprises free-forming, overlapping circles of singers and singing events once typical only in the Deep South but now increasingly spread across the globe. Word of mouth and interrelationships (aided by a widely distributed or online directory of singings), and not any single authorizing body, create and grow these loosely constituted networks.

A singing: A community singing event, a democratic gathering in which participants have the opportunity not only to join in the singing but to lead one or more songs from the songbook. Sometimes called "a sing." (One term is favored in some areas; the other, elsewhere. Both the plain noun and the verbal have language analogs. On the one hand: a dance, a ride, a swim. On the other: a reading, a meeting, a gathering. To my ears – accustomed to early and countless references to "a gospel singing," "a hymnbook singing," "a Sacred Harp singing" – the one term seems natural; the other, newfangled, a bit prissy. Whatever one calls the event, though, the singing experience is apt to be just as good.)

Convention: Dating from the mid-19th century, this use of the term applies to an annual (usually) multi-day singing event. Though in the early decades the conventions were often large three- or four-day gatherings, almost all are now only two-day events.

Singing "the notes": By earliest tradition, Sacred Harp singers, before singing the words, render a song first by vocalizing designated syllables (by what's known as solfege, solmization, "fasola" or "sol-fa"), according to the shapes the notes are printed in: *Fa* (triangle), *Sol* (circle), *La* (rectangle) and *Mi* (diamond shape). A practice that began as an instructional or self-instructional method for sight singing – by associating pitch with shape and syllable – this singing of "the notes" became a ritualized part of the singing experience, leading to the moniker *fasola singing*. All eight notes of the octave are represented, by a repetition of the first three shapes and syllables in this way (in a syllable system devised a couple of hundred years before the now more commonly known *Do-Re-Mi* system): *Fa-Sol-La-Fa-Sol-La-Mi-Fa* (for the major scale). All eight notes, then, but in only four shapes and syllables. More on this in the narrative.

Leading: The opportunity generally given each willing participant to conduct the singing of the song(s) he or she chooses. The practice varies from what will appear as authoritative and demonstrative directing to merely calling out a selected song number and then standing more passively in the center of the group, maybe beating time all the while, and letting the singers do their thing.

Beating time: The leader marking the beats of the music (in, for example, 4/4, 3/4, 6/8 time) with up and down, and sometimes sideways, hand movements – to keep the group singing together. The down- and up-beating of hands almost in unison across the group of singers – diverting or mesmerizing as it may be to a first-time observer – is a means of keeping the individual singer in sync with the leader and the others, and is a traditional manifestation. (Foot-patting slips in there, too.)

Keying or pitching: The process by which an experienced volunteer, or occasionally the song leader, sets the pitches for the just-selected song. Eschewing a pitch pipe or other mechanical device, the keyer relies on (one hopes) a highly developed sense of relative pitch, adjusting what might be called for on the songbook's pages to fit with the assembled singers' capabilities (for highest and lowest notes) at that point in the session. One of many impressive skills on display in this open community singing tradition.

"The hollow square," or just "the square": The open space across which the four seated vocal parts face each other, and in which the leader stands. The leader faces the *tenor* or "lead" part (the melody part, sung by both men and women) and any audience gathered to listen. The tenors look across to the *altos*. To the left of the tenor is the *bass*, across the square from the *treble* (in country parlance, "tribble"; also sung by both women and men). Because of the powerful quadraphonics converging there, the space occupied by the leader is acknowledged to be "the best seat in the house."

Class: The overall group of singers, or the singers of one of the four parts. "A great class today." "A strong tenor class." "I'll ask the class to sing this a little slower." Vestigial term from the days of the early American singing schools.

Lesson: The content of the leader's time in the square; the song(s) she or he leads, along with any remarks. "She led a short lesson." "I really enjoyed your lesson." Another carryover from the singing-school era. There's also the precedent, from at least a couple of centuries back, of a musical piece being referred to as a lesson.

Dispersed harmony: The catch-all term for the typical Sacred Harp sound and written composition: open rather than close or condensed harmony, with the chords made by the three upper voices often spread over an octave or more; with chords of fourths and open and parallel fifths; and often with polyphony and crossing of voices (a lower voice part occasionally going above a higher part, for example). The melodically independent nature of each voice part requires a separate staff for each and results in the songbook's distinctive oblong format.

Arranging committee: The person(s) assigned the task of arranging the order of leaders – typically, and as practically as possible, by calling on everyone present who is willing to lead. From a sometimes hastily assembled list, from registration cards filled out at the event, or from a careful and continual scanning of the crowd, the committeeperson calls each leader in turn, usually announcing the next-name-up as well – with an eye to variety by part, gender and home community. Ideally this all happens with as little time wasted as possible, so that, on an ambitious day, as many as 80 to 100 songs can be rendered.

Front bench: The first row of singers on a part, but mainly used to refer to the front row of tenors, who are most responsible for assisting the leader in keeping the group together, keeping up with the directed tempo and so forth.

Fuging (or fuguing) tune or song: The term used to describe the many songs in which the harmonic parts enter separately or successively, appearing almost to chase each other, as in a round. A simplified form of fugue, usually occurring in what would normally be the chorus or refrain, the latter half or two-thirds or so of the song. One of the most distinctive features of Sacred Harp style.

"Class song": A lively song, most often a fuging tune, one that registers on the foot-patting index and that is distinguished from the more staid hymns and anthems. A song, then, more appropriate for use by a singing "class" than for use in a regular church service.

Denson book, Cooper book, White book, Colored Sacred Harp: The informal names for the four editions of the Sacred Harp songbook continuing from the 20th century into the 21st. After the four successive editions of the original B.F. White *Sacred Harp* (1844 to 1870), the singing tradition in the early 20th century splintered, as singers pursued new and rival revisions.

The "James book" of 1911 (for its general editor, Joe S. James) gave way in 1936 to the "Denson book" (primarily the editorial work of brothers Thomas Jackson Denson and Seaborn McDaniel Denson and Tom's son Paine). Through several editions, that book evolved into the current red-backed "1991 edition." From the mid-'30s on, the Denson book has been the predominant songbook – especially in the traditional areas of Georgia, north and central Alabama, southern Tennessee and Mississippi – and is the one I first knew and used (and, unless otherwise noted, the one usually depicted here). The blue-backed "Cooper book" (for its editor, Wilson Marion Cooper), generally reigning over south Alabama, northwest Florida, east Texas and parts of Mississippi and Georgia, dates from 1902. Its latest edition is 2012. The 1911 "J. L. White book," compiled by one of B.F. White's sons, was fairly obliterated over time by the two other revisions. It survives today in small singings in northern Georgia and in occasional use elsewhere. Likewise, *The Colored Sacred Harp* (a slight compilation of 98 new tunes produced by Judge Jackson of Ozark, Ala., in 1934) hardly survives, as the classes that supported it in southeastern Alabama and over the border into Florida are now almost entirely gone.

The songbooks differ in a few major ways. The various editions of the Denson book have more consistently held to the ideal of dispersed harmony characteristic of the body of songs in the B.F. White editions. To varying degrees, the Cooper book and the White book have admitted and retained more songs in "close harmony" and of the "gospel" variety (ANGEL BAND, ROCK OF AGES, SWEET BY AND BY, as examples). The spread of Sacred Harp across the country and beyond near the end of the 20th and the beginning of the 21st centuries has found singing groups more open to use of more than one edition, though rarely a mixing of them in a particular singing event.

Sacred Harp Publishing Company: The non-profit organization that oversees the publication and distribution of the Denson or, currently, the 1991 edition of the songbook and that promotes the spread of Sacred Harp singing and tradition. (The company that produces the Cooper book is the Sacred Harp Book Company.)

Minutes or minute book: The annually published (or listed online) schedule of each year's singing events, along with the recorded minutes from the previous year's singing sessions. A useful handbook for keeping up with Sacred Harp activities.

"Been used": One of the most deflating terms in the lexicon, this is the phrase often sounded out to the leader who, because of late arrival or faulty short-term memory, has just called out the page number of a song already sung. Except in special cases – that of a child, a newcomer or an elderly figure, for instance – the leader should then choose another song. Most singers don't mind joining in on a song they have sung many dozens of times over the years; twice in one day, though – especially considering there are more than 500 songs to choose from – is considered once too many.[2]

And Essay Answers to a Couple of
Naturally Occurring Questions . . .

Not at all. There's no reason to think Sacred Harp events or organizations any different today from what Earl Thurman in 1952 said in summary about the Chattahoochee Musical Convention, the Sacred Harp's oldest institution. Thurman, the organization's longtime secretary, wrote then of the convention's "nonsectarian/non-denominational character." The Chattahoochee had "never concerned itself with dogmas, doctrines, or articles of faith. Participation in its activities is open to all, regardless of church affiliation." And anyway, he had added, "Feelings of prejudice and intolerance melt away under the spiritual warmth of songs like the immortal 'Ballstown.'" [3]

Members of rival singing traditions over much of the past century and a half might have been surprised to hear Sacred Harp adherents described in terms of tolerance or neutrality. The image they conjured might instead have been that of a somewhat stiff-necked people: welcoming, hospitable folk, no doubt, but – where their music was concerned – a people set in their ways, inflexible in their tastes. (Had they not been so, of course, their music would long ago have been mongrelized if not swept away entirely.)

But a tradition of tolerance has indeed held true through the many years and the many chambers of Sacred Harp history. The overall sentiment expressed in boilerplate language from the bylaws of 19th- and early-20th-century conventions still carries over to today: "This convention shall have no partiality for the different opinions which now affect the public nor any sympathy for any of the religious creeds that divide public sentiment."

Sacred Harp grew up in "an age of much singing," to use a phrase from one of the songbook's chief composers, H.S. Reese, at the end of the 19th century. It was also an age, and in a place, in which singing of *sacred* songs was common, and even expected, public practice.

As Sacred Harp communities and overall numbers dwindled almost hopelessly in the mid-20th century, it might not be surprising
that visitors and newcomers would have found a highly accepting attitude on the part of those most eager to preserve and extend their
singing tradition. Today, as the numbers are increasing again, Sacred
Harpers are more than ever a disparate lot, stretching the old boundaries of geography, demography and worldview. That people from
such different ways of life and thinking are able to join in social as
well as chordal harmony stems in large part from the generally nonjudgmental spirit with which all are greeted. So long as people are
civil and non-disruptive, the prevailing attitude has been: "Whoever
or whatever you are, we're glad to see you." There's no card check at
the door, or at the edge of the square: only perhaps a friendly inquiry
about whether you'd like to lead – and, if you're a newcomer, whether
you'd like to try treble or bass, alto or tenor (and if so, you might want
to sit with that part over there. . .).

IS IT A CULT?

Well, no. Or not exactly. . . .

Could typical Sacred Harp behavior *appear* cultish? Yes. If nothing else, there's that perhaps disconcerting sight of most participants
at a typical event waving their hands up and down almost as one. . . .

A couple of years back, a younger-generation member of my family visited a session of Camp Fasola – the summer camp to which
both new and experienced singers come to learn more about the history, discipline and intricacies of Sacred Harp. He enjoyed and was
impressed by the experience, he said, but was left with this lingering
sense: "It was a little like watching a science fiction movie. . . ." I think
I knew instantly what he meant: ordinary-looking people of various
ages and other demographic factors attending classes, having lunch,
going through perfectly ordinary motions – but somehow attuned to,
or led by, a voice the rest of the world didn't, couldn't hear. . . .

Sacred Harp doesn't set out to be a cult. There's no governing body or figurehead for the movement, no authoritarian principal. In basic form, it's self-directing participants acting democratically, coming and going completely independently: singing, traveling to singings, cooking for singings, eating well at singings and so forth.

Mind control? Well, only that participants are typically encouraged to "seek the old paths," to do things as much as possible in the traditional way – not just because following such would honor the tradition itself and those who forged it over the many decades, but because that tradition has bequeathed us such a clean and workable format.

No "brainwashing," then. But undeniably for most singers, there comes, over time, this desire to preserve and grow the singing tradition, these sounds and songs that have wormed their way into our souls. One wants to pass the gift on to as many others as possible. Somehow Sacred Harp tends to draw its adherents in deep – and hold them.

"Uncle Tom" Denson famously stated at the beginning of his early-1900 singing schools, "If some of you don't like this music . . . all I've got to say to you is you'd better get out. If you stay here it's going to get a-hold of you and you *can't* get away." Those words were surely half in jest, more boastfully descriptive than prescriptive. But Uncle Tom's warning still carries resonance into this century.

There's a sense, for those who have sung Sacred Harp for a while, those of us who have been steeped in its words and music, that we are somehow soldiers in a cause. It's not just that, maybe for most singers, singing songs of faith, of the hope of heaven, is itself binding; it's also that an emotional bond with fellow singers and with the particular tradition that brings us together strengthens over time. The songbook's extraordinarily high number of parting or farewell songs (and similarly themed texts included in as many other songs) is testament to these sentiments.

Here on the subject in the 1930s was Sacred Harp biographer George Pullen Jackson, who more than anyone else in his era drew the attention of the academic world to the already antique singing tradition: "When one singer calls another 'brother' or 'sister' and the older ones 'uncle' or 'aunt' it has a real and deep significance. It means that Sacred Harp singers feel themselves as belonging to one great family or clan. This feeling is without doubt deepened by the consciousness that they stand alone in their undertaking – keeping the old songs resounding in a world which has either gone over to lighter, more 'entertaining' and frivolous types of song or has given up *all* community singing."[4]

Nothing brings this feeling more to the fore than the traditional Memorial Lesson, that special time during many singings in which deceased singers from the past year are memorialized in song. Heart-tugs are felt for those we have sung and communed with, comrades with us in something that often seems to tower against the ordinary elements of life.

I remember, though, this cautionary word from an elderly Charles Kitchens, scion of one of the old singing families and himself an active singer: "You can make an idol out of anything – even Sacred Harp singing." Perspective, as always, must govern.

"The Sacred Harp *may* persist another century," Jackson observed on the 100th anniversary of the Sacred Harp in 1944. "But it will be a wonder if it does."[5] We're now well past the mid-point of that interval, and I don't believe an imminent demise for the movement is projected any longer – though in spreading abroad, taking itself to new places (musically as well as geographically), Sacred Harp could spiral out of its old moorings. Will it keep its traditional hold, still generate that distinctive emotional bond?

There maybe is the kernel of the issue. In the meantime, caught up somewhat helplessly in a nomadic weekend existence, does anyone seriously desire to be freed of the bondage?

1

To Start With . . .

A couple of decades ago I walked into a music equipment store in a suburb of Birmingham, shook hands with the young manager and handed him a Sacred Harp tape. We had previously talked by phone about his interest in Sacred Harp, and I had brought the recording for him to hear. He popped the cassette, already cued to the song STRATFIELD, into his player and brought the sound up agreeably loud and reverberant throughout the store. The two of us stood there luxuriating in the bright, powerful a cappella music – truly a thing unto itself. Just before the *fa-sol-la's* had given over to the words of the song, the front door opened and a young man walked in, headed back in our general direction and then paused almost mid-step with a quizzical look on his face.

"Is it *people?*" he asked.

The question – hanging naked there, seemingly free of context or opinion – tickled me then and amuses me still today. I of course gave the chap a Yes or affirmative nod, and, apparently satisfied, he went on about his business.

I use that brief exchange as pointer toward a larger question about Sacred Harp, about the source of its unique appeal for me and for so many others. How, against all odds, has this singing tradition, so fragrant of the rural South of the mid-19th century, not only survived but, now well into the 21st, greatly expanded its reach?

Sacred Harp, I could have told the young man, is not only people – and people only. It is today, as it was from the start, *the people singing*.

As much as anything else, that seems to me the essence of its power and charm, its magic, its durability. There's something stirring about the sound, and the idea, of a crowd of people singing. A veritable hillside of voices. Not a congregation shadowing the church organ's preponderances, not the trained choir's thinner, more rarefied sound – but the "bold, lusty" sound of strong, unaccompanied community singing. And at its height, in fact, people looking and sounding as if they were singing for their lives (which, in a way of course, they are).

Writers, observers practically fall over themselves attempting to describe the splendors, the rawness, the peculiar, transcendent sonic power of Sacred Harp. *The New York Times*: "unique sound, dense and almost eerily spiritual . . . Gregorian chant meets bluegrass." *Rolling Stone*: "the soaring magnificence of Southern sacred-harp choirs, a robust, harmonically intricate blend of country joy and unearthly drone." A Minneapolis periodical, *The Old Times*: "a ferocious full-volume nasal snarl with something of New England about it, and something of the South. Vowels narrow and intense, every consonant hammered home, it was the noise of a whole people busy being born." And then there's the line, attributed to both H.L. Mencken and folklorist Alan Lomax, about the singing sounding "like a cross between a steam calliope and a Ukrainian peasant chorus" (or "choir" or "melody"; I haven't been able to confirm it yet from either source, but somebody certainly said it!)

Newsweek, in a two-page spread in 1978, found that "The volume is turned all the way up, as if God might be a little hard of hearing; the pace of the majestic hymn is breakneck, as if God's patience were exhaustible." "The closest thing to a harmonic train wreck that I have ever heard," one blogger called it. Another writer: "Sacred Harp moves a room the way tectonic plates can move a city. . . . Nothing in music is heavier or more exhilarating, not Zeppelin or the Who, neither Wagner in his frenzies nor Beethoven in his throes."[6]

It's been referred to as "a human pipe organ," "a musical tsunami," and, maybe first by Chicago singer Ted Johnson back in the 1980s, "the old growth forest of American music." Another phrase, by Chicago singer Judy Hauff in the early '90s, made an immediate claim for most unforgettable tag: "the heavy metal music of the 19th century."

Mentioning that the notation "looks like unevolved hieroglyphics," a U.K. journalist opined: "The sound is like nothing I have ever heard before – and I grew up in a Welsh chapel. It's as deep as funeral music, but feels like a resurrection. When Michael [Walker] invites newcomers into the hollow square to get the full surround-sound experience, my insides crack like a flagstone."[7]

Closer to home, any number of first-timers have shared with me the reaction that "this doesn't sound like anything I've ever heard!" (That line, usually uttered with admiration or awe, is quickly distinguishable from another common reaction: "Well, that was really *interesting!*" – the politest version of "This just really isn't my thing. . . .")

Though we may find it reminiscent of Gregorian chant or bagpipes or gospel singing (without accompaniment) or the stadium singing of European football clubs (but with harmony), Sacred Harp has, finally – for observers across the spectrum – a sound like . . . well, like no other.

Years ago I asked one of my sons to sit for a moment and listen to a recording of a Sacred Harp song he had once singled out for a compliment. "Sound familiar?" I asked. "Dad," he replied, "they *all* sound familiar." I knew, of course, what he meant, pejorative or not – and knew that, in the way he put it, he had the target plainly in view.

I think, too, of a story a woman once told me about a child in her family who had found himself beyond weary with the *fa-sol-la* chords swelling all around them in a little country church that day: "They've been singing the same song all morning!" he protested.

The distinctive sound of Sacred Harp, this sound of *the people* singing: That sound, when I was about 20, called me out of my ordinary life and pointed me down a path of rich associations I could hardly have imagined. This book is a re-exploration of that path.

2

Granny Cobb – and the First Inklings

Sacred Harp slipped into my consciousness in childhood or early teen-age years through a few references to "fasola singing" or "old Harp" or "old-book singing," mainly by my paternal grandmother. She was born Amanda Bell Brown in 1895. She preferred Belle – and gritted her teeth when old childhood friends saluted her as Mandy. To our family, she was always just Granny Cobb.

Because I think she was the first person ever to mention Sacred Harp to me, she belongs as a beginning part of my story. But because she was such a character to all who knew her – rivaling any I was to meet later on the Sacred Harp trail – she deserves more than just a mention. In fairness to her great spirit, I feel bound to try to capture and share what Granny Cobb was like.

She had come up the hard way, on a farm in western Cullman County, Ala., the youngest of ten children. Her mother and father were 50 when she was born. (I note that the parents were born the same year *The Sacred Harp* was birthed, and I, a century later). She lost her father when she was just 14 and her mother when she was 17. When just a girl, she learned to take her father's place in the field, plowing with the mule or an ox. She also learned early on not to be intimidated, by others or by life in general. I don't know when she met her husband-to-be, a young dandy, already a noted gospel singer and singing-school teacher, but she married Joseph Franklin "Joe" Cobb when she was 19 and he was 24. After a few years they moved to the small city of Cullman. In time she gave birth to four children, two of whom lived to adulthood: Buell, my father, and Lillian – two bright, personable, worthy members of their community.

Granny was a person of marked contrasts. As mother and grand-mother, she was the she-bear, at once the fiercest to outside threats and the tenderest to her children and grandchildren.

Dignity was not the virtue Granny Cobb held highest in aspiration. True, she could grab some and throw it about her when pressed, when the situation required – she was an inveterate faker – but it was usually a last-minute or half-hearted acquisition and easily dispensed with (when the review board, the minister, the distinguished guest or host or whoever or whatever had passed). No, she much preferred free-and-easy fun, good gossip and spirited shenanigans.

She was a notorious mimic – what in those days was called "a monkey." And in that mimicry she played the broadest exaggerations. At the window, she would observe the comings and goings of others by the highway near her house. The details of this scrutiny fed an on-going monologue. "Who's that coming down there? . . ." she would mutter. "Oh, that's old so-and-so. . . . I wonder where he thinks he's going! Look at how he's walking! . . ." (followed by a high-stepping, low-shuffling or bow-legged imitation).

Later in his life my grandfather owned a neighborhood grocery, where I worked from childhood on through high school, and on oc-casion – especially when he had to be away – Granny Cobb joined me there. These appearances put customer service in jeopardy. Granny seemed to make little connection between customer happiness and the livelihood she and her husband depended on. She took these occasions as opportunities for the two of us to have fun. In my younger years, I more than once stood behind the check-out counter with her and watched a customer look up from rummaging in her purse to catch Granny in a momentary readjustment of her face from the comic contortion she had just put up for my benefit. Yes, when they weren't looking – but when she knew I was – she often made faces at her customers. That the business endured was a testament to my grandfather's pluck, stick-to-it-ive-ness and universally revered geniality.

Granny was incorrigible, always preferring the naughty to the straitlaced. She was pleased, for example, to pass on a mongrel mix of the gospel song LOOKING FOR A CITY and the *do-re-mi* syllables she and her childhood mates used to add in: "L-o-o-o-k-ing for a city," she would sing, "la-la-*tee-tee*, la-la-*tee-tee*."

The house at 1002 Interbitzen was virtually on the street, separated from it by only a narrow margin of ground that she filled with flowering plants. There, working in the beds, she would catch a car slowly driving by with its occupants staring back – and mutter to them a schoolyard taunt: "Y'got your eyes full, now open your mouth. . . ."

Once in elementary school when I had some assigned fund-raising project for class or band, Granny offered to walk to town with me to try to shake some contributions loose from a few of the local businesses. As I look back on it now: if Granny hadn't the sharpest sense of the business needs of Cobb's Grocery, it would have been a push to expect her to see things from the point of view of the store management we visited. Of what was generally an unsuccessful run, I remember only one little exchange from the haggling she attempted that day. Through a pained but smiling expression, the woman behind the service desk in this instance had just whined, "You know, you can't squeeze blood out of a turnip. . . ." Granny's response was swift: "No, but you can stomp the hell out of the greens!" I don't know that she stomped out of the store with me, but Granny left little doubt about how irksome she found the proprietor's convenient little piety.

She was a spitfire, always up for a good argument and, as loosely as she played with facts, frequently finding herself in one. There was a particular point in some of these little kitchen or dining-room disagreements (of no real matter) that I found fascinating. Granny was not much on logic to start with, and when the logic or the facts of her argument failed – her opponent thereby gaining the strategic advantage – she would quickly abandon her position and reply, to the other person's latest salvo, "Well, that's what I *say!*" This move, equivalent to snatching a club out of the opponent's hand and conking her over the head with it, would stun or at least confound the opposition. There was the briefest moment, you could tell, in which the other person tried to scramble back over the last few steps of the exchange to discover the point at which she had become confused, when the argument had fishtailed on her. The integrity of her own position was rarely that important to Granny anyway – she was just drawn to the scent of battle – and this tactic allowed her to gain at least a stalemate out of what otherwise would have been certain defeat. She could then quickly transition, breezing right on to another topic.

More fun, though, were the mock arguments that the Cobb grandparents conducted for the benefit of my brothers or cousins or me when, as youngsters, we spent the night at their house. Some remark or joking insult would start the two of them off on a series of outrageous threats of abuse to be foisted on the other: "I'll throw you so far out of this house you won't come down for a week!" "Oh, I'll knock a knot on your head so big you can't walk through that doorway!" and so forth. Pappa Cobb would laugh uproariously, the biggest of stage laughs, at Granny's latest, most extravagant claim and then try to top it with one of his own. We loved all this grandstanding – as much as we did the pan-fried chicken and biscuits and gravy, the pies and yellow-cake-with-chocolate-icing that Granny cooked up for us (amid a general dusting of flour over all the kitchen appliances).

Granny was not much of a housekeeper. Flowers were her passion. She could put a stick in the ground, it seemed, and it would green up and bloom. Outside she reigned over groupings of dahlias, cockscomb, salvia, roses. Inside the house she hovered over dozens of African violets, which she had crowded in rows on cookie or cracker racks discarded from the grocery store and now fixed against the window sills. When she was not watering these plants or pinching off faded blossoms or stirring the ingredients on the stove pan, she wielded a fly swatter in efforts to find and then finish off the latest member of a vast tribe of "dasted flies" that, gaining entrance by the loose-flapping screen door just off her kitchen, were the bane of her daytime existence.

She could brandish a pistol, too, when from time to time late at night, as our grandfather slept or was away, some drunk wandered up too close or too loud by their porch there on the fringes of town. The grizzled alcoholic next door, a disreputable veteran of the local pool and juke joints, joined her in occasional shouting matches, though overall she seemed to respect him as a fellow free spirit. She made nice with the preacher's wife and other church and community doers of good, but it was with rascally Wallie Weaver, a portly, sharp-tongued matron, that she was most at home. The bond between them had been deepened in 1942 when, as the war cranked up, each sent a son off to Camp Stoneman in California and then beyond. Their husbands were the most mild-mannered of men, but Belle and Wallie made a formidable pair, a front line that surely few assault forces would have had the temerity to test.

Granny never seemed much of a reader. She gave scant notice of the newspaper, which Pappa Cobb digested article by article and line by line each evening, as he listened to baseball games on the radio. Politics – local, national or international (past the war times) – did not engage Granny either. When I once mentioned what was surely news to her, social upheaval in China in the mid-'60s, the beginning spasms of the Cultural Revolution, it didn't take Granny long to sum up the situation. "It's just ignorance," she said. "That's all it is, just ignorance."

For all her naughtiness, her lack of depth in some areas, Belle Cobb was the most loyal, the truest friend; the quickest to feel sympathy for the wounded, the sick or the bereaved; and the most loving of wives, mothers and grandmothers (and of mothers-in-law? Well . . .). When one of my cousins said, "I don't know that anyone in my life will ever love me as much as Granny Cobb did!" the rest of us could know what he meant. She may not have loved more, but her love was *felt* more. It seemed almost a force of nature, a penetrating, elemental love that began in adoration, and in taking nothing for granted, and seemed only to grow stronger as she sensed the various possibilities of loss through the treachery of time. It was not unlike, it seems to me, the kind of intense love a soldier on the battlefield, surrounded by hazards, with life and death in immediate contention there, might feel for loved ones back home. Granny was a person of fun, but it was the fun of a great sentimentalist. No laughter she engaged in was very far away from the tug of her love-born emotions.

Belle Cobb with husband Joe and sons Joseph Doyle (left) and Buell (Sr.), about 1924.

Granny Cobb with Joe, Lillian and Buell (Sr.), about 1942.

Joe and Belle had seen a daughter die in infancy, but the great tragedy of Granny's life was the loss, ten years before I was born, of their eldest child, who, crippled and drawn from the effects of polio for most of his young life, finally succumbed at the age of 17. Joseph Doyle was by all accounts a saintly boy, generous of spirit and, though in pain much of the time, rarely complaining. He had a dog, a spotted mutt of likely bulldog and terrier lineage, devoted to him in the almost supernatural way pets sometimes are with an owner of great physical limitation. When Doyle died, the dog followed the funeral procession to the cemetery plot on a sloping hillside that could be seen from the house on Interbitzen Street. Day after day following that, Granny would look out the back of her house and see, on that near hillside, the dog waiting there by his master's grave. The grief she could never lose gained its sharpest focus through the prism of that dog's deathless devotion.

That was the Granny Cobb I knew and loved, this tall, proud, handsome bundle of contradictions, of town-and-country, sweet-and-sour mix – the one who first spoke to me of "old *fasola* singing." The intonation she gave that phrase bespoke affection for something she knew to be out of fashion. Her father, she said, had been a great bass singer in the old book in their little community of Jones Chapel, a noted incubation area for Sacred Harp. Her sister Martha, I later found out, had been a treble. But her husband, Joe, was on a more progressive train, leading singings in the "new book," the thin little Manila-covered Stamps-Baxter, Vaughan and Convention books that came out once or twice a year. She attended countless of those sessions with him over the years. Sacred Harp had by then become just a set of memories from her youth, another part of that early life now vanished.

Probably more than once, though, she sang for me just the littlest bit of the Sacred Harp standard THE GOLDEN HARP and a strand of THE MORNING TRUMPET: ". . . and shall hear the trumpet sou-ound in that morning." Those soft-voiced fragments remained in my memory, dormant perhaps but intact. They laid a thin, membranous foundation for what was yet to come.

What was to come, in part, was attending my first Sacred Harp singing, when as a teenager I accompanied my grandparents (surely at Granny's request) to a session of the big courthouse singing in Cullman on the second weekend in July and sat with them in the balcony that ringed the large courtroom. And about that event, I remain perplexed: perplexed in that almost nothing about the experience of that day called out to me. I noticed but wasn't drawn in by the ritual of it all – not the antique architecture of the square in the middle of the crowd of seated singers below, not the revolving parade of leaders, each of whom took a place in the center, and finally not by the strength or strangeness of the robust, layered sound that would later speak to me so compellingly. Amazingly to me now, no song reached out and tugged at me – not major or minor tune, not WORLD UNKNOWN or SAINTS BOUND FOR HEAVEN, not RUSSIA or SCHENECTADY. Maybe if they had launched into THE MORNING TRUMPET. . . .

I have, in fact, but one specific memory of the hour or so we stayed there. A young woman of some height – and girth – was leading a song I would later come to know as LAWRENCEBURG. She was relatively light of foot, as was demonstrated during her steering of the class through the song's exuberant chorus. What caught my attention was the repetition of a quirky little piece of choreography I have never seen the likes of from any other person in such a setting. I didn't know the words of the song, wasn't looking on a book, and of course wasn't following the music. I didn't know, in short, that the singers had come to the most playful section of music-writing by Tom Denson or any other Sacred Harp composer. As the singers ran their course through the alternating and repeating duet runs of the chorus – tenor with alto, treble with bass – the young woman performed an audaciously conceived little set piece of foot, arm and body movement.

It would be too cumbersome to lay out the words for a complete description of it – what I could demonstrate in person with but a few quick motions – but it involved her extending her arms like a windmill in opposite directions, then moving them 90°, rocking back on one foot while kicking the other forward in the air, then reversing her foot for the next two beats, then switching her arms back and repeating the set of gestures again, and then again and again.

I couldn't at the time have given a detailed description of what I had seen in that confident young woman's movements, but a few years later I had the good fortune to see that same scene repeated, with the same leader, when I was attending as a singer myself. Knowing the song, I could then enjoy taking in again what had once caught the eye of the mimic in me (one of the things I may have inherited from Granny Cobb). It was not just the leader's one-of-a-kind performance itself that I enjoyed, but the retrieval in full glory of the single specific memory I had of the first Sacred Harp singing I ever attended.

Before I leave the Cobb grandparents and the warm cottage on Interbitzen, I should mention another influence carrying over from my childhood. Pappa Cobb – "Uncle Joe," as he was to a whole community of relatives, acquaintances, customers and vendors – was a great storyteller. He loved a close-up audience, and loved to reminisce. If exchanging groceries for money, or credit, was the business of Cobb's Grocery, telling stories often seemed to be *his* business. Working beside him there for years, I came to pity the deliverymen who, weekly if not daily, had to come and go through the store's portals. Having distributed their wares, they then had to make for the door, empty crates or boxes in hand – and past Uncle Joe, who invariably would snag them with a question or emphatic remark that would lead in turn to a story, which he would bridge into still further yarns. He had mastered the art of transition and used it to full netting effect. Pressed to make their rounds, the vendor reps or deliverymen would try to edge their way to the exit tactfully, always seeming to enjoy the humor or history, but doubtless wishing hard for a customer interruption and a chance to dash to their idling truck or van. I was there as witness and side audience for many hours of this varied storytelling.

From an early age, I had found myself attuned to grown-up conversation – "Big Ears" adult members of the family called me, the first grandchild on either branch of the family tree – drawn always to narrative, to dialogue, to reflection and argument and colorful description: from Pappa Cobb, from my dad, from Aunt Lil – great talkers all – and, from the other side of the family, from Aunt Bonnie, Uncle Cecil and Aunt Fraz. How to account otherwise for my compulsion now to delineate a narrative? How else explain that it is always the spoken voice I hear, and insist on trying to bring through, in my writing? The simplest episode – what just or long ago happened – I find myself spooling out in detail. Family and friends often attempt, restlessly, to jump ahead to the bottom line, the waiting point of the narrative: So what did that mean? So what did you do? I find myself thwarting their efforts. Never mind the *point* – I'm getting to that, I'm getting to that! – I just want to tell the *story*. . . . I'm thus aware of a creeping and resistless horror: I am becoming my grandfather, heavily, heedlessly standing on someone else's sudden urge to get away! This book at least I find the healthiest approach to the problem – in the contract it implicitly represents, whereby the impatient reader can slam the thing shut and have done with it.

On the other side of my family, that of my mother's people, the McDaniels and Clelands, there was certainly plenty of talk – but, sadly, no record of Sacred Harp singers. All the family, though, knew of fasola singing in the Myrtletree community in upper Marshall County, where my McDaniel great-grandparents had lived, just up the road from the Holsombacks, the four spinster sisters – Miss Clara, Miss Alice, Miss Lissie and Miss Sarah – who, in our family lore, regularly swept the dust off the hard-packed ground around their home and pounced on every impertinent blade of grass, leaving only the pampered flower beds to show God's handiwork.

When my McDaniel grandparents moved to Arab ("A-rab") in western Marshall County, they became next-door neighbors of a Mr. and Mrs. Rains, who, family members would later tell me, often sat on their front porch in the evenings singing Sacred Harp tunes. Many years later, I would see their names among the song leaders at the Cullman courthouse conventions of the 1930s.

I used to visit my grandmother McDaniel in the summers as I was growing up, and both Granny Mac and Mrs. Rains were widows by then. I have no real basis for guessing so, but I picture Mrs. Rains as a treble – and not because of her behavior (even if the Star Trek series did nod in that direction with the name of one of its episodes: "The Trouble with Tribbles"). Mrs. Rains was capable of neighborly acts and was, I suppose, harmless in the main. But I knew her chiefly at that time as a sneak and a pilferer. My grandmother rarely locked her house when we walked downtown to shop, and it was not unusual for us to return and discover Mrs. Rains either poking around the back entrance to the kitchen or rummaging around in the basement, where Granny Mac kept rows of canned goods and miscellanea. There was never a confrontation: Before she managed to slip away, we would simply see this white-haired figure hunched over, trying to hide – either in the little hallway behind the kitchen or down in Granny's garden, framed among the corn stalks, the beans and the peas – or we would hear her bumping around in the basement.

Granny Mac, who had raised nine children and who had seen a good bit in her time, was an unflappable type who seemed always to carry in her perspective a little warm spot of amusement about the foibles of others. It wasn't, I think, the Old Testament instruction about leaving something for the gleaners and the widows that informed her default generosity, or lack of pique, in these instances; it was just an example of her live-and-let-live approach to things. And so Mrs. Rains, singer of songs for the righteous, got to indulge her persistent curiosity about the McDaniel household and to pick up, along the way, a few incidentals for her trouble.

Bessie Mae

One other memory from my childhood has a tie-in to Sacred Harp. We had an elementary-school music teacher whose given name was Bessie Mae. A figure of some ridicule among her charges, she had a stocky upper frame and carried on her backside a higher than average rump, which had the effect of tilting her forward slightly as she walked. She held her head high, though, and was forever exhorting us – in music class, now – to exhibit good posture, to walk healthily, swing our arms freely, step up on the balls of our feet, and breathe properly! All of this we as a unit ignored or disdained. Maybe if she had been named Linda or Gloria or Nancy instead of Bessie Mae, if she had not been so dowdy and old-fashioned. . . .

Now belatedly acknowledging respect for much of the overall message she brought, I think back to her introduction to us of a brief strain of music, the significance of which, for me, neither of us could have guessed. Among the themes Miss Bessie Mae explored with us over the course of one year was native folk music. As well as loudly insisting as a group that we get to sing, every time she came before us, the entire BALLAD OF DAVY CROCKETT, the ten-versed theme song from the popular Disney TV series of that time, we made our way through many of America's representative folk melodies – ballads, work songs, spirituals, courting songs and such.

Along the way, we tried out once or twice a simple little folk song that I can still visualize across a two-page spread in the music book:

> There were three crows
> Sat in a tree.
> And they were black
> As crows could be.

There were probably other verses as well, but only this first stanza and its melody stayed with me. Over the rest of my young life, I would occasionally, with no apparent prompting, think of that song and momentarily retrace its notes.

Why? What about it was beckoning? It was the simplest of melodies, a little stair-step exercise of only four tones, its words forming a simple, stark image, no narrative attached. I could have had no explanation at any of the times the song came to me for why it alone of all the new songs we tried out that season would linger with me long after.

When I came at last to Sacred Harp and the song TO DIE NO MORE, I found that little melody virtually intact:

> To die no more,
> to die no more,
> I'm going home
> to die no more.

Had I uncovered a genetic predisposition for pentatonic melodies? Had I come across in that simplest of folk tunes an early place-keeper for Sacred Harp song? I wonder still.

One series of episodes from that time perhaps also had a carryover effect for me. I had always loved music and singing, and it had never occurred to me that I didn't have a passably good voice or couldn't sing. I sang to myself regularly, whistled too, and my own ears heard a generally pleasing sound – not solo quality certainly but agreeable nonetheless, especially when blending with others or singing along with the radio. So when I had the opportunity with other third or fourth graders to join the school chorus, I looked forward to the tryout eagerly. Each of us was called into the room individually by Miss Bessie Mae and asked to sing a few bars of a familiar hymn with basic intervals (HOLY, HOLY, HOLY! comes to mind as a suggested piece) or maybe a bit of a foray into the national anthem. My voice sounded lonely in that setting for sure, a little naked and momentarily awkward, but I was confident in my pitches and, while I didn't think it sounded great, I also didn't think I had missed the mark. When I finished the brief exercise, she thanked me, opened the door, and I left, unselected.

At school assemblies that year and the next, I listened to the chosen chorus with admiration and envy. With very little, I could have sung along with them. When the next year's tryout came up, I presented myself again – to the same procedure and the same result. I can't say otherwise than that it was a hurtful, a most disappointing experience, a bit humiliating, too, walking out of the room and down the hallway, the door closing firmly just behind – and it made me question my own auditory perception. Was I truly this far off the norm, the standard – this much poorer than my fellows? Could I just not tell that my voice had an unpleasing resonance or little resonance at all? And in any case would my inadequacies not have been buffered or hidden by the group sound?

The third year I still had hopes. Maybe my voice had tempered itself or bodied up or something and would now be acceptable for mixing in with the others. But this time when I completed the little assigned vocalization, I stopped the process and – showing fledgling maturity? – asked for feedback. In what way, could she tell me, was I falling short? Oh, not at all, she responded, you've always qualified! Incredibly, this had somehow been an "opt-in" process, and that fact had just never been communicated to me, or I had failed to infer it . . . had failed, I suppose, to say, "O.K., can I join now?" (Since the tryout itself was voluntary, did my presence not indicate my intent?) But, oh well, I now was added to the group and got to stretch my voice along with the others and experience the pleasures of blended singing, as well as better acquire the discipline of sight-reading.

It seems to me now that the denial of the right to sing along with my peers in those formative years may well have strengthened my desire for the thing itself, may well have, in overcompensation, edged up my passion for group singing and for fixing my voice in the midst of a bright sound. And if I have sometimes squirmed when sitting next to someone at a singing whose voice seems incapable of moving up or down beyond a couple of tones, I try to remind myself of the egalitarian beauty of a singing tradition in which there are no tryouts and no one is turned away.

3

A Sustained Bolt of Lightning: the Sacred Harp Recordings

Throughout my high school and early college years, I gave no more than a passing thought to my sketchy sense of Sacred Harp – until maybe the summer before my junior year at Alabama College, now The University of Montevallo, in the small central Alabama town of Montevallo, and then only by what seemed mere coincidence (but now looks more like a stroke of fate?).

Montevallo, as we called it, was a nourishing environment, a small, public liberal arts college with a stately campus and red-brick streets and pathways. It was where I met my future wife and mother of my sons and where I formed many lifelong friendships. Among the good chaps I met there was Mike Hinton, who had transferred in from junior college. He, it turned out, was a grandson of the great Tom Denson, the key figure of Sacred Harp in the 20th century and the composer of that rollicking song LAWRENCEBURG and a number of other shape-note standards. At one point, Mike, after hearing me and some buddies singing a few gospel songs in a dormitory basement, pulled me aside. "I've got something you should hear," he said. Within a day or two, he handed me two record albums recently produced by "the Sacred Harp Publishing Company."

The lending of those albums turned out to be a transformative act. In short order, I turned the record player on, watched the turn-table begin to speed around, the needle arm finding its groove – and stood back, or quickly sat down, transfixed. In whatever ways I can't guess, I was now as primed as I could be for a life-altering sound and the body of music it carried along. Thunderstruck is what I seemed to be. There was nothing about the singing I heard that was less than engaging, and much of it was thrilling. Any imprecision in tonal reach or quality or blend, the twang of voices – anything in fact potentially negative to my ears – was swallowed up in a powerful, heavy-textured music with ancient-sounding harmonies, mesmerizing cadences and a pulsating beat that wouldn't quit (even when I at last, and on occasion after occasion, allowed the record player to stop). There in full and rousing form were THE GOLDEN HARP, THE MORNING TRUMPET . . . and so much more. I had never heard, and certainly never sung, so much minor music . . . the chords based on intervals of the fourth, the open fifth. . . . I was immediately drawn to it all. (I wouldn't, by the way, hold those studio recordings up as the ultimate in Sacred Harp sound, though I respect them still for being all of a piece, seemingly every voice within the group clipping along with the same accent, and all with Southern accent! The beauty and excitement of today's field recordings, in truer fidelity, is now more irresistible to my seasoned ear.)

This was different, in order of magnitude, from finding myself freshly enamored with some new popular song, some new singer or band. . . . It was like being rushed into an entirely new realm, and there discovering, musically speaking, the sturdiest architecture, spa-cious corridors, resplendent trappings. I couldn't recall coming upon vocal music so *grounded*. Amid marching chords that seemed so *right* and melodies spiraling out with the most appealing Celtic swing, each song, as if intentionally, plucked at strings deep in my being. As thoroughly old-fashioned as I realized this music to be, it seemed fashioned, in the moment, somehow specifically, majestically *for me*. It was like coming home – and in the most resounding way – when I hadn't realized I had been away. . . .

There was something else, too. Almost from the first, and un-expectedly, I found in Sacred Harp something beyond the great attractiveness of the music itself. Early on, it assumed for me a kind of mythic power. The big oblong songbook, the tradition and the people who were its standard bearers assumed larger-than-life character. In what I might now refer to as a kind of cultural nostalgia, I identified with an ethos that seemed bound up in so many of the texts, a spirit of triumph through travail. I responded, intellectually and emotion-ally, to what I knew to have been the hardness of life for so many of these plain-living, God-fearing people of the 19th and early 20th centuries. The fabric of this tradition had been woven with the lives of untold thousands of yeoman folk who had found in the music I was hearing not only essential entertainment and social bonding but spiritual sustenance. I joined them across the many years. . . . I would sing the songs they sang, and, I hoped, in the way they sang them.

Well: Like hundreds, maybe thousands, who would come after me, I was hooked. Claimed. As much as I had enjoyed hearing the "new-book" music of my grandfather's time or singing the well-known gospel standards of the day, I had jumped across the river now and would not be looking back.

My First Songbook – and Second Singing

My family then turned up a used songbook in Cullman, and I was shortly in business. Through them, I also made contact with the preeminent Sacred Harp figure in the area, Ruth Denson Edwards, Tom Denson's daughter and Mike Hinton's aunt. And on the second Saturday in July of 1965, I walked into the courtroom of the new Cullman County courthouse to hear, live, many of the 28 songs whose melodies I now knew by heart from many hours of record-playing.

The old courthouse, that magnificent structure built in the center of Cullman in 1912, had been demolished. (No one I've talked to in Cullman since can recall why, other than from some vague com-mitment to progress hovering in the air at the time and from the realization of a big money-making project by a few of the local construction honchos.) With the destruction of the old building went any chance for me to re-familiarize myself with the central chamber and its appointments – and to relive that visit with my grandparents to the singing convention some five or so years before, the only time I could recall having been inside the building.

A couple of blocks away from the former site, the new courthouse, big, boxlike and sleek with marble, had nothing of the distinguishing charm of the old structure. But it had on this occasion an old, and for me now wonderfully familiar, sound running down its corridors and up the stairwells.

The people in the courtroom on that Saturday were a mixture of town and country folk, generally in Sunday dress – the men in ties, many of the women with hats and gloves. They were predominantly, I would guess, 60 to 90 or so in age. I don't remember seeing youngsters. As I would later be able to tell, most were singers from Cullman or the surrounding counties, with a few visitors from Georgia or Tennessee.

I sat in the back with my songbook and followed along, gratified to have penetrated this amazing subculture, so workmanlike in its observance of old ritual, so ornery in its shunning of modernity. The pace of the singing was breathtaking – literally. Each song – loudly, almost punishingly rendered, it seemed – was no sooner brought to a close than the next leader and song were called out and a new song commenced. A skilled and hurried rustling of pages punctuated the brief silences between. The minutes would later show that 97 songs were summoned and finished off before the group adjourned for the day. No choral or band concert, no extended church service and no program I had ever attended had packed so much into a few hours.

I was at that point scarcely a participant, more of a dazed and dazzled observer, still in the fog of new love. It would be the following July before I would join their company again – but then as full-scale singer and leader.

Unlike most or all of the singers present, I wasn't really using the shape notes as an aid in pitch-placement. I hadn't after all learned to sight-read with shape notes. What sight-reading skill I had acquired came from singing in church (in a hymnal that used noteheads of the seven-shape variety, but without the instruction that might have accompanied them), from music classes at school, from piano lessons and from playing in band – and in all of that I had learned to determine pitch by note position on the lines and spaces. The singing of shape notes for me, then, was more of an add-on, an appliqué over a melody I could pretty well, with a little time, figure out on my own.

A triangle shape in a song will always now say *Fa* to me, but neither the shape nor the *Fa* – relative to the other intervals around it – calls up a note sound to my inner ear. Unconsciously over time, though, I came to rely on shape notes to orient my sense of pitch and of note intervals; I can certainly sight-read much better with them than without, the most immediate benefit being the indication, at a glance, of whether the song we're starting up is in major or minor key.

Newcomers may initially regard the practice of solfege or solmization (technical names for the process) as a pesky obstacle – "I keep singing a *La* instead of a *Fa!*" – but few if any veteran singers, having conquered the discipline, would vote to give it up, even when that regularly means, in the interest of time and economy, dropping a verse or two of the song. The *why* of that practice may still puzzle us: Why is it so appealing, so necessary? For sure, the singing of "the notes" gives a chance to "get it right" before the words are undertaken. But for the great majority of singers, and for the great majority of songs, rendering the tune by its shape-note syllables is more than rehearsal; it is somehow its own language – a language unencumbered by words, a language of the music itself. (To my ear, the *fa-sol-la-mi* names make fairly euphonious sequences. My bias shows through here, but I find the syllable sequences of seven-shape traditions – well, at least those *do do do's* – less attractive.) It functions like a musical ladder, by which to ascend to the chamber of meaning provided by the song's words. It is preamble and prerequisite; a cherished, and only occasionally dispensable, ritual.

My mission in those early days, like the mission of almost any newcomer then or now, was to spread the word, to share what I could only think universally appealing. Friends, family, classmates, professors - if not casual passersby - became the targets of my effort. You must come and hear this! Here, let me play something for you! Wanna try to sing this song along with me? If those efforts were generally unfruitful - beyond friends and relations productively adjusting what they considered safe distance from me - they did sharpen my appreciation for the tribe of singers still carrying on the tradition and for the few newcomers who elected to join us.

Among the probably hundreds I would speak with about Sacred Harp over the next dozen or so years were two noted Southern authors who had mentioned Sacred Harp in their writings and whom I had the opportunity to meet briefly. Given such an opening, I of course directed our conversations as quickly as possible to their familiarity with the tradition. Andrew Lytle, who had written admiringly of Sacred Harp practice in his contribution to the 1930 Agrarian manifesto *I'll Take My Stand*, told me in the late 1960s of being impressed by the great crowd at a courthouse singing in Guntersville, Ala., on a visit there in the '30s. More evocative still was a 1978 conversation with Eudora Welty, who came to do a reading at Montevallo and who turned out to have known maybe the leading proponent of Sacred Harp singing in Mississippi in that era, the affable Robert Archie Stewart, for 50 years a rural mail carrier in the northern part of that state whom I had met a few years before. (Not just Arch, but Mrs. Stewart had been endeared to me: in her case, for the tasty meal and especially the lemony iced dessert in a little pan taken from the freezer that she laid out for Hugh McGraw and me on our visit to their home, before Arch, that afternoon, led us to a singing.) Miss Welty, that writer of finest visual acuity, shared with me an image, stowed away from a courthouse singing many years before, of a baby, "at the breast," already "beating time" - seeming to take in, along with mother's milk, the very pace and pulse of Sacred Harp.

4

The Ring of Repugnance

The quiet, heartfelt struggle for Sacred Harp survival in the Deep South of the 1940s and '50s through, say, the '70s or '80s and even onward might now seem a little hard to imagine for more recent converts across the country and the globe. Well beyond that earlier time and limited region, the music and tradition of Sacred Harp can seem fresh, welcoming and inspirational. What, after all, is not to like? Spirited, engaging music; rich words to sing; spiritual nourishment; delectable food in abundance; and a warm sense of community.

A bitter truth, though, held fast through those years. For conveying the situation in a phrase, I long ago settled on a pungent metaphor: the Ring of Repugnance, the term scientists use for the invisible circle around a cow pile where livestock won't graze.

For a couple of generations in that era, Sacred Harp lay well within the South's ring of repugnance. Like other cultural carryovers from its rural past, "fasola singing" smelled of primitive, uncouth things, of tattered, old-fashioned ways. Dirt roads and old country churches. Outhouses and no air-conditioning. Predominantly elderly folk in unfashionable garb putting tunes up high with their cracked voices. Dinner-on-the-grounds, in the heat of the day, with flies and sweat bees and yellow jackets. The whole scene could seem to represent everything an up-and-coming youth from the area would want to leave behind – and did.

Several generations of singers had labored to keep their children and grandchildren in the fold – to little avail. New generations of potential singers abandoned old ways and the old places and what after all could be an intimidating musical discipline, and headed off toward more modern settings, easier fare and slicker, uptown entertainments. How, after all, can you keep 'em down on the farm?

Within a small community or family – with everywhere the tyranny of youthful peer pressure – it often took a healthy ego to turn against the trend. Thankfully, exceptions to that trend were possible within large, insulating families of singers or within smaller families whose elders had somehow instilled a core communal value, patiently, lovingly bringing their children or grandchildren along in a way that allowed the songs to seep into their consciousness and form a cluster of endeared memories.

A changing pattern of church-going in the region had also contributed to the Sacred Harp's decline. In the heyday of the tradition, the 19th and early 20th centuries, churches in the rural South were often served by circuit-riding preachers, with regular church services occurring only on the weekend or two of each month in which the preacher visited that community. This made the church building and its congregants available for an occasional Sacred Harp singing in the off weekends. With the increasing establishment of regular church services every Sunday in almost every community, congregants, especially those now recruited as choir members, found a conflict with traditional Sacred Harp events. (Incidentally, as many converts to the singing tradition can attest, Sacred Harp, if it is ruinous of anything, is likely to ruin one for choir practice. Singing dozens of songs once each – freely, with abandon – has immediate appeal over what, as "practice," can seem a tediously repetitive process.)

So in the time I came to Sacred Harp, I found few singers my own age or younger. It seemed everywhere a rapidly dwindling tradition. When I was compiling a master list of singings in both black and white singing communities for my 1978 history of Sacred Harp, I tabulated 25 annual sessions from Georgia to Texas on a single

Sunday in June! By the time the book was ready for publication, that number had dropped to 16, and today it is no more than a half-dozen. Similarly, the 1944 booklet "Report of The Sacred Harp Centennial Celebration" in Double Springs in Winston County, Ala., had listed 23 annual sessions in the Cullman County area; only seven of that number remain, and probably none close to their mid-1940s strength. With declining numbers overall and demographics overwhelmingly tilted toward the aged and the rural, many singers wondered, along with me, if the tradition they loved so much would last beyond the century.

A little singing I attended in the central Alabama countryside that first year of my involvement could serve to illustrate the point. A college buddy had heard about this particular event, got directions, and he and a girlfriend and I and mine excitedly struck out for the site. Inside the small country church that I remember as being fairly dark, we found a welcoming spirit – especially when the chairman heard that one of our group was from Cullman: "*All* those folks up there can sing!" A handful of mostly elderly singers formed the remnant of what had once been a robust community turnout. How far things had fallen off became painfully clear when I, invited to lead early on, called for THE GOLDEN HARP. With apologies, they begged off. They could no longer bring that one up, it had been too long. I chose another tune, and we limped along. A few years later, compiling my master list of annual sessions, I was not surprised to see that the little singing was no more.

As much of a worrying downward spiral as Sacred Harp found itself in during that era, I have been privileged not only to witness but to participate in its rebound over the last few decades, an upturn as heartening as it was unexpected. The Sacred Harp will never regain the prominence it held in the rural South before my time, but this durable songbook and distinctive singing style now are taking hold in places undreamed of in earlier times. It's as if two orbs – one a descending tradition, another an ascending set of circumstances and opportunities – in passing touched, and, in touching, reset the trajectory of the one upward again at last. My previous book was, almost necessarily I thought, tinged with an elegiac feel. This one I can write not only at a historically interesting and important juncture for the movement but from a vantage point decidedly more celebratory.

5

Transitions

The Years in Georgia – and with Hugh McGraw

By the time I finished my undergraduate degree in 1966 and enrolled in the graduate program in English at Auburn University, I was a full-fledged Sacred Harp singer. (My Sacred Harp experiences while at Auburn are the subject of the last chapter.) And when I left graduate school in 1969, I looked for a teaching position in a community where I could pursue singing activities. I had married while at Auburn, and within a couple of years Mary and I would begin our family – in Georgia.

An opening at what was then West Georgia College (now the University of West Georgia) in Carrollton brought me to an area close to the cradle of the Sacred Harp, and one with a good number of singings (most of them, unfortunately, now dried up). Not far from Carrollton – if, at the time, out a dauntingly elusive route – was Wilson's Chapel, a building constructed and used only for Sacred Harp singing, and a frequent home to the historic Chattahoochee Musical Convention, which dated from 1852. Holly Springs Baptist Church, a spacious, (then) one-room, all-wood country church dating from about 1880, and one of the great Sacred Harp sites, was but a few miles north of Carrollton and just shy of Bremen.

The move placed me within the magnetic draw of Bremen's Hugh McGraw, the major Sacred Harp figure in the second half of the 20th century and one of the most dynamic and commanding personalities I've known. In a position he would hold for more than four decades, Hugh served as executive secretary of the Sacred Harp Publishing Company, and for the seven years I lived in Carrollton, I acted as his unofficial assistant ("Answer this letter, Buell, and tell 'em we can send . . ."). Hugh was both friend and mentor. I had a standard invitation to accompany him and one, two or three other close friends on singing trips. He never accepted a dime in gas money, a notable concession to a financially challenged young instructor and then assistant professor. Usually with a small entourage, Hugh traveled widely in support of the tradition to which he had devoted his life. Being able to accompany him on most of those trips gave me unparalleled opportunity to experience the breadth of the Sacred Harp movement, not only in traditional areas and traditional singings but in the teaching and workshop sessions and singing performances he conducted across the country.

With vision and energy for finding new destinations, Hugh carried the Sacred Harp on his leading arm to places it had never been before. More than any other person in the last century, he was responsible for the spread of Sacred Harp outside its traditional borders. Wherever he went, Hugh was a gregarious, upbeat figure, and his enthusiasm for the songbook and its surrounding singing practices was infectious. He was particularly good at puncturing any latent snootiness in an audience. The more sophisticated the listeners or workshop participants - regional ministers of music, members of the College Music Society and conferees of the American Choral Directors Association as examples - the better his country humor and chutzpah played. Given a microphone or speaker's space, he always brought to the moment a brashness that proved disarming. Here, for example, was his quoted response to Joe Cumming, *Newsweek*'s Southern bureau chief, who, tracking him for a 1978 spread on Sacred Harp at Holly Springs, had just asked about participants' religious affiliation (this at a time when the national press *never* came to visit): "We get Southern Baptist, Methodist, even a lot of Catholics . . . You might even find some hypocrites here."

Lightning-quick in his decision-making and in his pronouncements, Hugh could also be intimidating. Few questioned or crossed him. In his post with the publishing company, he directed the strategies – and virtually every detail – of the publishing and distribution of the successor editions to the original Denson revision of the songbook. An honored shape-note composer himself, he led the production of three editions over a period of more than 25 years, including the creation of the monumental 1991 revision. He brought to that set of enterprises the managerial perspective and delegating skills he employed as longtime director of a local clothing manufacturing plant, as well as a canny understanding of people, a formidable memory and unflagging devotion to the task at hand.

In his prime, Hugh was also the most dynamic song leader I ever saw. He had mastered every song in the book – in all four parts, too – and seemed to know exactly how to send the class wherever he wanted them to go. He had no fear. When he was especially energized, his moves were dazzlingly quick and sweeping, and he could give the class a galvanizing jolt with a sudden stomp of his foot – a move no doubt picked up from having watched gospel quartets perform before he was drawn into Sacred Harp in his mid-20s. He was, among other things, a master showman. A little incident at Holly Springs roughly 25 years ago reveals the trait.

The church on this occasion was packed, the singing vigorous. At some break point in the late morning, Hugh, as chair of the event, announced that he had in his hand something no one had ever seen before! Stepping from around the large podium, he moved into the square and held out his clasped hand. For that moment of quiet, he had everyone's rapt attention, with observers in the far corners of the room craning to see. Unfolding his fist, he produced a peanut shell still intact, crushed it and held aloft the kernel, pink and innocent, for us all to behold. There was a general sigh of appreciation for the simple truth he had laid bare. "And nobody'll ever see it again!" he said, and popped it into his mouth.

In time, Hugh saw to it that I was added to the board of the publishing company and even, for a period, elected its president. Over the years, he and I had some mutually painful disagreements that spilled over into the broader community we both tried to serve. Through it all, I'm confident that neither of us doubted the other's sincerity or intent, in our differing ways, to do the best thing for Sacred Harp. And I appreciated the opportunity, if I chose to take it, to reason or make my case with him. Mellower with the years, we remain friends today. And all of us who care deeply about the Sacred Harp tradition and its future owe Hugh McGraw a great deal for his untiring work and statesmanship in taking our music abroad and making it both more widely known and more generally accessible.

A virtual Who's Who of singers in Georgia passed through Holly Springs and the other local singing houses in those years: Bud and Tom McGraw, Newman Denney, E.I. McGuire, Ellen Huggins Pate, Ludie McWhorter Lambert, Charlene Wallace, Carl Hughes, Hoyt and Mary Lou Cagle, the brothers Horace and Doris DeLong, Louis Hardin, Ellis and Ima Brittain, and, supremely, the magisterial figure of Raymond Hamrick, prolific composer of *Sacred Harp* tunes, including several of the songbook's best beloved. Once greeting Mrs. Brittain at Holly Springs, thinking at that moment (and always) that she had as sweet a face as I ever beheld, I was stumped by hearing from her a once-in-a-lifetime compliment about my own, which, she said, had "so much countenance in it!" Jim Ayers, blessed (and blessing us all) with the deepest, most powerful bass voice – he was truly a bass section by himself – then was cursed toward the end of his life by inner-ear troubles so severe that they ruined his sense of pitch, made his singing intolerable for himself and others and caused him to have to withdraw altogether from the thing he so treasured.

The front bench at Holly Springs, early 1970s: (of figures mentioned herein) Florice Akin, third from left; Loyd Redding, fourth from left; Lonnie Rogers, second from right; E.G. Akin, far right. (Photo by Betty Oliver)

Loyd Redding (honoree of Raymond Hamrick's song LLOYD), who loved minor music as much as anyone I knew and who had the absolute best touch for keying it, sits in my memory as he did on the front row of the tenor there at Holly Springs, with one hand cupped over an ear and the other broadly laying out the beat, and with one leg, under the bench, impossibly twisted about the other. Singing with him and a few others at his home in Bremen, I once appraised a just-finished song with "Pretty tones." Loyd's correction was swift but gentle: "Them *beautiful* tones!"

E.G. Akin, from one of the area's old singing families, was a jeweler in Carrollton; he and his dear wife, Florice (the two of them honored by Dan Brittain with his song AKIN), were trusted and generous friends. A great supporter of the singing both close in and far away, E.G. sang a really good tenor. He had a slight chirping quality to his spoken words, but it was *what* he said in one of our conversations that left an indelible memory. Mentioning some interaction with a singer who had ended up giving him a warm embrace, E.G., with a smug smile, reached for the intended word and landed improbably: ". . . she squazzed me." He seemed to enjoy a good story about as much as I did, and one he told had us both grinning big: that of a boy, maybe seven or eight, from their circle of family or friends who in his heart-to-heart prayer at the supper table was observed flexing already formidable negotiating skills: "And God, if You don't let me have [?], I'm gonna lose all the faith I ever had in You. . . ."

Charlene Wallace, Holly Springs, early 1970s. (Photo by Betty Oliver)

Visitors crossing over from Alabama made the singings at Holly Springs and other local singing sites more powerful still. Henry and John Kerr, Preston Warren, Ruth and Leman Brown, Millard McWhorter, Willie Bob Morrison, Forney and Clelon Cobb, Jeff and Shelbie Sheppard and many others regularly took up places around our square.

Jeff Sheppard, right, in synchrony with Tim Eriksen, State Line Church, 2000. (Photo by Laura Densmore)

Though not unexpected, Jeff Sheppard's death, as I was putting finishing touches on this book, left an enormous void in our community and leaves me thinking anew of his contributions to our singing in those years and all the way up to the present. Many others from places across the globe join me in certain knowledge that, in Jeff's passing, we have lost one of the giants of Sacred Harp in our time. Knowledge of the songbook in all its facets; the ability to sing, with great voice, multiple parts; an unfailingly spot-on keying sense; a superb feel for pace and of how to lead a class; along with the friskiest, most winning personality made Jeff an indispensable presence at singings both near and far from his home in Anniston. Deserving of special mention are his leadership of the Sacred Harp Musical

Heritage Association and his co-founding of the Association's Camp Fasola. Actively singing, leading and promoting Sacred Harp (with essential help from his family) up until weeks before his death at 82 – even when dementia had overtaken him – made him seem a natural wonder. In a tradition already renowned for hospitality, his – and Shelbie's – inexhaustible generosity over the decades set a sterling example for us all.

Writing a Book

Our two sons, Tad and Will, were born during those years in Georgia. Something else was conceived during that time as well. My master's thesis at Auburn was an analysis of Sacred Harp singing and tradition, and at some point I began to think of expanding the monograph into a book. Earlier studies of Sacred Harp, primarily those of George Pullen Jackson (and especially his landmark *White Spirituals in the Southern Uplands* of 1933), filled in huge gaps for an understanding of the history and early spread of the shape-note phenomenon. But so much of the Sacred Harp world in the time I had come to know it – the details, the current complexion of the singing, the differing manifestations of the tradition – awaited a more up-to-date treatment. So I plunged into that effort.

The book would eventually be published by the University of Georgia Press in 1978, two years after my family and I had relocated to Birmingham, where I began employment with South Central Bell Telephone Company – and later worked for its parent company, BellSouth Corporation. First, though, came a bit of wandering in the wilderness. While still in Georgia, I first submitted my manuscript to a university press in another state. The typical process for acceptance of a book by a university press required recommendation by two specialists in the field. The editor of this particular press, generally familiar with Sacred Harp and enthusiastic about the project, assured me he had in mind, for the first reader, a local scholar who would be perfect for the task. He then turned over to the reader my typed manuscript, the only one I (improvidently) had. What should then have been a waiting period of a month or two began to stretch out much further. One excuse for delay followed another. Then a home fire, in which the reader herself was partially burned, spared the manuscript but delayed things further. The reader insisted on keeping the manuscript and keeping to herself the task of apprais-ing it. All of this was, for me, a young and soon-to-be first-time author (then under the threat of "publish or perish"), like being put on the rack and gradually stretched to extremity. Each month of waiting seemed interminable. Having lost almost a year to this first step in the process, I was at last able to retrieve the manuscript and submit it to the University of Georgia Press, where, in Ken Cherry, I found an editor who was not only an admirer of the tradition the book described but someone who would skillfully manage the pro-cess through to completion.

"I can tell you almost exactly how many copies we'll sell to our traditional audience," Cherry told me, as the book rounded the cor-ner on the way to its issue date. "We'll sell to two percent of all the libraries in this country." But: "What we don't have any idea about is the Sacred Harp audience." I could offer little guidance on that calculation. At any rate, 2,500 copies of the hardback book were issued. In an early tip-off for gauging our special audience, Hugh McGraw showed up at the Holly Springs singing of 1978 with his trunk full of new books – and sold 50 on the spot. Within a year, an additional printing was necessary. In 1987 the press committed to do a soft-cover reprint with new preface, and in 1989 that paperback edition appeared. The preface updated the state of the tradition a bit but failed to peer very far into the future. Discussing the printed National Sacred Harp Newsletter of the time, it posed the question: "Through what other means would someone . . . seek out fellow singers in unfamiliar territory? How else communicate about any matter with shape-note loyalists across the nation?" As well as failing to foresee the Internet and what that might mean for connecting future participants, it also never contemplated a Sacred Harp wave touching foreign shores.

Blind spots and other limitations notwithstanding, the book did some of what I and others hoped it would do: make possible a greater understanding of a historic phenomenon and a music worthy of pursuit. Over the years, I heard stories from a number of singers about having come to Sacred Harp by way of my book. The most unlikely may have been the one from the late Jim Hearne from St. Louis. Making his acquaintance at the Midwest Convention in Chicago one year, I asked the usual question: "So how did you come to Sacred Harp?" Well, his story had started, he told me, when, on a business trip, he had wandered into a bookstore and seen on the shelf a narrow volume with the title *The Sacred Harp: A Tradition and Its Music.* He had found, then, something that might be of interest to his wife, a harpist. Later, at home, his wife gave the book the lightest once-over and declared (something to the effect of): "This isn't about a harp at all!" Determined, I suppose, to get a little of his money's worth out of an otherwise wasted purchase, Jim began to read – and then to find himself engaged. A subsequent newspaper notice of a Sacred Harp event in town allowed the completion of an arc: in short order he became a dedicated Sacred Harper.

An earlier acquaintance-making at the Midwest Convention also comes to mind. Keith and Jenny Willard, then from Minneapolis, handed over to me at that event in 1990 what would be for any author an implicit compliment, a dog-eared copy of a book for autograph. Our meeting there, at what would be their first of many Sacred Harp singings, represented a surprise for them; like perhaps others I would meet in that era, they had expected "an old man!" My book may have seemed old before its time, its prose (as I said to them that day) creaking with apparent age or infirmity – but I was then in my mid-40s and would have some decades of Sacred Harp yet to experience and to write about.

Birmingham, Mobile and the National Convention

My painful decision to leave teaching reflected a combination of factors: mainly, financial exigencies for a young family (exacerbated by a state education budget essentially frozen during seven years of ripping, and at times double-digit, inflation) and a nagging sense that I was not truly helping my students, a captive and, for the most part, listless contingent of freshmen and sophomores. (The difference between those teaching experiences and that of conducting Sacred Harp workshops over the years for eager, knowledge-thirsty participants could not have been more pronounced.) Awareness of my own writing gaffes over time hasn't prevented my savoring a few of the imperishables from those days of teaching freshman composition: from one chap's proud hoisting of an everyday cliché – "It's a doggie-dog world" – to the circularity of another's sense of early history: "Since the beginning of recorded time, man has written things down." (If pressed, I could produce a substantial chapter if not a slender volume of such.)[8]

So, with a truckload or more of mixed regret, optimism and excitement, I started out on a new career and in a new place. Birmingham became home for my family and me for a couple of years beginning in 1976 – and then home again more permanently shortly after that. In between came an assignment and move to Mobile, as close to the tropics as I would ever want to live. We never managed to appreciate what so many coastal residents seemed to enjoy, or at least not to mind: a daily pattern – spring, summer and fall – of baking heat and high humidity, with afternoons frequently given over to spectacular thunderstorms. The area is noted for beauty, and splashy azaleas grew everywhere like weeds, most winningly when they circled the big antebellum-style homes in and around the city. Huge live oaks draped with Spanish moss made picturesque backdrops. And indeed we had a magnificent specimen just off our back deck, though, practically speaking, the great limbs seemed to serve mainly as wide runways for supersize cockroaches to drop in among us! The absence of Sacred Harp singing in Mobile at that

Gallery of photos from the 1998 National: (from left) top, Rodney Ivey, Henry Guthery, Barney Roberson; middle, Freeman and Jewel Wootten, Edith Tate, Ruth Brown; bottom, Marie Aldridge, Peter Irvine, Karen and David Ivey. (Photos by Joel Cohen)

time added to my list of complaints. I made it back to singing territory for only one event during that stint.[9]

Through a zigzag of fate, a company position opening up back in
Birmingham cut my official Mobile time to but ten months, though
it meant for the family, who had to stay behind for a while, a scary
evacuation in front of Hurricane Frederic, at that time the costliest
hurricane ever to hit the Gulf Coast. The move back to Birmingham
put me again in the very center of Sacred Harp activity. Within a hundred or so miles in every direction, I would have no difficulty finding
a singing to go to most weekends of the year.

In 1980, the year after I returned, Hugh McGraw, Dr. William
J. Reynolds of Nashville and Dr. Claude Rhea, dean of the school
of music at Samford University, organized the National Sacred Harp
Singing Convention, with its first session to be held on Samford's
campus in the Birmingham suburb of Homewood. Modeled on the
conventions of old, it was set for four days, though in subsequent
years that number was dropped to three (and to the annual dates of
the Thursday, Friday and Saturday before the third Sunday in June).
It was originally conceived as an event rotating about major college
campuses; after Samford, the next two projected host sites were the
University of Texas at Austin and the University of North Carolina
at Chapel Hill. That rotation never happened. Stewards of the convention heard strong rationale from out-of-regioners that having the
convention in Birmingham, the virtual seat of Sacred Harp at that
point, gave them contact with the greatest possible number of traditional singers. And so metro Birmingham became the convention's
home.

It would be hard to imagine a more magnanimous host than
Samford proved to be. Through Dean Rhea and his successor, Dr.
Gene Black, the university provided magnificent, free and con-
veniently located facilities. It mailed out, at its own expense, two
promotional flyers a year to a list of roughly 2,000 and even for a time
provided chicken sandwiches for lunch out under the trees during the
convention!

But in the Sacred Harp aesthetic, acoustics is no trifling matter. And unfortunately, the quality and quantity of sound in and around the square in those years failed to measure up to Samford's many complimentary features. The stage at the fine arts center was plenty big enough to accommodate hundreds of singers, and indeed hundreds were there each of the first several years, including most of the best-known singers from Alabama and bordering states. For the spectators out in the spacious auditorium, from the front rows all the way up to the eagle's nest, the rising sound may well have been worthy of the great classes of singers who gathered below. The stage itself, however, failed to contain enough of that sound for the singers themselves, failed to give them back a satisfactory return on their vocal investment. Attendance dropped off steadily from the original registration of 761 (but with an estimated attendance of over 1,000) to, before the convention was relocated, a few hundred.

A recital hall on campus made possible beautiful sound for the 1992 session, but we were immediately then thwarted by having bumped up against the fire marshal's maximum attendance figure. The better the singing sounded, the stronger the likely attendance and the quicker the possibility of a shutdown. . . . And so, as I became convention chair in 1993, the first of what would be 15 years of my tenure in that position, we left Samford and began to cast about in a series of moves to other locales in search of that most elusive goal of all Sacred Harp pinings: the perfect convention site.

Through its ups and downs in that era, what the National did better than any other modern-day convention was to provide an unparalleled cavalcade of traditional singers, mixed in with participants from four corners of the country – and beyond. The year 1997 saw the first of many visitors from the U.K., with 14 in that group ("The British are coming!" the convention flyer had warned). And throughout, the National offered the best example of diversity within traditional Southern singing communities. Dewey Williams, Japheth Jackson and other African American singers from southeastern Alabama attended the first session and many others after that. Mississippi's black Sacred Harp community was soon represented by the father-son duo of Elmer and Aubrey Enochs and companions. Denson-book, Cooper-book, White-book and former James-book adherents were all there from time to time, and, along the way, predominantly *Christian Harmony* and *New Harp of Columbia* singers joined the musical mix.

A major gratification for me was seeing an influx of many hundreds of Birmingham-area or statewide participants (listeners, for the most part) – sometimes three to five hundred in a yearly session and perhaps 12 to 15 thousand overall – making the National the closest thing to the courthouse conventions of earlier decades. Curiosity about the unusual brought out many of those who attended; many more came to indulge a nostalgia for the shape-note music that Momma and Daddy, Grandpa, Uncle Frank or Great-aunt Martha used to sing.

My retirement at the end of 2009, after seven years of commuting weekly to the Florida Panhandle for work in real estate – along with my assuming a less active role in the National – gave me time to begin to record my Sacred Harp memories, especially those of some of the great figures I had known over the decades. Thinking of that reminds me of a line that Birmingham singing friend Jim Brown once shared from a conversation he'd had with famed Appalachian herbalist Tommie Bass. An old pear tree, Bass told him, would, about a year or so before it died, tend to produce "the awfullest crop of pears!" Whatever my metaphor here – being now out to pasture or being but an old pear tree in that pasture – I have gradually channeled my pent-up store of memories into book form. The following chapters here – reminiscences about Miss Ruth, Mr. Dewey, George M., Tat, Buford and all – came as a result of that seasonal change in my life. I offer them for viewing by the indulgent reader.

6

Taking Sacred Harp on Stage

It's often said, and rightly so, that Sacred Harp is a participatory experience rather than a performance activity. Singers' rather than listeners' music.

Participants, after all, are amateurs, self-selected singers, with abilities distributed along the whole range from something just below the Olympian all the way down to ground level (and occasionally lower?). And rather than singing outwardly to an audience, singers in traditional format face inward to the center from the four sides that represent the separate voice parts.

Then, too, what the mere listener hears at singings or in recordings is something of a vocal thicket of crossing branches, so that the song's "melody" is obscured. (Voice doubling – both men and women singing, an octave apart, on tenor and treble – further thickens the sound.) With each voice part being somewhat melodic – through what's known in the tradition as "dispersed harmony" – singers have the pleasure of hearing their own part stand out against this heavily textured sound as each singing line crosses both above and below that of other parts. Instead of a distinct melodic line supported by harmony, then, what uninitiated listeners receive out of all of this may be a mere clanging of closely repetitive chords, though usually with a beat strong enough to make them want to pat their feet on the floor.

And so: singing to and for ourselves. And yet if we're going to en-
ergize this tradition and extend the privilege outward, at some point
we have to take the music to the people. The courthouse singings of
old did that, though it was then more a matter of the people crowding
up close within hearing distance of the big-room singings. But beginning at least as early as the 1950s, providing a broad-scale, in-person
listening experience meant singers transporting their music a good
long way from home.

Marcus Cagle with his band of singers at the Waldorf, October 1952.

In October of 1952 a group of more than 40 singers from
Alabama, Georgia, Mississippi and Tennessee paid their own way
to appear at the Waldorf Astoria on the occasion of the New York
Herald Tribune's 21st annual "Building Leadership for Peace"
Forum. Led by A.M. Cagle of Atlanta, the undoubtedly dazzled
group of mostly country and small-town folk stood up front in those

smart, art deco surroundings to perform at the Second Session's evening program – in between presentations by Ambassador William H. Draper, CBS Chairman William Paley and heads of the New York Stock Exchange, Coca-Cola and Firestone Tire & Rubber. The singers stood facing an imposing audience, with the capacious auditorium's first floor packed and the second-floor balcony and third-floor boxes simply stuffed.

Before taking their first pitch, they heard Forum director Helen Hiett Waller introduce them as representatives of "a truly American institution," which, she said, "today . . . exists only in upland areas of the Deep South." She would use the now-familiar formulation first made prominent by George Pullen Jackson: "This is in no sense listeners' music; it is singers' music, sung for spiritual uplift and community fellowship. To really appreciate it, you would have to happen on an all-day singin' as I did in Georgia a few months ago." The audience was then asked to wait until after the sixth and final song before applauding. (And to go all this way – at one's own expense – to present only a half-dozen songs? Yes, but think of the thunderous, sophisticated applause. . . .)

A still-fresh anecdote from 98-year-old "Tat" Bailey gives a sense of the singers', if not the listeners', excitement that evening. Not actually a singer himself, Bailey was not along for the trip, but fellow Arab, Ala., townsman Coy Putnam was. Tat would always laugh convulsively in retelling the story his friend shared with him after returning from that highest-of-high-cotton experiences. Just before the performance, Putnam had ridden down to the auditorium on an elevator with a dressed-up New Yorker, who, seeing the name badge, had said, "So where's your 'Harp'?" "You'll see. . . ," Putnam had coyly replied. Tat's telling would grow almost joyous at this point. Per his account, when Marcus Cagle first threw out a down beat, Coy "just kind of squeaked! . . . He said he couldn't even make a sound, he was so scared!"[10]

A dozen years later, another group of roughly 40 singers, mainly from northwestern Alabama, brought Sacred Harp to one of the

big audiences at the Newport Folk Festival. In less highfalutin' surroundings this time, the fasola folk apparently had no trouble getting
beyond a squeak. About that 1964 trip, Smithsonian folklorist Ralph
Rinzler, who helped arrange it, wrote that "about ten minutes after
they arrived at Newport, they were all jammed into one sitting room
shaking the walls with their voices. . . ."

If singers are generally inclined to be, like Ms. Waller at the
Waldorf, a bit apologetic about such appearances – "It isn't, you understand, the *real thing* you're experiencing here. . ." – it has to be
recognized that many of the voices added to the growing Sacred Harp
chorus today arrived as a result of just such events.

Cold Mountain

The 2003 movie "Cold Mountain" was of course the biggest
of those events. At some point in 2002 I was approached by singer
and performer Tim Eriksen about joining a group of fellow Sacred
Harpers to record music for use in a film based on Charles Frazier's
award-winning novel about the Civil War. Through his association
with impresario T Bone Burnett, Tim, as well as lending his splendid
solo voice to the movie, was the person responsible for the incorpora-
tion of Sacred Harp into the film and subsequent events.

I hadn't read *Cold Mountain* and wasn't aware of the planned
film, but the project sounded intriguing. I arrived at Liberty Baptist
Church in Henagar, Ala., on the appointed June afternoon expecting to join a small group – and was surprised to find about 60 others
gathering there. Mostly from north Alabama, the group included a
number of skilled singers from out of region – altogether a balanced
and potentially powerful class. I also wasn't familiar with Anthony
Minghella, but the director soon stood before us to explain his reasons for bringing a high-powered recording crew from Nashville to
tape our country-church singing. He wanted to bring a "beautiful
book" to life through film, he told us, and in his extensive research – I
think he mentioned at one point having reviewed approximately 300

books about the South and the Civil War – he had stumbled upon Sacred Harp. I would later hear him say that when he heard Sacred Harp, he knew he had a film.

We were treated to a generous dinner-on-the-grounds at dusk in Liberty's beautifully wooded surroundings. And just before that, each of us, in exchange for our names on a dotted line, received two crisp 100-dollar bills. (Nothing in moviedom, I would find out, is free.) Back inside, Minghella, along with film composer Gabriel Yared (Burnett and actor Brendan Gleeson were there as well), had us run through several dozen tunes over a two-hour period, including the song that had piqued Minghella's interest coming in, the fuging tune LOGAN by Tom Denson. I could probably speak for most if not all who were there in saying that it was an exhilarating and, at times, euphoric experience: finding once more, and over and over again finding ourselves lost in, the driving, high-decibel, soul-in-the-throat singing we loved and love. Only later would we discover Minghella's and Yared's ultimate choices for the film: the songs IDUMEA and I'M GOING HOME.

I was particularly struck by one little episode from that experience. After we had finished and the crew was packing up equipment, I walked to the back of the church, where one of the Hollywood music consultants was helping tidy up. Another of our group, Elene Stovall of Birmingham, arrived just ahead of me and spoke first – and breezily: "So, whadya think? . . ."

The answer I heard was unexpectedly stirring: "I have worked with orchestras from all over the world . . . I've worked with 115-voice choirs . . . and I have never heard *anything in my life* . . . as beautiful as what I heard here tonight. . . . I . . . am . . . *ab-so-lute-ly* . . . *blown* . . . *away.* . . ."

Not everyone who saw the movie or heard the soundtrack would have the same reaction, but the two songs did resonate strongly with a great many who heard them. *Rolling Stone*, in its review of the soundtrack (whose contributors included weighty names from the music world), certainly got the picture: "Cold Mountain's salvation is the Sacred Harp Singers at Liberty Church, a shaped-note choral group that delivers its two hymns with an otherworldly intensity."

(But unusually intense for Sacred Harp? Oh, maybe not so much. . . .)

Through a gracious nod from Tim, I was allowed to squeeze into two trips to Hollywood as a member of a group of 30-plus each time for follow-up events to the film itself: first, a taping for the A&E Network's special "The Words and Music of 'Cold Mountain'" and then an appearance at the 2004 Academy Awards.

And here I could sidestep for a moment to say: If one is going to name-drop, might as well pull out the names of Nicole Kidman, Jude Law, Elvis Costello, Alison Krauss, Sting. . . . For the A&E program taped in December, 2003, our on-stage company, reprising the movie's exuberant rendition of I'M GOING HOME, suddenly included Kidman, Law, Minghella, Burnett and actor Kathy Baker – their hands joining ours in the trademark Sacred Harp slicing-up of time into down-and-up beats. (I was amused immediately afterwards by the luminous Ms. Kidman's hands-off signal to the smiling crowd of singers she found herself in off-stage: "Where's my handler?" "Here, dear" might have been several mumbled replies. . . .)

The Academy Awards experience was an abbreviated ride of highs and lows. The plan was for our group to back-up Krauss at the big event on Sunday evening in her performance of THE SCARLET TIDE (written by Burnett and Costello), one of the two songs from the movie nominated for Best Song – and also, and most important, to perform the Sacred Harp song LIBERTY, shape notes and all! The prior evening our group, joined by Krauss, Sting, Costello and Burnett, was to lead off with two Sacred Harp songs at the program for the Max Awards, the big internal recognition ceremony for Miramax Films, our hosts for the weekend events. First rehearsals for the Oscars production were in Studio B of Capitol Records, where we could humble ourselves amid the ghosts of Frank Sinatra, Nat King Cole and so many others of legendary voice. We, in all of that, filled our eyes with the world of movies and big-time music-making; at the same time, Hollywood peered ever so briefly into the world of Sacred Harp. The slightest symbol of that for me? Sting (Gordon Sumner), at our Max Awards rehearsal, had trouble viewing the songbook – so I lent him my glasses.

Being at the Academy Awards was a heady experience – and in a little twist on the word itself, maybe more so for me than for the rest of the gents. Back stage, in two opposite lines, nervously awaiting our entrance for the Krauss number, and flanked up front by those 20-foot golden Oscar statues, we were given a last-minute make-up check. As the cosmetician went down the row, faintly dusting the cheeks of our garbed-up womenfolk, she passed me, took another step or two, then, as after-thought, evidently fearing a reflected gleam off a too-smooth surface, backed up and settled a little cloud of powder on my ample forehead.

The Oscars event did end up representing the ultimate "near-miss" opportunity, as the performance of LIBERTY was scuttled the night before the performance, preventing the debut of Sacred Harp on the biggest of all stages: a TV broadcast to hundreds of millions worldwide. The disappointment of our troupe on hearing that news – knowing what that minute and a half would have incomparably represented for our music – I can only describe as crushing. (Burnett and Costello were said to have lobbied with producer Joe Roth deep into the night on Saturday in efforts to reverse that decision.)

The Oscars aside, though, this much can and should be said: more people came to know and to respond positively to Sacred Harp through the movie and soundtrack of "Cold Mountain" than through any other single source in history.

A few film documentaries over the years have also provided a window into Sacred Harp music and lore, none achieving more exposure or critical success than Matt and Erica Hinton's "Awake, My Soul: The Story of the Sacred Harp" (2006), which spread the word through Public Broadcasting Service showings across the U.S. and through special screenings both in and out of the country. Craftily weaving a variety of authentic voices, "Awake, My Soul" offers an excellent tutorial on Sacred Harp practices through compelling narrative and powerful footage of singings in Georgia and Alabama. Other virtual Sacred Harp appearances of note: extended segments on National Public Radio's "All Things Considered" in 1991 and 2003; in between, a shorter segment on NPR's "Morning Edition"; and a three-minute piece (late '80s/early '90s?) on ABC Television's "World News Sunday" with Forrest Sawyer.

The Festival Trips of the '70s

No one in the 20th century took more groups of Sacred Harp singers to more audiences than Hugh McGraw. I was along for the ride on three memorable performance trips with Hugh and others – two to Washington, D.C., for the Smithsonian Institution's Festival of American Folklife for five days each time in the summers of 1970 and 1976, and one to Montreal for the Man and His World Exposition for a week in the summer of 1971.

The first Festival experience sprang from an idea conceived by Ralph Rinzler and Texan Joe Dan Boyd, who had studied and written of the Sacred Harp tradition among African Americans in what's known as "the Wiregrass area" of southeastern Alabama (for the distinctively wiry clumps of grass that grow on the sandy plains there). Their notion was to bring two Sacred Harp groups – one white, one black – to share elements of their tradition with the crowds that frequented the great stretches of the National Mall during Festival week. Each group was to conduct a sort of mini-singing school, with a quick pass through some of the songbook's rudiments. Any audience milling about at the time would be encouraged to try out a few scale-running exercises, with *fa-sol-la's*, and then to join in on singing one or more of the better-known hymns: Amazing Grace, Wondrous Love, The Promised Land.

Hugh's group had four singers from Georgia (himself, Raymond Hamrick, Charlene Wallace and me) and eight from Alabama (Ruth Denson Edwards, Elmer Kitchens, Palmer Godsey, Toney Smith, Walter and Nora Parker and sisters Pernie Pelfrey and Ora Lee Fannin). (When we first arrived, a grinning 20-something Festival staffer told me how eager she and others had been to greet these people with such interesting Southern names! – my own maybe, but she at least mentioned those of Palmer Godsey and Pernie Pelfrey.) Bystanders, as we sang, would have noticed a wide range of ages, with me the youngest at 26,

Ruth and Palmer in their 70s and Walter at 80. (His was a young 80, though; Walter played golf into his 90s and lived to be 100.)

Hugh McGraw (front) with his group at the 1970 Festival of American Folklife. From left: Buell, Nora Parker, Ora Lee Fannin, Ruth Denson Edwards, Elmer Kitchens, Pernie Pelfrey, Charlene Wallace, Palmer Godsey, Toney Smith, Walter Parker; not pictured, Raymond Hamrick. (Photo by Joe Dan Boyd)

During my time at Auburn, I had sung a couple of times with members of the Wiregrass group, including their leader, the great Dewey Williams. But for the rest of our group, this was a first; and for most, it was a watershed experience. The differences in singing style between the two groups were immediately noticeable. Our group offered the straight-toned, no-frills, directly delivered version of Sacred Harp we were used to hearing back in Georgia and Alabama (though normally in the company of many more voices and usually in walled-in spaces that contained and magnified the sound rather than out in open air). The singing from Dewey's troupe was, I can say, more crowd-pleasing. It had swing to it, heavier vibrato, a bouncier beat, and, from their wide-smiling leader, decorative grace-note flourishes around the edges. (One of their staples – the Cooper book's I'M WANDERING TO AND FRO – also has to qualify as maybe the catchiest, most easily accessible number in any of the Sacred Harp books.) In his teaching remarks, Hugh was masterly, but Dewey was a charmer.

At the National Mall: Hugh was masterly, but Dewey was a charmer. Seated behind Hugh, Raymond Hamrick; standing behind Dewey, Alice Williams. (Photo by Joe Dan Boyd)

Considering persistent segregation throughout our region in that era, the convening of our two bands represented an important cultural encounter and exchange. It was as if two singing nations had been brought together, side by side. We rode the bus together between our lodging place and the Festival grounds, and in our off hours met and sang together. (The sound in the resonant rooms of our evening songfests remains a cherished memory. Dewey's heavily accented, staccato lead on the old gospel classic FARTHER ALONG remains at the top of my list.) Lifelong friendships were formed there.

Joe Dan Boyd, documenting and photographing the sessions each day, wrote this note, which includes a quote cast in language more typical of that era than of ours today:

Admiration had replaced aloofness by the third day. Then, during a shuttle run, Alabama white Sacred Harper Elmer Kitchens said to me, "It's the Negroes who are making this go, not us. We sing it so straight it nearly breaks, but you've got to mix a little of the rock and roll, and give the people what they like. When we first came up here, we kinda turned up our noses at Dewey, but now we're kinda taking off our hats to him. We talk about having the Spirit with Sacred Harp: Well, he has it."[11]

Yes, Dewey indeed had it. And for all their spirit, he and his group admired the greater technical facility and mastery of hundreds of songs by the members of our group. So after initial reserve or doubt, there was mutual admiration all around.

Let me draw up one little image, a special moment from our time together that first week in July of 1970. Ruth Denson Edwards, a reigning presence in our group, came from the most famous Sacred Harp family of the 20th century. Dewey Williams was the central figure, the unquestioned leader, of the singing in his area. He was 72; she that week turned 77. Now, the heat of those July afternoons was draining, nearly stultifying. For the very young and the elderly (visitors and performers alike), the hour or so after noon each day would have been conducive for a nap. And so it happened that on one of the afternoons, Hugh's big Oldsmobile, parked curbside close by the performance stage and slightly shaded by the trees, provided a convenient opportunity. With the car windows down and both doors open on the curb side, Ruth, probably with encouragement from Hugh, had stretched herself out on the backseat of the car to rest; Dewey, after carefully angling his long frame under the steering wheel, did the same in the front seat. In a time of racial and cultural turmoil in the U.S., I don't believe there could have been, along that heavily trafficked, noisily chatted stretch of ground, a better, a quieter picture of peace and harmony than this one of the two unlikely companions from small-town Alabama dozing in the leafy afternoon, their feet hanging out the car's open doors.

With Miss Ruth, sharing the music we loved. (Photo by Joe Dan Boyd)

My Weeping Eyes

It was not always so quiet thereabouts, though; and things were about to heat up considerably. On July 4th, a great crowd gathered before the Lincoln Memorial to hear a plea for national unity by evangelist Billy Graham. Protesters against the Vietnam War were there in numbers to demonstrate. Police were skittish. Skirmishes broke out, and suddenly tear gas was flooding everywhere. The panicked crowd began to flee. In all the confusion, and separated from the rest of our company, Toney Smith and I were somehow caught in the undertow. Our eyes stinging and watering from the gas, we made a dash for the Smithsonian, where our two groups had been given a gathering place.

We, though, weren't the only ones to see the Smithsonian as sanctuary. People running ahead of us had already pushed through the entrance, and many more were rushing behind. As Toney and I reached the main doors, the guards inside just managed to lock them – in our faces, and despite our pleas. We were then pushed up hard against the entrance by the surging group behind. It was a scary few moments before we could extricate ourselves, as the throng behind us began to peel off and run elsewhere.

The rest is a blur to me now – it was something of a blur then – but Toney seems to remember that the two us, further on down the complex, gained access to a corridor which led to our reserved chamber, where we could reunite with our companions and reflect on our relief.

Under the Dome

Between the two Festival appearances was another trip coordinated by the Smithsonian: the Man and His World Expo in Montreal in 1971. Two Sacred Harp groups were again invited to perform, this time under the umbrella theme of "Music from the Southern Mountains": a quartet from Georgia (Hugh, Charlene Wallace, Dan Brittain and me) and a foursome of the Wiregrass singers (Dewey Williams, his daughter Bernice Harvey, H.J. (Japheth) Jackson and his sister Dovie Reese). The venue was spectacular: a lofty perch in

Buckminster Fuller's famous geodesic dome. Our groups alternated performances each day with Roy Acuff, the Grand Ole Opry's "King of Country Music," and his Smoky Mountain Boys. (The ratio of those who knew the name Roy Acuff to those who recognized "Sacred Harp" would probably have been in the neighborhood of 1000-to-1.)

One of my pleasures with that experience was seeing at close hand the immediate and joking relationship between Roy, Dewey and Hugh. Roy and his band members were familiar with shape-note hymnody, and Roy not only respected Hugh and Dewey for their roles in the tradition but seemed to genuinely enjoy their company. The three of them typically hung out together between performances.

Almost exactly one year before our Montreal trip, having read in an Atlanta paper about an upcoming session of the Chattahoochee Convention, Dan Brittain had shown up at the event for his first-ever Sacred Harp experience. It was love at first hearing. With the U.S. Army Bands at the time, Dan was stationed for three years at Fort McPherson, just southwest of Atlanta. He was not only a facile sight-reader; he was one of those people who immediately "got" Sacred Harp, almost instantly appreciating its nuances, its rural roots, its democratic flavor. In no time, Dan was driving to singings in western Georgia and Alabama, helping to man the bass part and, at smaller singings where it was needed, giving the pitches for the music. We were often together on those trips and spent many hours singing and talking about Sacred Harp. (With his background in music and new knowledge of Sacred Harp, Dan was also an invaluable consultant as I was putting together my first book.) A gifted composer, Dan wrote a number of shape-note songs, four of which were ultimately included in the songbook's 1991 edition. Japheth Jackson, amazed at Dan's mastery of Sacred Harp by the time of our performances in Montreal, proclaimed him Rookie of the Year!

If for each of us the Montreal trip was a venture well beyond our normal sphere, it must have been for Dewey, an essentially uneducated 73-year-old black man from Ozark, Ala., and for his companions, a daunting experience. One little detail from that time lodged in my memory. Neither Bernice nor Dovie had a travel iron, and so, until

Charlene discovered the fact and loaned them hers, they had resorted to what may have been in many places around the world a time-honored practice for pressing wrinkled clothing: They spread their dresses out tightly between the mattress and box springs each night and slept on them. Each day, to me, they looked crisply attired enough to face the gawking tourists who rode up and down the airy escalators of the dome and in many cases stopped by to hear us sing.

Hugh sent Joe Dan Boyd a report that included the following description:

> The response from the crowd was wonderful. There were people from all over the world. The people like fast, peppy music best. They would get in the swing with you, clapping and rocking while you sing. After each performance, we would stay around and sign autographs, have pictures made and show them our books. At our last performance, we sang "Parting Hand," and I told them the traditional reason we close with it. The people had tears in their eyes as we closed. They hugged us and bid us farewell.[12]

Woottens and Watersons

The Festival trip of 1976 was maybe less eventful overall than the first one, but it did allow me to spend good time with two of the senior members of one of the great Sacred Harp singing families, the Woottens from the small northeastern Alabama town of Ider. Hugh had become acquainted with the clan in 1973 when he taught a singing school at their home church, Antioch Baptist. Soon after his return to Georgia with word of the singing prowess of this large extended family, several in our local community joined him in traveling to Ider to sing with the Woottens, their cousins and friends.

Somewhat like the Lee family of south Georgia (depicted in a later chapter), the Woottens had for several decades remained fairly isolated from the broader singing community. The older generation when we first got to know them – five brothers and two sisters – had grown up singing together almost every day of their lives. In an interview for Alan Lomax's "American Patchwork" series, which aired on public television in 1990, Chester (or as everyone called him, Check) Wootten described their upbringing in this way: "We grew up during the Panic, had a hard time living at home. But we would work hard in the field. We'd come in at night, why, we'd all get out on the porch after we eat supper. My daddy would start singing. Then we'd start joining in, and we'd sing till bedtime. A lot of time, we'd sing till our neighbors would drive in and help us. We'd have a singing before we went to bed." Their voices, gravitating toward a common sound, made a remarkable blend. With Postell and Mack on bass; Check, Carnice and Gertha on tenor; Olivia on alto and Freeman (and sometimes Carnice) on treble, they already had a full and balanced class. Now with children and grandchildren – all of whom, it seemed, could sing well – they had little need of outside help to create powerful singing.

Gertha and Olivia were gracious presences, but I was better acquainted with the five brothers. Carnice was an outstanding singer, a successful farmer-businessman and a father of three sons, who were themselves fine singers. Postell, a preacher, was earnest and unassuming, the humblest of men. Mack was one of the most charismatic and outgoing people I've known in Sacred Harp ("Hey there, good-lookin'!" he would say to a singing acquaintance and envelope the other's palm in his); no one within the sphere of his sweeping vision remained a stranger. Freeman, the one I sang closest to for years, was similarly friendly; through his carpentry work, he had traveled the most extensively and knew the most about the world outside their home community. Check, the eldest, was shyer than the others and, at singing events even at their home church, always more reserved. Within the family, though, he was always the singing leader.

When Hugh was putting together an ensemble for the 1976 Festival, adding at least a couple of the senior Wootten brothers must have seemed an obvious choice. So Freeman joined me on treble that week; Check was our pivotal lead. Hugh considered Check "the best tenor" singer he had ever heard, and, though I've sung with many brilliant tenors over the decades, I wouldn't disagree with that assessment. (If, by the way, Check's daughter, Syble Adams, is not the best Sacred Harp alto of our time, I don't know who it would be.) Check had great range, power, beauty of tone, a wonderfully ornamented singing style - and a lifetime of experience in honing those qualities to the highest level. The two Wootten brothers and I swapped yarns and did a lot of laughing that week, but a long, contemplative walk Check and I made to and around the beautiful Jefferson Memorial cemented a friendship that lasted until his death in 1988. From our earliest acquaintance and over many years, I don't believe that Freeman and I ever sat separate from one another at any of the singings we both attended.

From members of one gifted family of singers with exquisitely blended sound, I was about to walk up on members of another. Ambling through the Festival grounds one afternoon, I came upon a tented area, clearly a premier venue, with a good-sized crowd seated beneath the canvas top. Up front was a youthful quartet, two women and two men. The signage by the tent identified them as the Watersons from Yorkshire, England, a family group I would soon come to know as arguably the foremost British folk band of the '60s and '70s: sisters Lal and Norma, brother Mike Waterson and Norma's husband, Martin Carthy, probably the leading folk singer of the U.K. at that time.

I was immediately struck by what I heard: a warm, rich, darkly resonant sound. The experience of that moment was like expecting, say, a sip of tea and receiving instead a shot of liqueur. The unusual beauty of the quartet's singing, with their distinctive intonation and broad Yorkshire accents, I found beguiling. And their plaintive, yearning sound, mainly a cappella, inevitably made me think of, well, what else but Sacred Harp?

After the performance was over, I made my way up and introduced myself. Had they by chance ever heard of something called Sacred Harp? Well, only partly, and in an oblique way - from two 1920s cuts they had admired on a Smithsonian Folkways compilation: ROCKY ROAD and

PRESENT JOYS, sung by a group called "Alabama Sacred Harp Singers." They had heard, on those recordings, the singing of *fa-sol-la's*, but, as I recall, didn't know what that was all about. "Sacred Harp," then, was for them just some disembodied term, almost a throw-away. . . . As we talked, they seemed intrigued to hear that a full body of music beyond those two tunes lay out there before them.

I will step outside my story of the Watersons momentarily to borrow a Socratic metaphor. Beyond the enjoyment of singing and hearing Sacred Harp over the years, one of my great satisfactions has been what I've called a kind of midwifery – Sacred Harp midwifery. Having given birth to my own love of the music – from Mike Hinton's lending me two record albums all those years ago – I have taken pleasure many times in helping deliver someone else's discovery. I found out long ago that I can't make people in general love Sacred Harp as I do, but I have reveled in attending, even easing, the birth of someone else's fresh-spanked, bawling love of it.

And so it was in this case. My new acquaintances and I agreed to meet up again that evening. A couple of hours later I appeared with my songbook and another as a gift for them. For an hour or so, I led them on a spirited tour of landmark tunes, songs I thought would resonate with them, minor pieces especially: DAVID'S LAMENTATION, IDUMEA, THE MORNING TRUMPET, WINDHAM and so on. With excitement, the foursome welcomed, and conquered, each new tune. Norma and Lal seemed particularly smitten with the unfolding tuneful revelations and sense of the whole.

Then as we were about to say our goodbyes, one of the group mentioned regretfully that, as engaging as they found this music, they would not be able to perform it; they had made a commitment to sing only the native music of their region. This was crushing news: animated converts locked away at the start from something that seemed such a natural for them! We parted then, knowing it to be unlikely that our paths would cross again.

A postscript to this story is that in December of 1979 when I was in Vermont for a Sacred Harp workshop, my host, Tony Barrand, brought around a CD he wondered if I might have heard: something called *Sound, Sound Your Instruments of Joy* – by "the Watersons." Sitting close by Tony's wood-burning stove on that frigid evening, I was amazed to hear those unforgettable voices on four of the very tunes that, just over three years before, we had scampered through – as well as two numbers they had found on their own, GREEN FIELDS and CHRISTIAN'S HOPE. Their versions in each instance were not in the standard framework of four-part harmony – and no one in any case would have mistaken their sound for that of a traditional Sacred Harp band. Instead, each rendition was in the Watersons' distinctive style: part unison of voices and part improvised harmony filigreed around the strong melody. So in the year after I had met them, as they were considering a new recording, Sacred Harp must have worked on them, undermining a noble but maybe untenable commitment. . . .

When Mike Waterson died in 2011 (Lal had died in 1998), his obituary in *The Guardian* included this note about the group: "Their appearance at the American bicentennial celebrations the following year, where they heard a variety of religious music, inspired them to record an album of such songs, Sound, Sound Your Instruments of Joy (1977)."

Knowing I had played a part in this gift from our country to theirs – through the group the *New York Times* once called "the royal family of British folk music" – pleased and pleases me. In more recent years, I heard from two singers, one from Denmark and one from the U.K., lured to Sacred Harp by way of that remarkable Watersons recording. So the giving, the birthing, I'm proud to say, has continued.

∽ॐ∾

Of the various performance sites Hugh McGraw led groups to over the years, one more might catch a reader's eye: When I was still living in Georgia, a clutch of us were invited to St. Peter's church in

Rome to sing and share information about our singing tradition. And so we did. I wouldn't say we were awed by our surroundings or were particularly inspired or inspiring in our singing that spring day, but, yes, we were indeed there: St. Peter's Episcopal, Rome, Georgia.

Miss Ruth, in the only photo taken by the author.

7

Miss Ruth

Ruth Denson Edwards (1893-1978)

The lines she penned around 1970 seemed even then to have come from an earlier time:

> *Perhaps it will not be out of place for this writer to make a few observations on the subject of music, the greatest art and science to attract the attention of mankind since the advent of the human family into the world.*
>
> *Music is a God-given faculty that by sounding its melody and harmony opens the doors to human hearts and souls and brings man back to his first relationship with God. It is the sweet union which keeps man in close relation with the hearts of men while they live in the world and which will strike the sweet chords in that spirit land where mortality does not enter and where spiritual songs are sung throughout Eternal Ages.*

These passages are from the short essay "Music," written for the opening pages of the 1971 Denson Revision and carried still in the current edition of the songbook. For many singers who were never in her presence, the words she wrote may be the face of Ruth Denson Edwards.

The flowing cadences, the antique beauty of her phrasing in that piece seem to me the pure distillation of a lifetime of thought on this topic and on the special gift of Sacred Harp, the phenomenon she proudly called "Our American Heritage" in cover notes for each of the first five record albums of the Sacred Harp Publishing Company.

That was not the face of Ruth Denson Edwards I knew from my youth, though. It was not her *writings* or the several *songs* with her name on them, or her position of eminence and authority in the Sacred Harp community, that framed my early view of her. No, what I saw - at some distance - was something of a local curiosity, almost a relic from an earlier time. A longtime primary school teacher, she looked the part of the stereotypical spinster schoolmarm of the 19th or early 20th century and seemed to me an eccentric figure.

My view would not have been the view of everyone. To adults in Cullman, Miss Ruth was a venerable presence, almost an institution. It seemed she had taught everyone in town, or their parents (as she had taught my father, back in the '20s). She was like the mother of one's village, if not one's country, and an oxymoron: the childless matriarch.

It was in the barbershop of all places that I first remember seeing Miss Ruth up close in my early years. I had not been introduced to her, my family didn't encounter her at church or at the grocery store, and we didn't attend singings. At some point, though, I knew who she was, knew her name, and knew that she taught at East Elementary, the other elementary school across town.

While in the barber's chair, or waiting to be called there, I would see the door open, and in would stride this rather tall (as it seemed to me then), slender woman of a certain age. She may have had to sit and wait a few minutes, but I only recall her walking purposefully to the chair of a particular barber each time and having him quickly do the cutting. She wore her auburn hair always smoothed down. Parted off-center, it hugged the sides of her face in deep and uniform waves.

Seated in the chair, putting her plain, high-top, lace-up shoes on the footrest, she would lean her head forward and downward – Marie Antoinette at the guillotine – and bare her neck to the scissors. With her head thus extended forward, the barber was able to sheer off the locks just below the breaking point between head and neck. The effect was to leave the hairdo hanging at about ears' length. It seemed to me her hair then framed her countenance the way the ears of a setter or spaniel do its face. The little episode seemed to take just seconds: a firm, business-like whacking, with the gray-reddish strands tossed aside, and she would be on her way. I can almost see her opening a change purse, small as her palm, to award the craftsman his due.

Could any of this have been less a nod to the world of fashion? In that regard, she might as well have gone to a farrier to be shod. The whole image of her entering a man's world unembarrassedly, striding to the chair, having her hair lopped off and left as is – well, Miss Ruth, it seemed clear, lived by rules and customs that were higher and straighter, if also more eccentric, than those of society around her. And more than that, any action untoward, even frivolous, seemed beneath her.

That was the Ruth Denson Edwards I observed in my youth, a figure in profile only. When I discovered a love for Sacred Harp and came at last face to face with her, I found a person of graciousness and warmth. Her great welcoming spirit for Sacred Harp newcomers embraced me as it did many others of several generations who came to her for information or insight, or to touch Sacred Harp history, even celebrity.

She lived at Mrs. Myrtie Fisher's boarding house, a large, two-story, white Victorian – The Whitehouse, it was called – facing Cullman's 2nd Avenue West, which also served as U.S. Route 31. From that house, for the better part of 44 years, she walked to school each day or to church or to the department stores just a few blocks away. She was not a housekeeper, and rarely a cook, so the boarding house – and one so centrally located – probably suited her well. (She could no doubt have bought the house with her decades of payment for room and board.) Though I think she probably could have done her own baking from the kitchen there, she instead for years ordered elsewhere a big cake for the Cullman County Convention. For the annual singing at Shady Grove in nearby Winston County, a big pan of chicken and dressing, ordered by her ahead of time, sat steamed and waiting when Hugh McGraw, Charlene Wallace and other Georgia singers swooped by Cullman to pick up Miss Ruth and her special order. These were rituals strictly observed, handsomely paid for, classically finished off.

The Whitehouse
Cullman, Alabama

Ruth's residence for the better part of 44 years. (From the collection of the grandchildren of T.J. and Lola Akers Denson, used with permission)

Her greetings with the young that she knew and had affection for were, as I think of it, maybe old-fashioned in their physical nature. She would grab you by the upper arm tightly and give you a shake. When I would call on her at Miss Myrtie's, she would meet me at the door and, sometimes taking both my wrists in her hands, would lead me almost sideways into the parlor to sit down. She would seat me, pull a chair up close for herself and draw me into the conversation. I can't imagine there being a lull; she was never at a loss for words.

It was a light but penetrating course in Sacred Harp she would lead me through in those sessions – and not from the ordinary rudiments;

anyone could get those by a diligent reading of the songbook's first pages. No, the things she shared were from a seasoned perspective. From that, I can now recall only one specific suggestion. Pick a song for your lesson, she counseled, that not everyone else would lead. At one point, she turned to the song on page 339, WHEN I AM GONE, and said, "This is one you can lead for me when I'm gone."

A faint dusting of snuff showed on her collar or shoulder from time to time when I visited there. We all have our little vices, and in this one Miss Ruth was again old-fashioned. Many respectable ladies of an earlier era, in the countryside at least, were snuff takers. It was never acknowledged between us, but I assume that the nicotine powder, an old habit, provided comfort or pick-me-up for many solitary hours in her room in the big house. I'm somehow pleased at the thought of it now, maybe only as it gives dimension, even vulnerability, to the image of a person who seemed in almost all other ways above common need.

I used the word spinster in the description above, and yet that misrepresents, for Miss Ruth had had a brief early marriage, the details of which I never heard mentioned except in a version her niece Amanda later shared with me. When she discovered that he had been unfaithful to her – a dalliance or more with a girl or young woman – the husband, according to this report, came home at the end of one day and found his bags packed and waiting for him on the porch. Although Hugh never knew the reason for the breakup, he had at least heard the second half of that story. In his phraseology: "She told me when she run him off, she packed his bags and left 'em on the front porch."

It seems to me that in the resoluteness of her action, Ruth Edwards gave an early rendering of her character – and courage: divorce in her place, in the small-town milieu of that time, being highly unusual. I imagine the husband's clothing folded, if hurriedly, and all his personal belongings neatly, firmly, placed together in a still life of broken promises. All the makings for a dignified and shamed departure. And Mrs. Edwards thus returned to this closest approximation of spinsterhood, but with the marriage name and title she would carry always.

She had been given at birth the biblical name Jerusha (or Jarusha;

ironically, said to mean in Hebrew "married, a possession") Henrietta, and was called simply Rush ("Roosh") by family members. She must have found the name encumbering. And as Rush could already have seemed a toddler-talk version of Ruth, she didn't have to reach far to select another biblical name she could wear everywhere more comfortably. (Her nephew Mike's report is that the change was made when she was in school.)

Father, Mother and Family

The undetachable fact of the life of Ruth Denson Edwards, and the one she took greatest pride in, was that she was the daughter of Thomas Jackson Denson (1863-1935), the famous singing-school teacher, songwriter, leader and promoter of Sacred Harp.

The broad profile of T.J. Denson is easy to fill in: from a notable 30-minute lesson he led at the 1878 Chattahoochee Convention (when he was 15) to his founding of the Sacred Harp Publishing Company (1933) and the early work for the Denson revision of the songbook, which appeared in the year following his death. Aside from his compositions (eight in the current edition of the songbook), his legacy was spread over a reputed 25,000 students in at least five states in his more than half a century of teaching. Save for B.F. White himself, who produced the original songbook, no one else in the Sacred Harp world has ever had such an impact.

Earl Thurman, in his 1952 history of the Chattahoochee Musical Convention, summed it up well: "Like all leaders in a cause, Tom Denson had his critics . . . but critics unite with his friends in the unanimous opinion that he was the most dynamic figure that ever trod the Sacred Harp highway. There have been some in the Sacred Harp field who were more profound students of music . . . but in the history of the Sacred Harp there has not appeared the man who could create the inspiration and kindle the mighty flame of enthusiasm like the one and only 'Uncle Tom' Denson."

The Professor, T.J. Denson. (From the collection of the grandchildren of T.J. and Lola Akers Denson, used with permission)

A flowing and animated but always disciplined leading style that Denson taught his charges might be said to have revolutionized leading in Sacred Harp and surely influenced several generations of leaders. How recognizable was and is that style? At the 1998 National Convention, watching 78-year-old Myrl Smith Jones – a singer until then unknown to me but immediately one of the most beautifully stylish leaders I had ever seen – I nudged Judy Hauff sitting next to me on the far side of the front bench of tenor and said, "She went to school to Tom Denson!" At the next break, I hurried to Mrs. Jones to test my hunch. "I have to ask: Did you go to singing-school to Tom Denson?" "Yes!" she said, beaming with the news: "In 1930!" (when Denson made a landmark teaching tour across a broad swath of east and central Texas).

"We loved that man!" Myrl Smith with "Uncle Tom" and, right, Helen "Sunbeam" Smith (no relation to Myrl) at Garden Valley, Texas, 1930. (Photo courtesy of Myrl Smith Jones)

"To lift up with your hand, to pick up the part": Myrl Smith Jones, 81, at the 2001 National Convention. *(Photo courtesy of Myrl Smith Jones)*

At almost 94 at this writing and with memory amazingly sharp, Myrl Jones remembers that singing school at Garden Valley when she was 10 and another taught by Denson in 1933, when she was 13.[13] "We loved that man!" she said. "He taught different from anything we'd ever seen! His renditions were just so different. He turned our singing upside down here in Texas!" Prof. Denson evidently shared that opinion. In late April of 1930, he wrote his brother-in-law Joe Akers from Mineral Wells, Texas: "I shore am having a time out here you can read this clipping & see what we are doing." And with some of the playful personality he was known for: "I have Texas by the tale & a down hill [pull]. I hope that you can get your vacation the first of August & bee here the 8 9 & 10 so we can show these Texas folks that we sing in Ala."

Yes, they could sing in Alabama – and teach. But how and what exactly did he do to achieve that distinctive leading style? "He taught us to direct the music *as it's written*," Myrl said. "To have [without the book] one hand behind us when we went to each of the parts [for their separate entrances]. To lift up with your hand, to pick up the part – just like you were picking something up. He always had us to put one hand, at least the left hand, behind your back. I couldn't do that, though – I had to have both hands out in front of me! It was just so different, though. . . . We had four teachers that continued to teach in his methods, in the same manner, here in Texas – my sister [Myra Palmer] and three of my cousins."[14]

A letter from Denson, from Garden Valley in July of 1930, to the Alabama State Sacred Harp Musical Convention meeting at the courthouse in Birmingham the fourth weekend of that month, and included in the convention's minutes, brings additional perspective to his teaching tours. "My teaching in this new field has so consumed my time that I am unable to attend your present session," he wrote, "but I am with you in spirit. The 'Old Sacred Harp' is spreading all over Texas,– a great State and a great people,– and may this quicken your lives and efforts in our common cause." A second letter read to the convention, from wealthy Dallas businessman W.T. Coston, president of the Texas Interstate Sacred Harp Association and the financial sponsor for much of Denson's work in the state, reinforces the point: "I am glad to report that some progress is being made in Texas in the line of Sacred Harp singing and work. During the Spring just passed, much interest has been manifested in our section of the State among the young people in Sacred Harp music, under the leadership of Prof. T.J. Denson, of Loretto, Tennessee, who will perhaps remain here until the latter part of September."[15]

The professor's confidence in and care for his former students show through in this 1932 letter to Mr. and Mrs. Coston regarding the upcoming Texas Interstate convention (and included in its minutes): "I know that you singers out there will have a good time. I know also that my children can stand their hands with any of them out there, old or young, if they can get a fair chance, and I also know that you will stand behind them at any and all times. I am depending on you to help them put it over."

When Tom Denson died in 1935, just hours before he had planned to go to another singing, grief issued forth across a whole region. His funeral, held the next day, was attended, the local Jasper paper wrote, "by an immense crowd, estimated to number from 2,000 to 3,000."[16] Sacred Harp annals contain many myth-making demonstrations of singers defying the limitations of time and distance in order to join with others in that "common cause." But nothing, to my mind, comes close to what happened on and leading up to that occasion. For a description of Tom Denson's spontaneous "singing funeral" in my earlier book, I was able to speak with more than one participant or observer who had been moved by what had happened that day. It was, necessarily, an outdoor service, with the casket positioned outside, the family seated nearby and floral wreaths banked against the church building there on the outskirts of Double Springs.

News of Denson's death had been broadcast on several radio stations throughout the region, and telephone operators across several states must have found their arms busy plugging in the many calls that spread the word to the hinterlands. Many singers from outside the state had driven all night to be there the next day, lining cars and trucks and wagons up as far as the eye could see. Following the reading of scripture and prayer, the presiding ministers "gave it to the singers," as one observer told me. Uncle Tom Denson, they all knew, had represented everything to their movement. As the president of the Alexander City [Alabama] Sacred Harp Singing Convention would write in tribute in its 1935-36 minutes, "No representative convention of Sacred Harp singers was complete without him." And the assembly that day certainly knew what would be appropriate for them to do. For roughly two hours they sang. Rarely were the great singings of the past conducted outdoors. But did any plain or hillside of shape-note singers ever produce such a sound as that which must have wafted over the Fairview cemetery and beyond that afternoon? I hope those many hundreds, crowded up in mid-September sun, were rewarded for their devotion with at least some cloud cover, a cooling breeze and songs that tapped their sorrow and solidarity.

There was also apparently a memorial singing held early the next month in Jasper. About that event, Wilber E. Morgan of Atlanta wrote Denson's widow, Lola: "We had such a wonderful time Sunday, seems like Heaven and earth just met. Those wonderful songs sung by all those Denson Boys, if we could have had some one to have made the talk that was worthy of his life of influence, that would have painted a picture that would have made the young life of our generation sit up and take notice. I was very glad to have had part in that appreciation service, though I felt that I had followed my blessed Master at such a guilty distant I was not worthy to take part."

Morgan then attached a eulogy, possibly a copy of what he had said or read at the service. In it, he described a "life of service to God and humanity." "He was a man of unusual ability, perhaps somewhat limited in his education," he wrote. Yet: "His presence in a class of singers was a leaven that permeated all of the audience." Prof. Denson, Morgan wrote, "often recalled how his sainted mother and kind old father sang these sacred old songs for him in the tender years of his life. Thousands of people will rise up and call him blessed because of their own musical training. . . . Tom Denson taught the first singing school that I ever attended. He was a young man then, full of life and vigor. The class would do their best to help him sing and he would play games with them during the noon hour."

A portrait of Tom Denson as teacher, then, begins to round into view. But the more intimate soundings from that charismatic figure's life have until now remained beyond us. A crumbling clipping from the *Decatur* [Alabama] *Daily*, in what must have been 1926, brings fresh detail to that life – and does so in Denson's own words. (The article, in several little pieces, was lent me by Denson's grandson Richard Mauldin.) I will let the interview speak for itself, and for the interviewee himself.

"You want to know about the Sacred Harp organization, where it was founded and what is the mission?" said T.J. Denson as he looked straight into the eyes of a Daily reporter seated across the desk from him. Professor Denson is the Lawrenceburg, Tenn., leader of Sacred Harp music who is here for the purpose of leading the North Alabama assemblage of thousands of people on next Saturday and Sunday at the Morgan courthouse in an annual meeting.

"Why sonny, it's going to take some little bit to tell you all about this organization," said the 63 year old leader as he settled back into his chair.

Mr. Denson has been here several weeks, leading singing of the old rural familiar hymns at Primitive Baptist Church, Albany [originally a separate city adjoining Decatur and later subsumed by it] and remaining here to enjoy the "spiritual feast of song and religion" on Saturday and Sunday. J.T. Ryan, Albany chairman, has taken all necessary steps to make the two day session a success and has received unlimited support from the business classes of these cities.

[Denson then walks the reporter through a brief history of the songbook and the organization surrounding it.]

. . . Mr. Denson declared he had been in service since 1882, having taught out of the old book as far back as that date. He has been teaching one to eight schools each year since that time.

Every bit of the music is inspired, said the gnarled teacher in his deep bass voice.

"The old hymns were inspired," said Mr. Denson, "and they reach a tender spot," he said as he touched the bosom of his shirt. "Hit'l get it," he said as he indicated his heart with a tap of his hand on his breast. "You can feel it, instead of through the ear. Why the old book will never die. People have been singing these old songs for over 80 years.

࿐

"Why anybody can join the organization," replied the teacher to the question of membership qualification, "anybody who is spiritually inclined, who is a lover of music["] and is not an habitual swearer or an habitual drunkard. "Just anybody can't get in and sing with us, they have got to be clean folks on the inside."

"I've been at this singing since 1876. I've walked 15 miles to get to one of these singings, carried my Sunday shoes under my arm, not many boys could do that today.

"I can remember when I use to study by the light of pine knots when I used to lie before the fire and study the music in my own way." The old gentleman's eyes filled for the moment as he spoke of his mother. "Mother used to mould candles together that I might see how to study this work, you see they had been in the work before me, dad had two brothers who led the singings."

࿐

"I'm just serving the Lord the best I know how, I like the modern book, but the Sacred Harp book is the best. Music will never be revealed to us til we reach the glory world."

In 1878, when he was only 15, T.J. had married 17-year-old Amanda Burdette, sister of his brother Seaborn's wife, Sidney. Ruth would then be the sixth of seven children her mother brought into the world. After two children died in infancy in 1879 and 1880, while the family lived in Arbacoochee in Cleburne County, Paine was born in 1882, Anna Eugenia ("Annie") in 1885 and Margaret Frances ("Maggie") in 1887. Ruth was born in 1893 and then Howard Burdette in 1897. T.J. and Amanda also raised Amanda's nephew William Thomas ("Pansy" or "Pan") Mitchell from the age of two when both his parents, Amanda's sister Ida and her husband, along with grandfather William Howard Burdette, died, all apparently of typhoid fever.[17]

After Amanda died in 1910, Tom married the just-older sister of the young man who would become one of his sons-in-law, Marcus Cagle. That ill-fated marriage was brief. Tom's subsequent marriage to Lola Akers, after Ruth was already grown, gave Ruth and the others three half-sisters. I would know them later – the only siblings of Ruth's I would have the chance to meet – as Vera Nunn, Violet Hinton and Tommye Mauldin, lovely spirits all.

Ruth would lose her mother when she was 17 – and very likely away at school. Mike Hinton shared with me a letter from Amanda to Ruth, dated only "Mon 9th," that may have come in one of the last winters or early springs of the mother's life. Like so many letters surviving from that era, it presents a challenge to the reader or transcriber. Here, a bit disjointed and scant of punctuation as well as of a good many initial caps, is an abbreviated version of my attempt at deciphering Amanda's letter, from more than 100 years ago (the only one known to exist and, though written in graceful hand, now so faint on the creased pages that it's almost gone):

Well Rush I have thought I would answer your letter that we received last Friday was a week ago. We thought then that we would come over there last Wednesday the 4th but it was to damp you know the damp weather hurts my lungs worse than freezing. After it faired up your Pa was gone and it was to late then. Thursday I would not go because we have had to started back Saturday I would not go to stay that little while. We are

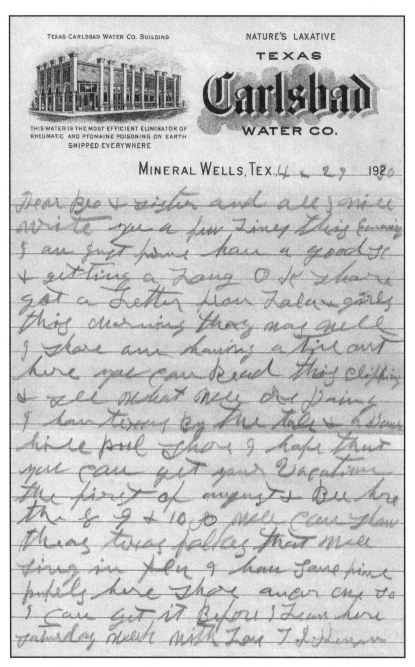

Tom Denson's letter writing: *"Now it's up to them to read it!"* (From the collection of the grandchildren of T.J. and Lola Akers Denson, used with permission)

coming before long . . . . I hope this will find you well and enjoying your self well satisfiede and learning fast The school went out here Friday . . . . I wish I could see you I missed worse yesterday than I ever have since you been gone but I want you to learn all you can from your books I want you to learn what I can't learn you I can learn you to cook and wash and scour and iron and keep house and sew all you can get to make she says two lessons a day one in the bible every morning and some time through the day in some one of her books you must write to bob he looks for a letter every mail You told Annie you had a new brown silk waist you get you a skirt to sew at night . . . . I will get a [fine?] dress of this goods you know a skirt of this would not suit a brown waist . . . . write soon and a long letter to your loving mother Amanda Denson

A greater challenge than representing that ghosted letter is deciphering some of those from "the Prof," T.J. himself, three of which I have been given copies of – and at first, in each case, almost despaired of reading. He may at least have had some sense of that challenge: Mike told me his Aunt Ruth once said that her father, slipping a just-finished letter into an envelope, had said, "There, I wrote it. It's up to them to read it!"

In an unforgettable memorial lesson in 1972, related in my earlier book, Miss Ruth had quoted her father using the word "Babe" in speaking to her ("Babe, there'll come a time when you'll think that's the sweetest lesson of all.") Denson was said to have used the term almost universally in addressing his female students (as he did "Son," in speaking to the boys and men, of whatever age). A letter to Ruth (again courtesy of Richard Mauldin), written in Loretto, Tenn., in December of 1923, lets us see more of the father's affectionate term. Solicitude on behalf of the reader – and on behalf of the letter-writing reputation of a peerless teacher – has me correcting the spelling and providing punctuation:

Dear Rush, I will write you a few lines this morning. They are all busy & can't write. But I can sure ["shore"]. We are all well

& looking for the time to come when my old Babe will come. Now it ain't long sure. We will have [?] to eat & butter to share & sweet milk & [?] nuts to eat & we will have a good time there talking & eating. We got the box sure O.K. When is Paine going to send them other things? You have them sent & I will pay the bill when you come to see us. I don't guess Paine has got the money to send them. [Financial difficulties seem to have been a theme throughout Paine's life!] What is the use of waiting so long about it? I would send the money to send them but don't know who to send it to tend to that. Now Rush, I can't write much. I am in a hurry. Write us & tell us when to meet you at St. Joseph [Tenn.] & I will [be] standing right there when the train gets there to meet my old big Babe. Answer soon. With *Love* [this word stretching halfway across the little page] T J Denson

To have grown up as (at that time) the youngest daughter, the "old big Babe," of Thomas Jackson Denson must have been an extraordinary gift – and responsibility. The rest of her life would show that, as tireless keeper of the flame, Ruth was up to the challenge.

Another letter – amply punctuated and perfectly spelled – that Ruth wrote to her younger brother in 1931 gives a glimpse into early life in the Denson household: a special occasion when Ruth herself was only four.

Dear Howard,

Thirty-four years ago today, I spent the day at Uncle William Denson's. Late in the afternoon Pan came after me on Old Selim. I rode home in front of him.

On the way he told me that Dr. Freeman had <u>that day</u>, brought us a little baby brother.

I could hardly wait to get home to see "it." Surely enough, there it was! A little red-faced, wriggling thing, oh, so tiny!

Grandma Dunnegan was there. She and Dad-Thomas showed me the "valise" that Dr. Freeman brought the baby in. An old black patent-leathery-oil-clothy-looking thing. Dr. Freeman left the "valise" there.

I was glad Dr. Freeman brought us that little baby brother, I'm still glad.

I loved the little brother, then. I love him, now, but my love has increased with the years.

"You" are that baby brother, and I wish you "a Happy Birthday"!

Your sister
Rush

With one hand behind the back, the three Denson-Burdette sisters: (from left) Annie, Ruth and Maggie. (From the collection of the grandchildren of T.J. and Lola Akers Denson, used with permission)

Ever thoughtful, the tireless keeper of the flame. (From the collection of the grandchildren of T.J. and Lola Akers Denson, used with permission)

Ruth grew up going to singings with family in Cullman, Winston and Walker counties and loved that best of all. As well as relishing the music and the company, their family heritage, she and her siblings jostled with each other in securing a place for themselves in this adult-heavy phenomenon. Once as children, while riding to a singing, Ruth and her sisters had been singing tunes from memory – according to a story she related many years later from the square. STRATFIELD was attempted and then interrupted, she said, as Annie and Maggie disputed whether the treble or the alto was next up after the tenor entrance in the chorus. With a book opened to see who would prevail, they laughingly discovered that the two parts entered together. In another scene, Paine and Annie, the two older siblings, were arguing over who was the better leader. Future attorney Paine may not often have been bested in an argument, but Annie, it seems, finished this one off with a claim lifted by a useful distinction: "I can't beat Paw, but I can beat *you*."

In those early years, treble was Ruth's favored part. At least at a point, though, alto better suited her voice, and so that's where she made her presence around the square when I knew her – but close to the treble always if possible.

The School Years

A graduate of Cullman High School, Ruth attended Livingston State Teachers College and began teaching in the Cullman County school system before completing her degree. After six years in the county system, she began a 40-year teaching stint in the City of Cullman school program. She completed her two-year teaching degree at Jacksonville State Normal School in Jacksonville, Ala., in 1929, reportedly as valedictorian of her class. (There Archery, her choice for a required class in Physical Education, proved the toughest obstacle. The thought of her drawing bow and arrow to focus on distant target is stirring.) She would ultimately obtain her bachelor's degree at George Peabody College for Teachers in Nashville.

As she was to tell me later, the compact she made with the school authorities in the City of Cullman had an unwritten clause with a sting in it. Founded by German colonists in the 1870s, Cullman in the early 20th century still had an unusually large Catholic and Lutheran population, but also had by then far more Baptists and Methodists, as well as a good many representatives of the smaller denominations. And, as in most other Alabama communities, the power structure in the city was mainly constituted of leading citizens from the two major protestant churches. According to Miss Ruth, it was the Methodists who held sway in terms of school appointments. And it was made clear to her in being hired to teach in the city system that she would be expected to conduct Sunday School lessons on a regular basis at the downtown Methodist church, where she would also serve as member of the choir (ah, that old church-and-state thing. . .).

So for the better part of her adult life, she was consigned to staying home on weekends and doing her church duty. She was free on Saturdays, of course, but didn't drive and was only occasionally able to accompany family members to two- and three-day singings and conventions out of the area. There were doubtless gratifications with this service, even occasionally transcendent ones. But tending a different vineyard on many occasions would have been her choice. Much later, she would tell a reporter from the *Atlanta Journal and Constitution Magazine* (1972), "I serve the Lord in song more than I do in church. I expect to be buried from a Sacred Harp singing."[18]

During those years, I suspect she simply fulfilled her duty rather than complain about it to fellow teachers or church members. She let me know, though, that she was made captive by this arrangement and resented it. When she at last retired from teaching, she was free – and felt herself free. Free, in fact, to attend the Chattahoochee Convention in Georgia every year, the one dear to her because her mother had attended it when Ruth herself was an infant, an arrangement made possible because the family was able to find a wet nurse for her to stay with in the area while mother joined father at the big singing.

Phillip Denson Aaron, grandson of Annie Denson Aaron and great-nephew of Miss Ruth, once told me a little anecdote from his youth about a visit with her that, in the eyes of a child, captured something about her, a flow of action somehow writ larger than the immediate scene. His family in Addison in nearby Winston County, Phillip said, would sometimes drive over to Cullman, and when they did, would almost always go by to see Aunt Rush. She would meet them on the porch of the Whitehouse and either visit with them there, one or more of them sitting in the swing, or they would go to the car and sit.

On this occasion, Phillip had asked his mother on the drive over if they could go by Yost's department store in downtown Cullman to get candy from the tempting array in the glass bins there. When they met up with Aunt Rush, she suggested a ride over to a park. Once they were parked in the shade and were talking, Miss Ruth, knowing children as she did and having taken account of the day's needs ahead of time, took out a little bag of candy to hand to Phillip. But he said, "I don't need any candy *now. . . ,*" by which he hoped to convey to his mother that he preferred instead to go to the store to pick out his own. As he watched, Aunt Rush, with one swift movement that bespoke finality, and without dropping a word in her train of conversation, popped the candy back into her purse and closed it. It was the smallest of actions to be remembered over so many years, but in such details can inhere if not character exactly then a typifying behavior, the aspect of personality and will.

Rules were rules in Miss Ruth's world, and always for a reason. No one who knew her would be surprised to hear, for example, that she believed speed limits should be plainly obeyed. Mike recalls a duty that he and Richard often had to render: picking up Miss Ruth to bring her to the town of Jasper for family gatherings. "When we 'boys' were old enough to drive," he said, "we would laugh about who 'had to go get Aunt Ruth.' She watched the speedometer and if you got one mile over the speed limit, she delivered a swift slap to the driver's leg along with a verbal reprimand!"

Ruth never saw a need for speed in the songs she led and equally failed to appreciate such out on the roadways. Along with her nephews' renditions, we have her own words on the subject. In what could be a letter to Paine or to sometime-brother-in-law Marcus Cagle in the mid-'40s (the recipient is addressed there as Gustus; nicknames for family members and close friends were standard practice for her), she mentions riding home from a Sacred Harp event with an "Ivy" (probably Ivy Hendrix, a friend of the family from Anderson, Ala.): "Yes, Ivy & I made the trip home in short order. Too short to suit me. He started out at 60 miles per but I objected & he let me set the rate of speed. I set it at 40."

Well, Ivy, as we see, didn't get a pass, but Hugh McGraw, who arrived on the Sacred Harp scene a decade later, always did. To Ruth, Hugh must have seemed a gift from heaven. Here was someone, with Sacred Harp pedigree, who had mastered the music as thoroughly as anyone around and who, along with his extraordinary musical talents, brought strong and innovative leadership to the publishing company her father had founded and to the cause it served. In her view, it seemed, he could do no wrong.

In the years of their devoted friendship – Hugh was known to have phoned her virtually every week for decades right up to her death – Ruth was often a passenger in his comfortable sedan. Hugh's vehicles always ate up the miles with ease, and as this twosome and their companions rode, talking and laughing, I'm guessing Miss Ruth avoided so much as a glance at the driver's panel.

The Old Hoop

A tussle surely playing out in many replications over the decades was the tug of war and wills between a school mistress and her young male charges: the teacher trying to effect progress, to maintain discipline and academic rigor, with the school boys often more intent on expressing their individual liberties. (At that age, girls were collectively, we can no doubt agree, more compliant and studious; Becky Thatcher vs. Tom Sawyer?) If in this contest the teacher had the incumbent advantages of authority, higher access to parents, and manifestations of corporal punishment – with switch, ruler, paddle or practiced hand – mischievous boys did find some compensation. There was the retaliatory satisfaction of branding the teacher, among themselves at least, as "that old battle-axe" or the phrase's innumerable local variations.

Miss Ruth, I would guess, could sniff out trickery as easily as the next teacher, could readily spot a rebellious youngster at the classroom's edge or down a long and narrow hallway. But that didn't keep the groundlings from assigning her a name that brought pleasure to the users by the sheer iteration of it. "The Old Hoop" came to be the code name for Mrs. Edwards. However it came to be associated with her, the term has a comically derogatory ring, a sense somehow of the hopelessly old-fashioned figure she no doubt appeared to those who chafed under her close supervision, many of whom would come in time to appreciate the discipline she enforced and the lessons, and life lessons, she taught them.

And so The Old Hoop it was. But Miss Ruth didn't know that. Didn't know it at least until her hearing was, in later years and right miraculously so, surgically improved. Like her sister Annie, Ruth had a congenital hearing limitation that worsened over time, and she wore hearing aids for years. Then a renowned surgeon in Memphis performed a procedure on one ear that gave her new dimensions of sound. A similar procedure on the other ear furthered the gain. As Mike recalls, his Aunt Ruth was elated to experience sounds that had been denied her up until then: setting her alarm clock in the early morning hours, for example, so she could hear the birds chirp and sing outside her window. The school boys, though, failed to know she now had gained an extrasensory power, and so it was that she discovered her nickname from one of the careless. Per the report, she, upon discovering it, "cleaned his clock."

For most of those years, she taught the fourth grade, that pivotal time when children have more noticeably begun, in mind and body, to stretch into young people, and when the academic disciplines seem to come hurtling at them. When Mike asked his Aunt Ruth why she always taught the fourth grade, why she didn't request a change of pace and scenery, she replied, "Well, I didn't want to." And then, cupping her hands: "I *wanted* to teach them, to mold them and *make* something out of them."

The payback came not just in the molding experience itself but in its sometimes long afterglow: the cards she received from former students now spread all over the country or beyond; the parents who, having been taught by her, now made special arrangements to have their own children placed at the school where she taught, even when that required extra miles of driving for them. Former students, now parents, would ask what she needed, and she would tell them. At least two parent-made classroom tables were fashioned for her (one, inscribed for her underneath, is still in the family's possession).

An uncle of one of my uncles told his family about returning to the area to call on Mrs. Edwards about 50 years from the time he had sat in her classroom. Answering the door bell, she saw him and immediately said, "Wait a minute. . . . Now don't tell me. . . ." With her lead finger now brought up against her face, she studied him for a moment and then, brushing away the years, retrieved the memory: "Gilbert Kennerly."

The point is not an elderly figure's remarkable memory or a former student's unforgettable face: it is that Mrs. Edwards, in a way that would draw admiration and gratitude from her charges for decades afterwards, elicited or, where necessary, *forced* an engagement with almost every student, a bridge by which knowledge was imparted, discipline imposed, values set. Long after being in one another's presence, many of those students reached out to renew that engagement, to cross once more that bridge.

Ben Padgett, a student of Miss Ruth's in the '50s and then for most of his adult life a minister and hospital chaplain, told me many years later about his previously one-sided relationship with her. "She gave me a spanking every day, it seemed like," he said. "She used a little 12-inch ruler. She would take me into the cloak room – we don't have cloak rooms anymore – but she didn't want to embarrass you." There she would apply the little wooden enforcer to a stretched-out pink palm or soon-to-be-pink back of calf. "She was very strict," he said. "She was very caring but very strict. She never quit liking me, though. She never quit caring, she never gave up on me. She wanted us to work hard and be quiet, and I wouldn't do it."

But if slow to fall in line, Ben found a hugely formative power at work in his relationship with Miss Ruth. "Character, that's what I think of when I think of her," he said. "Her character was so powerful." Many times later as a teenager, he would stop to visit her at Miss Myrtie's, stop and sit with her there on the front porch. "Over the years, she was one of my favorite people. I didn't regret my spankings, I earned 'em. But she's one of the few people I've carried with me everywhere I've ever been. I've used her to my benefit so much over the years!"

Miss Ruth was runner-up in the search for Alabama's favorite teacher in 1960 and, according to her obituary in one of the Cullman papers in 1978, "was also chosen by the National Quiz Kids as most helpful teacher." "Mrs. Edwards," that article continued, "has the distinction of beginning the city's recreation program. For many years she was the supervisor of play for Cullman children during the summer." (But was archery one of the scheduled sports?) A member of education honorary societies Kappa Delta Pi and Delta Kappa Gamma, she served for four years as president of the local chapter of the latter organization, as well as president of the local organization of retired teachers.

The director of the band program in the city schools of Cullman, accustomed to a considerable wash-out rate among grade-schoolers who initially thought they wanted to play the trumpet or the flute and march in a parade, once remarked that Ruth Edwards had been unerring in sending to him prospects for band. I took that to mean her recommendation not only zeroed in perfectly on musical talent but also reflected discernment in terms of work ethic and compatibility.

This will seem strange to consider, but for all the anachronisms of speech, manner and dress one observed in her, part of what characterized Miss Ruth's conversation, her presentation, was a kind of girlish charm: the way she leaned her upper body forward, arms folded across her chest but hands free as she conversed or took her lunch by a table under the trees. The way she would tilt her head back and freely laugh. Or just the cleverness of her remarks. She was at once ingénue and elderly aunt. Until she became feeble, she would walk with long strides, head down often as if she were in deep thought. Suddenly, when she came upon someone for greeting, she was erect, stationary and all smile.

Deliberate Steps

She died at 84 but was active into her early 80s. "The Loom of Life," a metaphor she used in a memorial lesson (the notes for it were found in her Bible when she died), seems appropriate here. The life she lived in her retirement, before her decline into poor health, seemed indeed like a tapestry that she wove, her foot on the treadle, her hands on the shuttle, feeding one thread and then another. Her steps were deliberate steps. It was clear that she had thought through, and doubtless prayed about, the decisions she made.

When she set her mind to something, it was as good as accomplished. Whatever she planned or schemed for seemed to have the weight of destiny. When she picked up the phone or wrote a letter – to public officials, to influential persons in town, county or singing society – the outcome she sought seemed already to be materializing before her. She wouldn't have settled on something injudicious or wrongheaded to start with; nor would the writing of a letter have been an idle exercise. And when she called in a favor or made an official request, who would have offered an excuse? Who would have told her no?

I've represented that her steps were deliberate, purposeful. There was one exception I observed, a pattern a little comical in retrospect but, in the moment, frightening. In our 1970 summer trip to D.C., we frequently came upon escalators in the Smithsonian buildings. In those instances, the one or more of us accompanying Miss Ruth found ourselves challenged. She had encountered escalators before

- surely in Birmingham's major department stores of that era, Pizitz and Loveman's (which in the '20s proclaimed itself "The largest store south of the Ohio"). And she regarded them the way a hiker would a rattlesnake. It was a simple mechanical principle she had failed to grasp, and she would not be instructed in it. Confronted with the steel-toothed gap opening before her, she would try – despite our best efforts – to step *over* it all. What any passerby then saw in silhouetted motion was a dangerously splayed figure – and one or more desperate hangers-on.

Miss Ruth took pleasure in having received a joking compliment from George Pullen Jackson, maybe when they were together during the 1944 weeklong centennial celebration of the Sacred Harp in Double Springs, Ala. At some point, when the two of them had been with a group of singers, some of whom must have been momentarily boisterous, Jackson had said, "Ruth, you're with this crowd, but not *of* this crowd." Set among her sterling traits and virtues was this bit of pride, of vanity. Yes, she was always a cut above the general crowd, knew it and was pleased that someone else of distinction would say so.

According to a family story, there was one incident from that weeklong event in Double Springs that gives life to Jackson's snapshot analysis. But first of all: when had or has there been such an event in Double Springs, one that would bring in hundreds of out-of-town visitors? It was then and is today a very small town, offering little in the way of public accommodations. So it was not surprising that Newton and Annie Denson Aaron would invite to their big house on the hill a sizable contingent of singers from distances too far for daily trips (and at a time of gas rationing). That group included notables from the singing world, Cagles and McGraws from Georgia as well as other family members.

On one of the evenings, Newt Aaron arrived late at his home to find liquor and its effects broadly in evidence. As chief deputy (and former sheriff) of this famously dry county, he was not of a frame of mind for compromise and not in a mood for additional hospitality. There was no suggestion that his sister-in-law Ruth was part of this. Presumably she and sister Mag were in their room reading, reflecting, maybe pressing a dress for the next day. At any rate, Newt called Ruth out to the porch to speak to her.

"Rush," he said, "I'm going back to town [to his office there]. I'll be back in 45 minutes. When I get back, if everybody's not in bed and all this mess cleaned up, I'll find 'em a place to sleep *up town*" – by which it was understood he meant the jail.

This would not have been the first or last time Miss Ruth was called upon to broker a peace, enforce a principle or wrestle a collective will into submission. One can imagine her making the directions plain. At any rate, when Newt returned, as the story goes, "everybody was snoring."

Two stalwarts: Paine and Ruth. (From the collection of the grandchildren of T.J. and Lola Akers Denson, used with permission)

The Scriptures say it, and we're familiar with the pattern that prophets must often look beyond home-country borders to find the honor due them. This seemed true in the way some Cullman and area singers regarded Miss Ruth and others of the Denson family, at least early on in my experience with them. Paine Denson had the reputation of being somewhat arrogant, and truthfully one or another of the large family had misbehaved or squandered goodwill. It may well have been that at least a few Sacred Harp "commoners" in the immediate area resented what they perceived as highhanded ways from some members of such a high-profile clan, born to Sacred Harp privilege as the later-generation Densons were. Ruth's letter to "Gustus," again mentioning Ivy, hints at her awareness of something like this: "He surely is a friend to you & to the Densons. Guess that explains his unpopularity with that other crowd." Ruth was often not present at local singings (that she had Sunday assignments instead would probably not have been commonly known), but did travel to big singings out of area – and would then appear at the Cullman County Convention on the arm of visiting dignitaries. I don't know that I ever heard such resentment verbalized, but a vapor of it seemed to be in the air.

One example sticks out to me: an occasion in which Miss Ruth stood before the class, and of course immediately in front of the first-bench tenors, including well-known Sacred Harp composer John Hocutt, who was keying. She mentioned a recent singing she had attended and said, "It was a *good singing*" – and then, almost as afterthought, as she looked down at him – "wasn't it, John?" "I've never been to a bad one," he quipped, not looking up at her. It was a discordant moment – a bit of a slap, I thought (and the only action or comment from John I ever found to be out of line). Caught in that moment, she pushed her lips out, swallowed the slight and continued with her comments. . . .

As she moved into older age, Miss Ruth, I'm glad to say, seemed to gain everywhere at home the revered status she and others of her family had always held abroad.

A Royal Line

Mike tells of visiting with his Aunt Ruth, along with Hugh and a couple of others, in a motel in Nashville in the mid-'60s. Hugh announced to Ruth on that occasion, "I've written your epitaph: 'Here lies Ruth Denson Edwards, the Queen of Sacred Harp – don't you know!'" Ending the line with one of her favored expressions drew a laugh from all in the room. I heard that same line, without the "don't you know," from Hugh more than once as well, and knew it to be his actual intent. He did at last have the back of her tombstone engraved with the words: "Here lies a queen of Sacred Harp, who, like her father before her, has devoted her life to the improvement, advancement, and perpetuation of Sacred Harp music." That maybe over-the-top tribute does point to an essential truth: Ruth Denson Edwards was as close to Sacred Harp royalty as we knew in those times.

On many occasions at breaks during singings I had the privilege of seeing her hold court. The crowd in general, including the alto singers around her, would have dispersed. She would remain in her seat in the front row facing the square, opening her purse for a quick errand and then snapping it closed again, or bringing her handkerchief to her face, a quick dab, and then slipping it back to her waist. In the interim a number of people from the back or the sides of the church would make their pilgrimage forward to be received by her. It wasn't a line that formed usually so much as individuals or twos or threes that would make their way forward, one after the other, to see her. They had made her acquaintance before, their parents had sung with her or her family, she had previously made remarks in their presence that signified – whatever the source of their connection or admiration, they now needed to come and tell her so, to receive her benediction.

She would sit, head up, smiling, and take the proffered hand in both of hers. At a slight distance from this, I could then hear her conversation bubbling like a brook, with little ripples of laughter or inflections of pleasure or recognition. No one left this encounter, I'm confident, feeling less than elevated, less than blessed.

Very much at home at Holly Springs, in the early 1970s. (Photos by Betty Oliver)

In her late years – most of the years really that I knew her – whenever she stood before us to lead, we were brought to a moment of attention. She would always have at least brief comments to make before she led her first or only song. With so much accumulated perspective, so many reminiscences called forth, how could she not remark on the occasion, on the song, on this still moment in the passing scene before her?

All eyes would be on her, all ears attuned, as she planted her feet at the center of the square, straightened her dress and cleared her throat. Well, except occasionally, as she began talking, when she would pick up, at maybe the far corners of the hall, low background interference – someone continuing to mutter to a neighbor. At that point, she would simply stop and stare in their direction. That put a stop to *that*. A moment of absolute quiet would follow, though with probably a few grins around the square. She would then turn her view back to the center of the audience, smile, her hands clasped (always without book, of course), and freshly begin again or resume her comments as if she had never been interrupted. If the courtesy, in other words, was not universally observed – as of course it should have been – why then she would *enforce* the observance.

We were again in school to her, to this proper and all-seeing schoolmarm, this figure somehow taller at the moment, more erect than life. The misbehavers had just had their knuckles rapped, and we could now go on with the lesson. As her beloved niece Amanda would often say about some situation that Miss Ruth had just concluded, heavy-handedly or not, "Aunt Ruthy just taught school!"

She had *presence* – how else to say it? And as much as anyone I ever knew. When she spoke before a group, she spoke emphatically – and was content to pause to gather up a new thought or invigorate the one she was currently stringing through. She was no hick, and didn't talk like one. But her speech did have a twang, an unmistakable flavor of the provinces. With her distinctive drawl, it was as if, instead of small, quick pumps, she would, every few words, push her foot down *hard* on the pedal. And probably from her early teaching days, she employed a little percussive aid to emphasize her remarks. She would pop the index and middle fingers of her right hand into the cupped palm of her left, with force, making a *loud, smacking* noise. She would sometimes use this device swiftly *three, four, five* times in a row, punctuating exactly the words in a string that she wanted received, implanted. (When I used to visit her and she had pulled her chair up close to mine, she would, as she talked, whack me on the knee with those same two fingers, to the same effect.)

In reading her always gracious, hand-written correspondence, you can almost hear, in her bold underlining of certain words, those same little palm-pops, as in this line from a 1970 letter to Larry Brasher: "I took up a collection for books for you & your group. Those present were quite generous & soon you will receive <u>three</u> '<u>brand</u> <u>spanking</u>' <u>new</u> <u>books</u> & an album – S.H. Vol 103." She knew how to deploy a simple declarative sentence to strong effect, too: "I attended a good singing yesterday. I wished for you." "They are my good friends." "He is my heart." (Who would not want to have as correspondent some-one who could spread words with such winsome personality, as in this line from the letter to Gustus? "This is a poor letter in answer to a good one but I'm sitting on a low limb.")

Miss Ruth and Uncle Bob

I well remember Miss Ruth and "Uncle Bob" (Robert E.) Denson attending a singing at Ider, home of the Wootten family, this place that had not been on the Densons' circuit over the decades. The oc-casion was like a visitation by heads of state. The crowd in general knew that the appearance of the two, well into their old age, was a favor bestowed on this class and this day. When Miss Ruth stood up to begin her lesson, D.T. White, from Tuscaloosa, sounded a request: "How about letting Uncle Bob lead with you? . . ." It was an endear-ing, a crowd-pleasing idea – the two old veterans and cousins standing and leading together. Miss Ruth snapped that off in a second. "No, I don't want to lead with him," she said. The startled crowd barked out a laugh – her unexpected reply was so sudden. "He can *beat* me too bad," she added. The laugh rolled away, and the class reset itself for her instruction. She had humorously deflected the request, and there was no question about who was in charge at the moment. Her time in the square was *her* time, as Uncle Bob's was with his turn. It was not shared. She knew what she would lead (selected song with backups), and did so in the way she wanted it led.

Ruth and Bob: As close as brother and sister. Denson Memorial Singing, Addison, Ala., 1960s. (From the collection of the grandchildren of T.J. and Lola Akers Denson, used with permission)

The loving, joking relationship between Ruth and Bob was an affecting sight. Double first cousins (Bob was a son of Seaborn and Sidney Burdette Denson), less than a year apart in age, they were as close as brother and sister. In their later years, Bob would drive over to Cullman from Addison to see and spend time with Ruth, often once a week. And they rode together to countless singings over the decades.

I long ago heard it said that all the Densons could "cry at the drop of a hat." And surely none among them shed more tears in all his public goings than Uncle Bob. Hearing him lead the prayer at singings was like overhearing his private entreaty to the Lord. In those prayers, he seemed to follow thoughts the way he might have wandered in the woods, turning here and there, now again going straight, finding his way on the well-worn path. His hoarse voice straining, he would cast his pleadings up like birds released to the sky.

Mike has reminded me of something we and many others heard Uncle Bob say. He was prone to talk, to "testify" in his time in the square. Red-eyed from weeping, sweating steadily, he would swab his face with a handkerchief, clench and unclench his teeth, and pour forth the words that had settled on him. In these remarks he said on more than one occasion that, like Moses, he was not a gifted speaker. "But," in Mike's words, "he would 'sorta' point to Aunt Ruth and say, 'but Moses had Aaron to speak for him and I have Ruth!' Then he would laugh and tears would roll down his cheeks."

Hugh tells a story, from many years before, of stopping by Addison to see Uncle Bob: "And Aunt Belle said, 'Well, he's down at the chicken house with his songbook.'" At the chicken house, with his *songbook*? She had an explanation. "He's down there learnin' a song by heart, so he can lead it without a book." Even a Denson had to practice to achieve perfection. Hugh's impression, though, was that Aunt Belle rather enjoyed lifting the curtain a bit on her husband's method of accomplishment.

Practicing, so as to make it look easy, is one thing. Still I never had the impression that Uncle Bob gave any thought to the potential verdict of the class or any person on his song selection. The page number he called, the song that spoke to him compellingly on the occasion, seemed to come from the heart. For all the hundreds of songs he knew through and through, the many appealing melodies he had immediate access to, he minded not at all calling over and over again, for example, 558, LIVING STREAMS, the song by his old friend Tom McGraw: "Yea, though I walk through death's dark vale. . . ." I never saw anyone for whom singing, and especially *leading* in singing, appeared more of a catharsis. By the end of the singing, he seemed wrung out, but thankful and spirited, ready for a laugh.

Later in life, Uncle Bob was accompanied on most of his singing trips by Irene Kitchens Parker. First- and second-chair treble were always reserved – or suddenly made available – for the two of them. Affectionate friends, they had sung together side by side for many years. When their spouses died, it seemed only natural that they would marry, and they did. While their spouses were living – both were non-singers when I was on the scene – Miss Ruth would point out good-naturedly that she had accompanied Bob and Irene "as their *chaperone*."

Uncle Bob's presence in the square, in those years, was all emotion. Miss Ruth's was controlled, audience-focused, and, as Mike has said, "just a little shy of regal." At a singing many years ago in central Alabama, Maudie Frederick, a singer maybe midway between my age and that of Miss Ruth, placed her hand on my shoulder from her seat in the row behind and whispered, as Miss Ruth began leading a song, "You just watch her – when she finishes that, it'll be *just right*." I never had the sense that Miss Ruth revved up or slowed her song as she sang – she was almost metronomic in her pacing – though it might have been that the class would at last have come in sync entirely with her. But I could appreciate the sentiment: it would be a moderate tempo for sure, but it would be pure Sacred Harp, deeply stroked, and exactly what she intended; it would be, in short, *just right*.

On Sacred Harp matters, Miss Ruth was of course a classicist. Though words were not spoken between us in this case, a little episode one year at the Cullman County Convention serves as a good, if oblique, illustration. She was seated at the back of the alto in the courthouse that day, and I was on treble, maybe the second or third row. One of the local-area singers was leading 421, SWEET MORNING. The lady was not a sophisticate, probably wasn't well-educated or well-traveled, and certainly wouldn't have been as well-equipped as Miss Ruth to render judgment on the layered tradition and etiquette of Sacred Harp. But it soon became clear how much she was enjoying the song and the moment.

Having exhausted the notes and then the two verses of the song, with chorus, we were all no doubt surprised to hear the good woman ask that, for yet another verse, we use the words "If you get there before I do (And we'll all shout together . . .) / Tell all my friends I'm coming, too. . . ." With hardly a moment's hesitation, the accomplished class began to sing the request.

Miss Ruth slowly turned her head in my direction, found my face and delivered a deep, heavy-lidded wink.

The good-humored eloquence of that act, the mischievous eye in so august a figure and the secret sharing between us across a back corner of the square gave me a memory of Ruth Denson Edwards I will carry with pleasure as long as my mind can still reel back the frames.

Miss Ruth – and young man in short pants. March 1970, Georgia State Convention, Poplar Springs Baptist Church, Tallapoosa, Ga. (Photo by J. Lawrence Brasher)

Like a beaming sidewalk vendor: Dewey at the National Mall, July 1970. (Photo by Joe Dan Boyd)

The most charismatic leader I ever saw. (Photo courtesy of Bernice Williams Harvey)

8

Dewey Williams

Dewey President Williams (1898-1995)

"Anybody who don't know more than's in the rudiments ain't learnt but mighty little."

"'Dear friends, farewell' – they wouldn't let you sing that in the mornin'. . . . I tell 'em sometimes, 'that's a closin' song, we're not ready to close.' Really and truly, that's the way they sung. They sung them good old songs in the mornin' and gettin' down songs in the evenin'."

Dewey Williams had a way with words. Like a beaming sidewalk vendor, he mixed his observations – part narrative, part philosophy, part gag line, but wrapped always in fresh, locally grown metaphor – and dispensed them to a public captivated by his presentation. It might have been in church or singing class that he was holding forth – maybe on the radio or local television, on stage in some distant venue or just close up in conversation. But that way with words, like his way with music, won Mr. Dewey many a listener's ear.

Here he is, with typically colorful language, talking about Sacred

Harp in the late 1960s with Joe Dan Boyd, as quoted in Boyd's 2002 book, *Judge Jackson and The Colored Sacred Harp*:

> You eat a good bait of peas and collard greens and drink you some good buttermilk, and you got a meal in you – you ain't apt to get hungry for the next five or six hours. But you go in there and drink you a bait of soup and you just as well drink you a glass of water, near about it, because that's what it is – with a little salt and grease to make it good. There ain't no strength in soup, but there is food value in peas. Sacred Harp singing is like that: You go to an all-day singing and, by the middle of the next week, those songs will still be ringing in you. There's something to that. Music is one of the greatest things I know of; it's sung with a joyful noise – so much so that it raises the hair on your head once in a while and makes you feel like you got a hat on. It sorta stirs you up. But now, lots of folks is just squalling and hollering – singing just to make a fuss. That's like eating soup instead of a good meal.[19]

Peas and collards and buttermilk, then, were not just restorative in food value for Dewey; they were serviceable for conversation, for making a point. And he never seemed to lose appetite for any of it – the food, the talk or the handy, table-ready analogy.

The grandson of slaves and a sharecropper for more than half his 97 years, Dewey President Williams – despite the boost from his middle name – grew up with the deck stacked against him. But he had song, a willingness to work hard and always a winning presence. Blending those strains, he persevered and attained in old age both honor locally and a measure of fame beyond.

He was born in 1898, one of eight children, in the Haw Ridge area of Alabama's Dale County, about seven miles from Ozark, the small city in the southeastern section of the state where he would spend the rest of his life. He fell naturally into the pattern of farming and singing set by his parents, June and Anna Bruner Williams. He met his wife-to-be, Alice Casey, at a singing, and they married in 1921. Eight children in time would give the family several more adept song-sters, to use the term favored by black singers in that area.

I first met Mr. Dewey in 1967 at the 45th session of the Alabama and Florida State Union Sacred Harp Singing Convention in Dothan, a mid-sized city a half-hour's drive south from Ozark. We then sang together in performance groups in D.C. in 1970 and in Montreal in '71. And we met up at least annually at singings – usually either in Birmingham or in or around Ozark – for almost all the years up until his death in 1995.

That 1967 trip for me, a second-year grad student at Auburn, was an adventure for sure. Separate traditions of black singing still re-tained a foothold then in southeastern Alabama (spilling over the border into Florida),[20] northern Mississippi and eastern Texas. With few exceptions, the Sacred Harp of that time was strictly segregated. From local-area white singers in the Wiregrass area, I had heard re-ports of African Americans singing Sacred Harp. I was keen to look into their world, to experience the inevitable differences with the singing and tradition I already knew. Tipped off about the conven-tion in Dothan, I struck out for the Adams Street Baptist Church on a late September Saturday. I joined up with Adams Street off from the church a good bit in a fairly seedy-looking industrial area. Two or three black men were walking nearby, and I pulled over to ask direc-tions. The reply was tentative: "Now, that's a *black* church. . . ." Yes, I said, I knew that it was. They pointed me in the direction and I was soon there.

Inside the church, I found a large gathering and heard familiar yet different strains of Sacred Harp. The singing was at a much slower pace and with a more ragged overall effect than I was used to hearing, but the sound was immediately appealing. I heard my first Sacred Harp blue note there, as well as much more natural vibrato, and saw for the first time leaders "walking" the time – stepping about the square, or sometimes just marking the steps in place, with each beat of the music.

Mine was the only white face looking into a songbook there, and no doubt some in the congregation found my presence presumptuous. I had simply appeared, unknown, unannounced and uninvited. (And after all, how many white singers then went around inviting black singers to their all-day singings?) Then, too, my visit was at a time of high racial tensions across the country and especially in our region.

It was exhilarating to be there and to hear an intriguingly different sound, but an incident from that day brings to mind something of the awkwardness I also felt. Daylight saving time was a recently instituted practice in the state. And when the chairman of the event, an ancient man, tall and lean, stood to direct everyone to the dining hall below – at what clearly seemed to him an unnaturally early dinner hour – he prefaced his invitation with the humorless note that "these white folks have got us on *fast time. . . .*" (I couldn't begrudge the sentiment on the part of this venerable figure, who had doubtless suffered a lifetime of racial indignities beyond my imagining.) Of all in attendance that day, though, no one was more welcoming to me than the tall, wiry figure with the infectious smile introduced to me as Dewey Williams.

At one of the breaks, Mr. Williams called me over to his seat and made an exploratory pitch of sorts, using the long, arthritic fingers of his right hand to help lay out his vision of a bigger and better Sacred Harp in his area, a wider spreading of the word. Though he may not have mentioned such at the time, it behooved him always to be on the lookout for sponsors for his monthly radio and TV programs. He had evidently sized me up as a young man of means (though I was hardly that). And even in that early meeting, I could see at work the entrepreneurial spirit, could feel the persuasive power of his presence and his wandering, soft-syllabled spiel. Anyone listening in on us might have conceived the recruitment of an extra-generational co-conspirator in a plot to extend this music well beyond its natural base.

'The Outstandingest Music'

Sacred Harp singing – which he called "the outstandingest music in the world" – was Dewey's life, his calling, his ministry. And he had a gift with it unmatched by that of any other singer of my experience: He was the most charismatic leader I ever saw stand and move and sing in the square. A lyrical quality to his singing voice, a beautifully rhythmic interpretation of Sacred Harp and old gospel tunes and a knack for knowing when and how to exhort singers and audience formed the core of his gift as an inspirational leader.

Sacred Harp went back a ways in his family, he told Chicago singer Ted Mercer in an extended interview in Ozark in 1987. His grandfather, born in slavery in nearby Barbour County, was also a singer – this man who, he said, "had the biggest hands in a man you ever saw." "Yeah, he fooled with this same music we're singing. . . . Grampaw, I can remember when I was a young man, and he was a deacon in the church, and he sung Sacred Harp music. He didn't do a whole lot of *leadin'* Sacred Harp, but we went down there and sung."

"He died in '28. Christmas night," Dewey said. Based on what the grandfather had said, Dewey believed him to have been 75 when he died. Dewey's father, too, sang: "He sung this book. He sung this song, 116 [I Will Shout and Sing in Glory, in the Cooper book, the version of Sacred Harp used in that area of the state]. That's his song."

But as with many others in his community of that time, Dewey's early experience in Sacred Harp was almost entirely oral, bookless. And he remembered first starting to sing, he told Ted, when he was about seven or eight. On the morning following a singing session that his daddy and "some more folks" had had the previous evening, he and his older brother, Telly, would get in the kitchen, "get on the floor . . . and we'd sing the songs that they sung that night." "And we'd sing maybe an hour," he said. "As long as they'd sung, we'd sing, too. And I done it until . . . I don't know . . . we got too big to go in the kitchen, I reckon. And we quit singing it then and got to singing behind them at the churches a little."

"Makes you feel like you got a hat on." (Photo by Kim McRae)

The singing by that older generation was mostly in informal gatherings without songbooks, sessions that were often, Dewey said, "peanut shellin's" – "peanut shellin's where they would sing. . . . They'd have a hand-shellin'. They'd go and give a shellin' maybe here at my house at night, and all the people'd come and the house'd be full and when they'd leave, there'd be peanuts all over the floor, everywhere. They didn't have nowhere to put 'em. They'd shell sometimes three or four or five bushels." And singing all the while.

"More or less, I sung by *guess*," Dewey said. "We didn't have a book down on the floor when we'd sing it. But sometimes we didn't know whether we were right or wrong, but we'd sing it. I couldn't tell nobody I was singing according to *time* [with metrical discipline, by beating time]. And a lot of those folks what sang at night didn't sing according to time. . . . But they sung, and had good singing."

The pull of memory of those singings was always strong for Dewey: "I don't know what I'd *give*," he said, "to go to one of them old-time singings like we had, one of the white and black singings!

"Lord have mercy, they [at the black singings] had some of the best basses you ever heard in your life! They didn't *know* music, but they *sung* it – I know what I'm sayin', I aint' guessin'. They *sung* it. And some of the best tribbles . . . altos . . . . They didn't have just two or three, neither. They'd have a *houseful* of them folks singin'. And children, 12 or 14 years old – they wouldn't allow them to sit on the front, they'd make them sit in back. Of course now, everybody now can get on the front that wants to, 'cause we ain't got many no-how – we don't want to lose none.

"Well, I tell you what. . . . Back then, if you got out there on that floor and didn't know your song, they'd have you go sit down. . . . Tell you to go back home and *learn* it, and then come back and let you lead it. You'd better learn how to lead your song before you left home. If you don't, you're liable to be sat down. . . . I told somebody the other day: I wouldn't regret $50 to go to one of those old-time singin's, what we had back then. Those people would sing, they'd sing out of their soul, and they knowed how to sing more, in a way, than we know."

"I used to water the white folks' singing," Dewey continued. "That's where I'd learn. And when I'd get enough water there for 'em to drink, I'd go in and listen at 'em sing, and sometimes I'd sing with 'em. I done a lot of that while I was coming up."

An influential figure in the local white community was song leader and singing-school teacher Robert M. Davis, who contributed at least two songs to the Cooper book. Along with black patriarchs Judge Jackson, compiler of the 1934 *Colored Sacred Harp*, and Thomas Y. Lawrence, both of Ozark, Davis took an interest in young Williams and helped fill out his musical education. As well as employing Dewey on at least a part-time basis, Davis gave him the copy of the Cooper book he used in those early years. "I've sung in every room of old man Davis's house," Dewey told Joe Dan Boyd. "If there wasn't enough light to sing in one room, we'd go in another."

Dewey's eldest daughter, Bernice Williams Harvey, well remembered the relationship between those men of two generations and two races. Her father, she pointed out, was a "special farmer." And the older Davis, she said, came to rely on him and his agricultural knack: "Mr. Bob Davis, if he was going to buy a hog, he'd have Pappa go with him, have Pappa weigh the hog, tell him which one to buy and so forth." At one point, though, Dewey had to draw the line with his patron. Davis on this occasion had taken Dewey along with him to a "Mr. Whitehead's place." There a festering disagreement between Davis and Whitehead broke out as loud argument, she said. On the way home, Williams told Davis, "If you all got somethin' goin' like that, don't you take me with you! I coulda got killed. . . ."

Joe Dan Boyd quotes black singer Columbus Sistrunk, who was born in 1884, on singing collaboration between the races in that area in the early 20th century: "Mr. Cooper [compiler of the Cooper book] and Mr. Pat Poyner [writer of a couple of dozen alto parts] spent a lot of time teaching colored folks to sing. There was a lot of mixing between black and white Sacred Harpers before all this integration stuff came up."

Dewey was often at the center of any biracial singing in the area.

"We'd meet on the street there in Ozark on Saturday evening, and we'd sing there on the street," Dewey said in the 1987 Mercer interview. "And Mr. Davis'd always have me to lead. There'd be a *gang* before we quit. Sometimes they crowded there just like they do for a singing convention."

Just out on the street? "The sidewalk, and sometimes we'd be on the courthouse lawn, but we'd be singing there on the square or somewhere about the square in Ozark. We done it until . . . I'd say we sung pretty good until Fort Rucker come to Dale County and Coffee County [about 1938 or '39, he said]. Then people got so busy, and ever since, money been floatin'. And it's interesting, singing as it was when they's singing for the grace of God to come in . . . now they got money, and they ain't got time to stop to sing, 'cause they got to go spend their money."

Dewey had begun leading singing at church when he was about 18. And in time he became the master leader at area singings as well. As he often said, he sang all kinds of music in those early years – including the blues. "I was a whiskey drinker around then," he told a reporter from the Evanston, Ill., *Review* in 1992.[21] "I could sing stronger when I was drinking whiskey. But I didn't realize it was bossing me." About the time he stopped drinking whiskey, he stopped singing the blues: "I realized what I was singing and who I was singing to." From then on, singing and leading sacred songs became his focus.

The *Review* reporter also elicited from Mr. Dewey some fine detail about his early habits: "Williams recalls that he quit drinking in 1939 on the second Saturday night in August. He quit smoking cigarettes in 1947, and he hasn't taken Castor Oil in 60 years. He attributes his longevity to all of these factors equally."

Throwing the Book at 'Em

Since Dewey was already 70 when I first met him, I once asked Bernice what her father was like in his prime. She then related what she said was a typical scene from that earlier era. Dewey would frequently also sing from the seven-shape tradition, using the little paperback books published by Stamps-Baxter and others, and Bernice was with him on this occasion at a seven-shape singing in a big Baptist church in nearby Enterprise. When it was announced that "Brother Dewey Williams" would be up next to lead, she said the big room filled almost instantly, as no one wanted to miss what was coming up. When Dewey finished his stirring rendition of some song, she said, "he threw the book across the audience, he was so happy. . . . He'd throw that book, and just thrill those folks!"

Bernice made another point about her father. He was, she said, "a community man," and she mentioned two examples. No one in the little black community around them had a radio in the 1930s. And in 1937 when Joe Louis was to fight in the title match for the world heavyweight boxing championship, Dewey Williams went out and bought a radio. (He after all could feel a kinship with Louis, who, like him, was an Alabama native, the grandson of slaves and one of eight children born into a sharecropping family.) Dewey then invited "the whole community in" on that June night to listen to Louis win the match. "Oh my Lord!" Bernice said. "We hailed it as much as the people with [Louis] there – and couldn't see picture one!"

The second example was from a later time in Dewey's life. When he was no longer farming and had no livestock of his own, Dewey would scour the area, Bernice said, in search of somebody with a cow that produced "good buttermilk, good butter – even somebody with layin' hens. He loved that country milk and butter!" When he came upon such a source, he would "announce it to the community – he would tell everybody about it. And when he went to get buttermilk and butter, he would take orders for others."

About 1955, Dewey and a group of singers, including Judge Jackson and his son Japheth, began a monthly to twice-monthly Sunday morning broadcast on WOZK radio in Ozark. They decided to call themselves the Wiregrass Sacred Harp Singers. They would sing mainly from the Cooper book, but would also include songs from *The Colored Sacred Harp*, as well as an occasional gospel tune.

Four years later, Dewey arranged for a twice-monthly, and then later monthly, program on a Dothan television station as well. About the program on WTVY, Dewey told Ted Mercer: "I sing Sacred Harp altogether, unless I might let a sermon come in, a short sermon. But I won't let them preachers can't preach . . . unh-unh. I ain't gonna have that program messed up." His directing of the radio programs lasted almost four decades and of the TV performances more than three.

With a foot in both the black and white singing worlds in the early years and later, would he draw some distinctions between them? "Well, the white folks, I say, sing it faster, and the black folks sing it slow," he said in the 1987 interview. "Black folks try to get *all* the sweetness up out of that note before they turn it loose, and white folks [chuckling now] try to turn it loose before they can get any sweetness. . . . Now, I tell you one thing, there's one thing about white folks: Now, I sit and listen; you won't find no *discords* among the white folks. . . . [and as his interviewer demurs at that] Now, wait a minute. When one chords with the cue chord, they're all in that *same chord*, that's what I mean. They're not like we is – like horses and mules pullin'. They don't do that. I ain't been able to get it, and I've been goin' to singings a long time. Sometimes it ain't the direct tune that I'd sing it in, but the tune that *one's* got, the whole crew's got it. That's what I mean. That makes the music good."

A longtime singing-school teacher, Dewey stayed pretty much in teaching mode all his adult life. Again in that 1987 interview: "Now, music is not what most people say it is. Music is a pleasing tone, correctly rendered, directly served. . . . You don't sing music with a fuss, with anything *like* a fuss. . . . You can take a stick and throw it down on the floor, and it'll make a fuss. But music is a *tone*. And when you're out of tune . . . you just ain't in tune! It's just like your car. You carry your car and get it out where it's got a skip in it. . . . Sometimes you got to put new spark plugs in it, and sometimes in singin' music, you're goin' to have to get a new keyer to get the tune right, and then it'll all *sound*."

As he frequently pointed out, though, the music he loved was about more than tone. "Sacred Harp music is written from the Bible," he told the *Evanston Review* reporter. "When you sing a good song, the spirit comes in you! It's somethin' that feels good. Like a chicken pie."

And in the 1987 interview with Ted Mercer, he expanded this point: "See, this Sacred Harp music is *Bible*. When they set out to make it, the first thing they drawed up was two kinds of music. One would be major, one would be minor." It wasn't difficult for Dewey to find biblical precedence for that basic difference in sound, there being, as he pointed out, both "major prophets" and "minor prophets" in the Old Testament – "and there's more major songs in this book than there is minor."

"The next thing they written was four notes," he continued. "And four notes – I said this, and can't nobody disagree with me, I know what I'm talkin' about – they're written from the four Gospel writers of the Bible: Matthew, Mark, Luke and John. Sol, la, mi, fa – all *them* carried from this Gospel. And the keys are seven. There's seven churches in Asia – in Revelation you find that. They got them seven keys. . . . And so, where you goin'? Tell me somewhere to go, and I go. . . . That's *Bible*. And when you're singin' Sacred Harp music, you're singin' Bible."

That Amazing Grace

Well, surely any panel of musicologists or biblical scholars (or numerologists) would have awarded Mr. Dewey points for creativity for the above analysis. But he was quickly on to the next point – and to more conventional thinking: "And when you get down to that Amazing Grace . . . Christ told Paul, 'My grace is sufficient.' I don't care what you got to do or where you're goin', how bad it is, if you got grace from God, you got somethin' *sufficient*. And that's the reason I love that old song – I just love it."

That old song brought him new fame. When Bill Moyers put together his acclaimed PBS documentary on the history and power of that best-known of all sacred songs, he discovered in Dewey Williams an entrancing presence, someone the camera, on the occasion of Dewey's 91st birthday singing, would find irresistible. The preview of the 1990 film led to Dewey being feted at Lincoln Center in New York City. Dewey had already in 1983 been named a National Endowment of the Arts "National Heritage Fellow" in the second year of that prestigious program (along with John Lee Hooker, Almeda Riddle and other notables) and had received – president to President, as it were – a letter of congratulation from Ronald Reagan. He was profiled, and with a darkly rich photo, in *National Geographic Magazine*. The rural blacktop road circling by his home had been named Dewey Williams Road, and in 1988 the Ozark mayor had designated an annual Dewey Williams Day.

All this for someone who had had to leave public schools after the third grade to help with the family's sharecropping and who had been a small-time farmer for most of his life. "It was tough back there in '30, '32, when Mr. Hoover was in full charge," Dewey reflected in the Mercer interview.

I made a crop for $2.50 a month. You wouldn't go to town and get your dinner tomorrow for $2.50. You'd just stay at home and get somethin' to eat. But one thing we had the advantage of that we don't have now, we had wheat in the field, bread in the field. We had syrup in the bottom, taters in the hill, and milk cow walkin' around there. . . . [It would] go out in the mornin' clean and would come back with a bag of milk. We had the advantage of things like that. But now if you don't go to the store and get yourself some milk, you don't have no milk. And if you don't go to the store and get some meat, you won't have no meat. You don't get you some syrup out of the store – it ain't good, no way – but if you don't get some, you don't have no syrup, no potatoes. But we had all that when we sat down at the table. In a way, we was blessed. We was. Above where we is now. Now if you ain't got it, you don't get it.

Mr. Dewey clearly enjoyed delivering such testimonies. Interspersed throughout his conversation was a distinctive chuckle – a quick snort or little shuddering sigh of a laugh, partially swallowed and barely audible, as if allowed out only for a private sharing. It drew you to him.

There was often, too, a noticeable pattern to his patter – not an equivocation exactly, but a hedging. He wanted to steer a straight course, and that sometimes meant pushing off from both sides. "Well, yes and no . . . ," he would often say in starting the answer to a question, or "No and yes." Or: "We wasn't direct singin' in a way, and we was, too. . . ."

That same cautious approach, a deference to both sides of an issue, must have helped Dewey ease his way through times of racial tensions and through the challenges of leading scores of songsters in performance, with many of his companions doubtless carrying their own views of how and what best to present.

"I ain't never cussed no one out, and nobody's put a scratch on my back," Dewey, at 97, told a reporter from the *Birmingham Post-Herald* in 1995, just weeks before his death. "If my daddy was here, he'd tell you I never give him any trouble. I've always tried to live right."[22]

He didn't mind dispensing strong medicine along the way when he felt it was needed, though – and often did so, right at the bottom line, with a little side jerk of his head for reinforcement. "I tell my people, 'If you want to get to heaven,'" he said to me once, "'you're gonna have to learn to love white folks!'"

As the indisputable leader of the singing in his area, Dewey had to employ skills as both negotiator and take-charge director. At a number of the black singings in and around Ozark over a period of years, I got to see those skills in action. The chair of almost any singing always has multiple interests to satisfy; so, too, the arranging committee – the person(s) assigned the task of calling the leaders, from the dozens who would like the chance to lead. It sometimes fell to Dewey to perform both functions. The events he presided over, and often called the leaders for, then pressed him to satisfy these sometimes competing requests, to squeeze everything into a tightening box of time. These scenes, as I watched them, often seemed to play out as in a highly choreographed dance.

The typical pattern I saw would be something like this: Dewey, now an elderly figure, would be just off from the bass toward the center, facing the main congregation, his lanky frame folded into a chair, with one bony knee atop the other and angling up toward his chin. The advanced age of most of the participants would inevitably slow the proceedings down and create a less streamlined process than I typically saw at other singings, with many more side conversations taking place and a little more noise and confusion between songs. Now, many, maybe most, of the participants would be non-troublesome types, singing and tending to their own business. But at every break and even during the singing itself, one or more emissaries would approach Dewey with suggestions – typically, requests for *themselves* to lead a song or make remarks, and maybe at a specified point in the proceedings, if not immediately – with the closing hour looming just ahead. A singer might approach Dewey to say he'd been asked to sing a certain song on behalf of someone not able to be present – sometimes, and obviously, when the request could have been handled in the singer's earlier appearance on the floor.

Politics, as we say, in everything. . . . I was always amused to watch Dewey react to all this posturing. He'd frequently not say a word – of assent or denial – scarcely even giving the petitioner the encouragement of eye contact, but would sometimes reach up with those long fingers, grasp the knot of his tie and, pulling it looser, exaggeratedly stretch his neck and lift and shrug his chin. The body language may or may not have been communicative, but surely it was the manifestation of decisions being formulated, of difficult choices being sorted out. Dewey's subsequent calling out of names, mixed in with the regular order of events, would reflect whose importunings he had chosen to countenance.

Such was the burden of princedom. An ordinary chair or committeeperson would doubtless have found himself beleaguered by all this lobbying and grandstanding, but Dewey seemed to take it all in stride. Wily in his ways, he knew people, he knew politics and he knew when to stand firm and when to step aside and take a glancing blow (but didn't take many, in my observation).

"And if you don't know what love is . . . ." (Photo by Melissa Springer, Ozark, 1987, courtesy of the Alabama Center for Traditional Culture)

Alice Williams, unlike Dewey, was always quiet, had little to say in public. She was dutiful where her husband and children were concerned. "He suits me," she said simply, in the 1995 *Post-Herald* interview with the two of them. "I didn't marry him for everybody else, but I don't mind sharing him."

Alice outlived Dewey, dying in 2000, just weeks shy of her 99th birthday. But she had become increasingly childlike in her later years. "I don't care where Pappa went, Momma always wanted to go," remembered Bernice. "He would say, 'I'm goin' over to town,' and she would say, 'I wanna go-o-o . . . .' Just like a child. . . . He would say, 'Now Alice, I'm just goin' to town. . . . Well, come on then. . . .'" And so off they would go, the business-driven man, who never lost his spark or vision, and the unleavable Miss Alice, who at least didn't mind sharing her husband with the wider world.

Just a Little More Time . . .

Over the years, a gospel song Dewey always gave a spirited version of, LORD, GIVE ME JUST A LITTLE MORE TIME, became, next to AMAZING GRACE, the song most often associated with him. Requested of him at singings anywhere he ventured, it seemed a fitting expression of his situation:

I've got a lot of things I need to do
Before I leave this earthly clime.
I'm ready (anytime) when you call me, (Lord,)
But give me just a little more time.

One of the people I most enjoyed in Dewey's company, one of the very few male trebles I ever knew in that community, was a fellow by the name of Gordon Jolly. Enjoying chatting and singing with him as I did, I was not unaware of some chafing between the two longtime town residents and singing compatriots. I had the sense, that is, that Bro. Jolly functioned somewhat as a gadfly to Dewey's leadership, made himself a bit of a burr under the saddle. Gordon was once standing beside me at the end of a session when Dewey rose, half-bent over, to lead that requested song. "Yeah, he *needs* just a little more time. . . ." Gordon muttered. Politics, as I say. . . . (When I once mentioned Gordon to Bernice and commented that he was "a character," she added simply – and discreetly – *"Amen."*)

But indeed it seemed clear that Dewey *could* have used more time – time to work his particular magic. The Sacred Harp tradition he had devoted such effort to in the black community had increasingly fallen on hard times. Younger generations of singers in the area had failed to take it up; older singers were dying off. "It's gettin' weak, to tell you the truth, and I work at it all the time," Dewey had told Ted Mercer in 1987. "That's all I can do." And again in his 1992 interview: "I don't want to quit. I'm not ready. When I get to the point where I can't help somebody with my singing and talking, then I'll be ready to go home."

The unforgettable composite image I have of Dewey Williams compresses countless scenes with little variation from the more than 25 years I saw and sang with him: a tall, angular figure leading the singing, with joy flashing on his face. Caught up in the spirit of it all, he would frequently stop singing and sway, rocking back and forth, like a reed in the wind. And with his book under one arm, he would often put the other hand out and wave it broadly as if in ecstatic surrender. With beauty and truth converging there in what the songsters gave him, how could he not bask in the glory of it all? It tickled him, thrilled him – and he sent those thrills back across the crowd like the little paperback he used to toss at the song's end in the old days.

To use his words, the best of this singing would "raise the hair on your head . . . and make you feel like you got a hat on." He sometimes couldn't resist preaching a bit as he led, too, exhorting all in the crowd to *love* one another. "And if you don't know what love is," he would say, "I ain't got time to tell you. . . ."

9

Roy Avery

Elder H. Roy Avery (1906-1999)

It's a sight now all but vanished from the American rural landscape. But if you tried to imagine the ideal itinerant salesman, a seller of home wares to country folk in the mid-20th century, you could hardly do better than bring forward the figure of Roy Avery – a man honest, friendly, funny and wise, who had the gift of talk.

Selling products from the trunk or back seat of his car in farming communities in east-central Alabama was what he did for most of his years. But as almost anyone who knew him would say, it really wasn't what he was. When I think of Roy Avery, who lived an active life to the age of 93, I think of him always as a shepherd tending his flock.

He was, deeply, a Primitive Baptist, and beginning in his mid-20s, he preached the gospel for 70 years, appreciatively wearing, like other ministers in the church, the biblical honorific of Elder. He served upward of 15 churches in the region, and as many as four at a time on successive weekends – but always the home church of Rocky Mount, near the little town of Daviston, just a few miles from where he was born and raised. Two months before his death in 1999, Elder Avery stood in the pulpit of Rocky Mount and, in his typically conversational way, taught a lesson that lasted about 45 minutes. As always, songs from *Lloyd's Hymnal*, many of them sung to tunes from the *Sacred Harp*, preceded and followed his remarks.

Charm in Roy Avery was a natural gift. (Photo by his grandson, Cary Estes)

Rocky Mount Primitive Baptist Church, this place that Roy remembered riding a mule to once in 1924, had been torn down and then rebuilt as a simple oblong structure with white siding set against a backdrop of trees and cemetery. It had been home to Roy's family for generations. Marshall Avery, Roy's younger brother and, like him, a Primitive Baptist preacher, once said to me, "I knew the words 'Rocky Mount' almost as soon as I knew any others." He pointed out that his and Roy's grandfather, great-grandfather and great-great-grandfather on their mother's side were all buried in the cemetery there. The tombstones, placed in the 1930s, showed that these Price ancestors fought in the Indian War of 1835 (great-grandfather) and War of 1812 (great-great-grandfather). It was not clear where some of the wives were buried; the great-grandfather had said that when his mother died, they tried to bury her close to her husband but in their digging came upon a big rock and had to choose another grave site close by.

Harvey Roy Avery was born in 1906 to Robert Harvey and Willie Martha ("Mattie") Price Avery. The immediate family included two children who died as infants and eight who survived to adulthood, three of whom lived to old age, with Roy, the eldest, always the leader.

From early on, the sound of Sacred Harp was often in his ears. Speaking of the song WONDROUS LOVE, he once said, "I've heard my mother sing it out working in the field, and I've heard her sing it while she was sweeping the floor. That's one of the things I like about Sacred Harp singing – I'm singing the songs my mother and daddy sang."

When he was 20, he married dark-haired Elma Duck, then just 16, of Eagle Creek in the same county of Tallapoosa. She sang a pretty treble, her daughters remember, but preferred always to stay in the background and, when I knew her, generally sat back in the class during the singing. Roy and Elma had six children: one boy, who died at the age of four, and five girls, all still living at the time of this writing.

Sacred Harp had, at its foundation, a system and discipline that Roy excitedly learned and then for the rest of his life enthusiastically shared. He taught his first Sacred Harp singing school in 1931 when he was 25, maybe a couple of years after he had begun preaching. His name became more familiarly intertwined with Sacred Harp across the broader territory when two songs he wrote found a place in the black-backed Denson Revision of 1960. One of them, MY HOME, has remained in each edition since.

As the Great Depression set in, the young Avery family grew, surviving some lean times. Roy and Elma's daughter Nell Estes, recalling a family story, says that for one stretch they had nothing to eat but potatoes. One Sunday dinner, Mrs. Avery had served mashed potatoes, boiled potatoes and potato soup - really, broth with two potatoes placed in the middle of each family member's bowl. Her young daughter Frances sat on her lap during the blessing of the food. When she lifted her head up, Momma Avery saw that little Frances had quietly eaten one of the potatoes from the bowl in front of the two of them.

Early on, Roy operated a commercial loan business in Lanett, a small town bordering the Georgia line along the Chattahoochee River, but found that regular office hours interfered with his growing ministerial duties. Traveling, by his own schedule, worked better. Meeting, greeting people, tending to their needs, suited his style and his interest. And it got him out among his flock.

In the mid-1950s, he and the family moved to LaFayette, the county seat a few miles to the northeast. From that base, Roy sold insurance and two kinds of home products: J.R. Watkins Products, advertised as "natural apothecary," and Rawleigh Products, which touted a line of "salves, ointments, spices & extracts." Vanilla, black pepper, pie filling, tonics, liniments and rubs were supplies he sold to area families who found it burdensome to go into town and who appreciated buying from and visiting with someone indefatigably cheerful, someone they could trust.

Charm in Roy Avery was a natural gift. There was an endearing, father-like quality about him. It's difficult to imagine him ever raising his voice, or needing to. He had a finely honed sense of human nature, and used it, sometimes mischievously but always lovingly, to press all the right buttons in his interactions. He had a sly sense of humor that reached around behind you and tapped you on the shoulder.

He was a tall, lean, long-armed man. With bright, twinkling

eyes, he had a countenance that always looked to me – despite his being almost 40 years my senior – a bit like that of a youngster who had just waked up and was ready to take in the world. When he talked, he tilted his head down, so that his eyes looked out from a position of leverage. He had what was not exactly a lisp, but somehow a hitch between his tongue and lip, so that his speech slipped a little as it came out. But if the oracle stammers a bit, do we heed the message less?

"Apt to teach": A preacher of the gospel for seven decades. (Photo by Cary Estes)

Congregants at Rocky Mount or other churches he served in those years would have had no difficulty seeing these scriptural words applied to him: "And the servant of the Lord must not strive; but be gentle unto all men, apt to teach, patient . . . ."

Apt to teach. Ah, yes. When he taught from the *Sacred Harp*, to him a sacred charge, he brought personality to bear, along with plain speech, humor and of course a good knowledge of the canon, with examples. His serviceable chalkboard was "full of the rudiments": staves, notes, measures and symbols so crowded the oversized board, top to bottom, side to side, that trying to move it, even with careful fingertips, risked smudging one or another of the figures.

For his singing schools, but even more at singings at Rocky Mount, Roy was always looking for visitors to help man the bass, bolster the lead or bring brilliance to the treble. The alto he could almost take for granted because of the strong alto class resident in the area, including at any point some combination of the following: Daphene Causey, Louise Dean, LaRue Allen and the sisters (and Roy's cousins) Erma Mann Jones and Ila Mann McGhee. There were other altos there over the years, too, none more eminent than the legendary singer and singing-school teacher Moses "Lee" Mann, who died in 1982 at the age of 93 and who all his life sang alto – as Daphene said, "the only man I ever heard sing alto in the woman's range."

Lee, Erma and Ila were children of J.B. "Tobe" Mann[23], notable for having lived to be over 100 and for having married, in turn, three sisters from a big singing family: the first Yates sister, Joda, who died in childbirth with their second child; the second, Lula, who gave birth to Moses Lee, Erma, Ila and four others; and when Lula died, the third, Nina, whose first husband had also died. About that un-usual grouping, a family member's wry remark from decades back has survived: When someone asked what had happened to the Yates girls, whom they had married, or some similar question, the relative said, "Well, two of 'em married Morrises. The rest of 'em married Tobe Mann."

At the singings he presided over at Rocky Mount, Roy always narrated the day, splicing in commentary as he noticed or thought of things, and generally preaching or making extended welcoming remarks just before the noon hour. A lead entry in the minutes for the February 1996 singing there is suggestive: "Elder H.R. Avery cel-ebrated his 90th birthday. Through the day he spoke several times."

In those sessions, a proper guest was always properly acknowledged.

While the rest of the congregants continued singing or talking among themselves, Elder Avery would leave his place at the edge of the square or in the pulpit area and go out and greet virtually every arrival. Each stalwart, each new visitor, came under the warmth of his enfolding wings. In that respect, I have never seen his like. He had a knack for making you want to be at your best. And in the light of his focused attention, you, the individual of the moment, simply shone.

These traits, not surprisingly, brought extraordinary loyalty among the people in his church and singing family. More than in any other singing community I knew of, a cult of personality developed around this charismatic figure. The singers in his territory were Roy Avery people, Roy Avery's singers. It was as simple as that.

Like communities in the Cooper-book territories further south, area singers published their own minutes book ("Minutes of the Annual Sacred Harp Singing in the First District," representing seven counties – Chambers, Clay, Coosa, Lee, Randolph, Talladega and Tallapoosa – later dropping "First District" and the list of counties and substituting "East Central Alabama") rather than joining with the main Denson-book minutes, which already covered a five-state area. And at a time when the Sacred Harp Publishing Company was producing six record albums with large groups of selected singers, the east-central singers, under Roy's direction, again went out on their own, producing two recordings. Field recordings made in this way, with smaller groups in which blend is difficult to achieve and individual voices stick out, inevitably come off as rougher products. But I have full confidence that the Avery-area singers savored their home-grown fruit.

Maybe because most of them were members of his singing community *and* members of the church at Rocky Mount as well, singers from close around rarely traveled to singings in other areas – and Elder Avery himself was committed, for most weekends, for services at one or more churches or Primitive Baptist Association meetings. Visitors from outside (from north Alabama and western Georgia generally) were always royally greeted and made to feel welcome. But there was little reciprocal visiting, the mutual back-scratching that singers throughout the Sacred Harp world depend on for building up or maintaining the strength of their own singings. For understandable reasons, the singing in this circuit was inwardly focused. But, for reasons just as understandable, would the singing community there not have profited by more outward focus? I always wondered if this stance or tendency was not a strategic mistake for the singers in the area, especially for Roy, who so valued fine singing.

In any case, with natural attrition occurring in his as in almost every other Sacred Harp community during that time, the singing grew steadily weaker in Elder Avery's circuit in his later life. And where there had been more than 30 annual sessions listed in the early minutes book I had from the "First District" area, today there are ten or fewer.

One casualty of that era was the singing at Wehadkee, just out from the small community of Rock Mills. The church, an admirably proportioned, high-peaked white wooden structure in a deep grove of trees, was one of the most beautiful country churches of my experience. It burned, an apparent act of arson, in 1995. The annual singing there each November had been the pride of Roy's beloved sister Lydia Hawkins, another figure of magnetic force and tremendous will (just try telling *her* you mightn't be able to make the next session . . .). It was, one year, the site of the smallest singing I ever attended, as evidenced by this distinction: the only bass we had for the morning session was a woman – who normally sang treble, but who carried the part that morning surpassingly well.

The first singing of the year in the area, the fourth Sunday in February, had been proclaimed the "Elder H.R. Avery Birthday Singing" long before I became aware of it. Meeting originally at several locations, it found a permanent home at Rocky Mount in the 1970s. In 1990 the date was moved to the second Sunday, bringing the event closer to Elder Avery's actual birthday.

Also in 1990, as accommodation for their old age, Roy thought it best to relocate, so he and Elma moved from the big, two-story house in LaFayette to a more modest one-story in Roanoke in the adjoining county to the north. From time to time, Roy continued to teach singing schools, the last into the 1990s when he was in his mid-80s. Up until the end of his life in 1999, he kept merchandise in his home for longtime customers who wanted to come by and replenish their cupboard. Elma survived Roy by four years, living to age 93 as he had. She was remarkable as well for having naturally dark hair into those late years, with only a few strands of gray beginning to show.

Roy and Elma at home, about 1986. (Photo by Cary Estes)

Below are notes taken from four of the February sessions at Rocky Mount in the 1990s, including the one just four months before this pivotal figure died. I hope they suitably flesh out a singing-day portrait of Roy Avery – teacher, kinsman, country impresario and vigilant overseer of his flock.

FEBRUARY 13, 1994

Brother Roy preached. Said he couldn't remember when he first believed in God, but could remember the first time he ever prayed: "It was only about four words."

It was in 1918, during World War I, and he was 12. His father had wanted to be "a foot soldier with a rifle" and so had gone to be. In those years, the light they had in their home at night came only from the fire they kept and from kerosene lamps. When they found themselves out of kerosene at one point, Roy was sent to town with their mule wagon to get some. He got the fuel in what he guesses now was a quart jar. On the way back, in the dark, he had to negotiate the wagon around many bumps and holes in the road. He cradled the jar carefully throughout. Close to home, there was a little gate he had to unfasten. He did so, and when he had brought the wagon through it, went back to secure it.

Knowing they were close to home, the mules at that point "decided they would go on" – and took off. He ran after them, fearing the worst. When he caught up, he vaulted onto the wagon – and found the jar of kerosene intact. *"Thank you, Lord, forever!"* he said.

Now more than seven decades later, though the objects of his gratitude were deeper, more substantial gifts, he didn't have to say that the tenor of his message was the same: Thank you, Lord, forever!

On this his birthday singing, he stood at the end to sing a couple of songs of his choice. Several voices recommended 159, WONDROUS LOVE, his mother's favorite song that he had led so many times before. This time, though, he had other songs on his mind. He asked for JESTER first, recalling it not by name or number but by the fragment of words: "If our mothers want to go, why don't they come along?"

And then he wanted to remember and honor his old singing-school teacher and cousin, Lee Mann (Lee's sister Ila and three of his daughters were present that day). "In all the years we sang together [more than half a century], I never called and asked him to sing at a funeral that he didn't make it. Not once. Never asked him to do anything that he didn't come through with. You learn to appreciate somebody like that.

"I remember him leading FILLMORE once: 'Thus will I sing . . . .' I want to sing that now. What is it, 434? And let's *go* with it!" He popped his hands together smartly as he said it, and we started off. He led without a book. On each upbeat, he brought his hands almost together, thumb to thumb, up almost to his face. With the downbeat, he sent them down and off to the side, a deep stroke, like a bird would make in flight. The old-time way. The old-time song. Singing with fire and sweetness, recalling another figure leading that song years, maybe decades, before. That was a fitting way to end a birthday singing, there in the presence of those who loved him and loved the one he sang for.

FEBRUARY 12, 1995

It had snowed in north and central Alabama, and the crowd was down. Elder Roy addressed the group about the difficulties for some in getting there.

"Some could, some couldn't, and some just wouldn't. Same as it's always been."

He preached, and told about volunteering for the war back in the '40s, after his brothers Ben and Bill had already left for service in Europe. He went to town to sign up and was asked by the official there how many he was supporting at home. "A wife and five daughters," he replied. "You've got your own war at home," he was told. "Go on back."

FEBRUARY 11, 1996

Elder Roy would be 90 in just days. His voice was fainter than before, his speech slightly indistinct. But he still gave the right pitches. When he missed one, he would recognize it, back up and sound it again. He mentioned that he was there despite having to leave his wife at home. She was unable to get out, but insisted that he go.

His birthday, he reminded us, was on Valentine's day. "And my wife was born on February second – Groundhog's Day." He grinned slyly. "A valentine married to a groundhog."

"We've got a good class here today," he said. "Some of the best you'll find anywhere . . . *anywhere.* 'Course, now, I'm not talking about most of us. But it takes all of us to make it. When you make a cake, you put dough in along with the sugar, don't you? That's what makes it good, puttin' all of us together."

He fumbled at the pages of his book, not in any rush. "They're making this print smaller every year," he groused.

Several kin pressed him with recommendations of his standard tunes. But he waived them all. From the wide meadow of his memory on this morning, he had sighted a couple of reminiscences that drew him now.

"PRESENT JOYS – what number is that?" 318 was the reply. He flipped the pages in that direction. "For present joys, for blessings past, and for the hope of heav'n at last."

The ones he wanted to remember today were Erma Jones, this great stalwart in his singing life who had died the previous year, and her brother Lee ("Moses Lee Mann"). About Erma, his voice broke. "The Lord only knows how much I miss her."

A little later, just before lunch, he told the group he would spend about 15 minutes preaching – and did so. It was a simple, all-encompassing vision he spread before us. The role for human beings: "To keep ourselves clean, love God and each other, be happy here and happier still over there."

After the meal, he talked to me about Lee Mann. He had given or swapped Lee a calf one time, he said. Later he and Lee were to-gether out in the field and came upon the calf lying on the ground. Roy stood over it, straddling it with his legs. Abruptly it woke up and lurched forward. "Threw me back over my head," he said. "I didn't know that yearling had gotten so big! Lee Mann *laughed* . . . he may be laughing still!"

We were standing on the church's front porch now, between the two restrooms. He looked out across the road to the woods sloping down there.

"One time years ago at a singing here, there was an old man stand-ing here on the porch, asked me where the bathroom was. I told him down in the woods. It was *pouring* down rain. He just stood there and looked. . . .

"I made up my mind that day we were going to build some bath-rooms. I went to Erma and told her what I had in mind. She said, 'Here's $500.' A few more gave money like that, too. And we not only built these bathrooms here, but used the money to add on the kitchen in the back."

I can't resist sharing another moment from that same singing: In the afternoon session, a woman I was sitting next to leaned in to tell me about a relative of one of the singers who had just come up to lead: "John had several kids. This fellow that hadn't seen him in a while saw him here at the church one day with those kids and said, 'Well, Johnny, look at all these kids. If you don't stop, you're gonna have a houseful!' 'Well, I'm not gonna *stop*,' he said." She chuckled heartily.

FEBRUARY 14, 1999

Brother Roy turned 93 on this day.

During the singing, he got up twice and went out into the congre-gation to greet new arrivals. When preaching, he looked at his watch several times. He had again allotted himself 15 minutes and didn't go over it much.

His memory seemed acute as ever. At the end, when it was time to close out the session, he led 143, PLEYEL'S HYMN, the young woman's favorite song, for a 21-year-old who was tragically disabled in an automobile accident 15 years before.

During the lunch hour, he and I talked about John Ramsey. Previously a professor at Auburn University (less than an hour's drive away), John had started singing there at Rocky Mount and, with his powerful deep voice, came to be a great help at area singings for more than a dozen years before he moved out of state. During that time, John was groomed by Roy to be first his backup and then his successor as singing-school teacher; John fulfilled that promise by coming back to Alabama and Rocky Mount several times to teach.

Roy told me again the story of John's first appearance there. He had looked around during a break at a small singing session one evening, he said, and saw this big man come in – and then heard that big, grave voice: "'I'm looking for Elder *H.R. Avery*,'" he mimicked. "Uh-oh," he thought, "the FBI." But then John introduced himself and said he had been told that Elder Avery could "teach him to sing." So began their friendship and John's launch into Sacred Harp.

Hugh McGraw, when he got up to lead, told a story about coming to LaFayette back in the early '60s for a singing and then spending the night with Roy and Elma. The large house with balcony across the front was just a block up from the school building where the singing was held. "I had to sleep on the floor," Hugh said, "but I wasn't the only one. There were about a hundred others that did the same thing! Women in one room and men in another." He said there were mattresses spread everywhere (I was to find out later that Roy had for the occasion rented them from a mattress factory in a nearby town). As Roy was out of the room when Hugh was speaking, I asked him about it afterwards, and he said he remembered that night, said there must indeed have been 50 to 60 who slept there.

"Roy's house was one place where you had music 24 hours a day,"

Hugh continued. "He had tapes playing all through the night. I don't know who got up and changed 'em at three and four o'clock in the morning." One of Roy's daughters whispered to several of us, "Daddy always was a night person!"

Roy later mentioned the recordings to me. "'Course, you couldn't get through my house now. I've got 8-track, cassettes, reel-to-reel. You're a young man still; you could grow old and die and still not listen to all of 'em."

✌ ✍

Nell Avery Estes told me that in the last weeks of her father's life, when his health was obviously declining, the family noticed that the tapes were not being played when he went to bed and knew then that the end must be near. For the bulk of his life and deep into old age, she said, Roy Avery went to sleep every night listening to his recordings.

> Then to my ravished ear
> Let one sweet song begin,
> Let music charm me last on earth,
> And greet me first in heav'n.

Awed by his imprint, I miss the man himself. And I regret that those well beyond his territory, and especially a younger generation of singers in general, never got to see and hear Roy Avery lead a class, never got to know the encircling charm of his conversation, the quiet, winking pleasure of his company.

10

Lawrence and Lula Underwood

They were from the Liberty Hill community, a few miles east of Boaz, in northeast Alabama.

Lula was a good-looking woman, short and dark-complexioned, often with a knowing – or guessing – smile on her face; a wise-cracker, the kind you instantly knew would give as good as she got.

Lawrence was the better singer of the two, having been taught as a boy to sing by the great song-master of that area, Uncle Henry Hallmark, whom Bud Oliver once told me his daddy had called "the best there was," someone who knew the key for every song in the book, and, without ever opening the book, "could hit it."

As an adult, Lawrence had left Sacred Harp for a while to pursue gospel music, but, according to Bud, "it didn't take him long to see he was with the *wrong crowd*. Saw that that was *all show*." And so he returned to the Sacred Harp community – and stayed there the rest of his life. (He died in late 2001 at the age of 90, with Lula dying in early 2002. His tombstone shows his official name to have been Larnce, though we and the Minutes, even when Lula took them, always recognized him as Lawrence.)

It was clear to see that Lawrence and "Luler" enjoyed one another's company. When called to lead together, they stood side by side, both without a book. But when it was just Lawrence, it was a different sight.

He was a great leader of "class music," usually fuging songs (though often it was page 170, EXHILARATION: ". . . and then my troubles will be over"). To start with, he might, with a grin, say, "We're gonna go pretty fast now – just slip your shoes off so you can run faster."

Lawrence, with Lula, not surprisingly, looking over his shoulder. (Photo by Linda Thomas, 1995)

As he stepped about the square, he would lay first one and then the other of his stubby hands against the flat of his back, while with the other, only inches from his belly, he would point at the parts and stir the music. It was not a sweeping or dramatic style but quietly, beautifully textured and, it seemed to me, all of a piece with the songs, the pacing, the wooden floor, the shuffling of the pages, the simmering heat of the day.

On warm days or cool, Lawrence always kept a little crackling fire of humor going, and was eager to spot one in others. I had once shared with a group of singers an embarrassing moment for me at another session. Singing treble on the song Victoria, while savoring a big cough drop, I had opened my mouth wide for a push to achieve one of the high B's in that song and suddenly felt the cough drop separate from me, heard a rattle somewhere about the place, but never saw the cough drop again! Lawrence, years later, out on the grounds at Pine Grove Church on Lookout Mountain, grinned and repeated that story to me. He was always, as the saying went, "studyin' foolishness."

But he had a much better story to share with me in 1995, the one time, I think, I attended his singing at Liberty Hill: a great little story of country courtship.

As the noon-time recess began, he and I met up at the back of the church and then turned to make our way to the dinner table. As we started out, side by side, he reached and took my hand with his, held it lightly, and we walked on together that way. As we walked, he began to tell me how he and Lula had gotten together, past their middle age.

It was not the first marriage for either. He had lost his wife in 1975 and was lonely. He knew of Lula or had been in her company previously, many years before, knew that she had brought up several children by herself after her husband died. She had, in other words, given a good account of herself. She was working then at a convenience store in a nearby community. And so he went there to pay a visit.

When he entered the store, she saw him, knew who he was, and may have guessed that something was afoot.

"What are *you* doin'?" she said. His rendition of her greeting was the verbal equivalent of a cat swatting something, but maybe with its claws retracted.

He must not have expected such an abrupt beginning. His friends knew him to be a man of few words, and few occurred to him now as he tried hastily to make his case.

"Well, just to be straight with you," he said, "I'm lookin' fer a wife, or a girlfriend or a cook. . . ."

"Go on outa here!" Lula said, quick as a cat's slap.

At that point a sound at the door drew his attention. Several customers entered and started to mill about.

"Well, I won't hinder you. . . ," he said, and turned to go.

"I get off Wednesday at noon," she said.

"I'll be here," he replied.

He gave me a nudge with his elbow. "And that's how we got started."

11

Japheth Jackson and Family

Henry Japheth Jackson (1916-2010)

When Japheth Jackson was a boy, he traveled with his family on a visit from their home in Ozark, Ala., across the state line into Florida. The next morning, when he was out to play, mixing with new-found buddies in the neighborhood, it was maybe only natural that at some point he would throw out some *fa-sol-la's* or refer to what he assumed a universal pastime, Sacred Harp. He never actually told me, and may not have recalled, whether what he got from his mates was funny looks, laughs or just puzzled silence.

Their reaction, though, brought him up short – and probably helped to harden his identity for a lifetime. For the first time in his young life, Japheth Jackson that day realized that not everyone spoke his family's, his little community's, language. Growing up with Sacred Harp as he had – singing with brothers and sisters around the kitchen table and with townsfolk at area churches – he had thought it a common heritage.

His was a special heritage, though, as he would come in time to appreciate. His father, Judge Jackson, was the compiler of that historic shape-note volume *The Colored Sacred Harp* and the preeminent figure among African American Sacred Harp singers.

A self-taught, self-made man, Judge Jackson (1883-1958) had left home at the age of 16, with, as he later wrote, only a small bag of clothes and 50 cents. Through farming – first working for the man, and then assiduously saving money and learning to work for himself – he in time became a significant land-owner in Ozark, a builder and owner of rental houses.

Japheth and Gussie Jackson, with his father's milestone compilation. (Photo by Joe Dan Boyd, 1968)

Over time, 12 children were born to Judge and Lela Campbell Jackson. Following the example of the biblical Noah, Jackson named three of the sons Shem, Ham and Japheth (Shem Campbell, Judge Ham, Henry Japheth). It wasn't an ark he was laboring at in those years, though; it was a songbook. He layered his collection with several dozen songs of his own, one co-written with daughter Pauline and others by singing companions – even one by a white friend from a neighboring farm (a well-to-do banker, who, with the reported gift of a thousand dollars, would subsidize the book's publication).

That he was able to put together this collection and have it published in 1934, in the depths of the Great Depression, says a great deal about the uncommon determination that marked Judge Jackson's life. Though only a 77-page soft-cover compilation of 98 tunes, *The Colored Sacred Harp* was a remarkable achievement for a man in his time and circumstance. And if the songbook's title now makes people wince, it's fair to remember that the author was using the designated terminology available to him in that era. For his family and for descendants of his singing friends, Judge Jackson's extraordinary investment in the project, his contribution on behalf of his race, hallowed the name of the songbook itself.

A note under a photo of the "associate author," Bishop J.D. Walker of Dothan, gives perspective to the book's birth: "We ask your cooperation both White and Colored to help us place this book in every home. That we may learn thousands of people especially the youth how to praise God in singing."

If the "little book," as it was often called, never displaced the Cooper book within the black community, it remained a companion collection used both at singings and in performances, on distant stages as well as on local radio and TV.

Henry Japheth – but always just Japheth, or "Japhus," to his family and friends – was the ninth of the Jackson children. And his life was lived humbly yet proudly in the deep shadow cast by his father's figure.

I first came to know Japheth in 1970 in our summer Smithsonian trip and to enjoy his genial company again at the Montreal Expo in 1971. Of "the Wiregrass singers," he was the one I was closest to over the years. And getting to know him in depth was an enriching experience for someone who grew up in a town with, improbably, no black folk at all. (Well, the one exception proving that benighted rule was, for a time, an old retainer on the estate of the mother of Cullman's mayor of that era.) As well as singing together in the Ozark area, Japheth and I often met up at the National Convention, when, over a 27-year period, he and a carload or two of his family or friends would make the four-hour drive north to Birmingham to join the large company there.

Japheth leading PANTING FOR HEAVEN *at the National Convention. (Photo by Joel Cohen, 1998)*

We almost lost him in 1989. As he was receiving horrific news by phone – about the rape of his older sister Emma – Japheth, already with equilibrium problems, reached for a stool to sit on, staggered and fell and broke his neck, injuring his spinal cord. The recovery from paralysis was slow and arduous. A few years later, following triple-bypass surgery, he became paralyzed again and had to go through another lengthy, difficult rehabilitation. He never regained much mobility and continued always to drag his feet behind a walker, if not struggling along with the aid of a cane. For virtually everyone who knew him, Japheth's courage, his indomitable will to triumph over the many challenges placed before him, evoked a kind of awe. I respected Japheth Jackson as much as anyone I ever knew and could wonder if I had ever been acquainted with a better man. He honored me by sharing his trust generally and, on a few quiet occasions, painfully frank comments about the difficulties he and his father before him had had to bear and ultimately to surmount.

Humor was part of what bound the two of us together – and especially, from him, the gentlest, most winningly self-deprecating humor. At the Dewey P. Williams Day singing in downtown Ozark in March of 1999, that humor was, as ever, like sunshine peeking from around the clouds. I was standing with Japheth during a break as he greeted young, local white singer Stanley Smith. First acknowledging the several close calls he'd had with his health over the years, Japheth smiled. "I should already be dead," he said, "but I'm just too stubborn, I'm just like old Bermuda grass." Stanley, he joked, wouldn't know about farming, about pesky old Bermuda grass, so he drew the picture for us: "Old 'muda grass, you dig it up and turn it over, it'll turn brown. Then two days of rain and it'll turn green again. That's the way I am."

Just after the close of the 1997 Jackson Memorial Sing (honoring his father), as he and I stood in the parking lot outside the church, Japheth, then 81, had pointed out his grave site. The plot had just recently been fixed, the headstone already in place. "I know I don't have many more years," he had said. "I'm on the downward slope now. 'Course, we all want to live as long as we can. . . ."

A wearying challenge for the main man: "You can hardly get 'em started sometimes, and then you can hardly get 'em to stop." (Photo by Steve Grauberger, 1995, courtesy of the Alabama Center for Traditional Culture)

The inimitable Dewey Williams had for decades been the force behind Sacred Harp activity in the black Wiregrass community, the one everyone depended on for direction. Japheth in all those years had dutifully served as right-hand man. With Dewey's passing, the burden of leadership fell to him.

At the 2000 Jackson singing, as we visited in the dining area downstairs, Japheth reflected on his old compatriot and on how things had changed in their singing community over time. He laughingly told about a singing performance the two of them had been involved in somewhere years before. He said that Dewey, leaving the stage on that occasion, had "hollered out" – and Japheth shouted out in imitation. "Mr. Dewey," Japheth had shot back, "why are you hollerin' out like that?" "I've been singing all my life," Dewey had answered, "and nobody's ever paid me to do it before!"

My question: Was I ever acquainted with a better man? (Photo by Melissa Springer, Ozark, 1987, courtesy of the Alabama Center for Traditional Culture)

Now the coordination of singing activities was Japheth's to over-see. On this day a number of requests for songs to be led came in a flurry in the closing minutes of the session, almost 4:00 in the afternoon. Trying to direct this singing traffic so that visitors from afar could get started on their drive home, Japheth, like Dewey before him, found the task vexing. Afterwards, he chuckled apologetically about how "you can hardly get 'em started sometimes, and then you can hardly get 'em to stop."

In his last trip to the National Convention in 2006, Japheth, then 90, had once more appeared with a Wiregrass contingent and stood before the congregation in what many that day would hold as an enduring image. Called to lead, he had risen from his wheelchair to a walker to lead a powerful version of 384, PANTING FOR HEAVEN, and then, toward the end of the session, 400, STRUGGLE ON, the song of implied trials he'd led so many times before:

Struggle on, struggle on,
Hallelujah,
Struggle on, for the work's most done,
Hallelujah.

As always when he led, he propelled the group forward with strong, quick movements of his right hand, but also threw his voice up loudly, thrillingly, in the unabashed way a child might do, the way he must have sung all his life.

It would be difficult to overstate Japheth's love of Sacred Harp, his daughter Janice told me after his death. In his last weeks, she played Sacred Harp songs for him each night until he went to sleep. Over and over again as a song ended, she said, he would smile and say, "That's a good-un!" When he was at last unable to speak, Janice would speak for him: "That was a good-un – wasn't it?" She sensed that he agreed.

Japheth had been married for 71 of his 94 years. "As to his children," his obituary read, "he provided the resources for six of the seven to attend college." [The eldest son, the only one who chose not to enroll, had also helped to send the others on.] That could not have been easy for a day laborer. It meant working multiple jobs for decades - as farmer, timber salesman, truck driver, painter, maintenance worker and carpenter. I've no doubt Japheth Jackson acquitted himself well in all those endeavors.

Miss Gussie

Gussie Jackson, Japheth's wife, was a lovely, sweet-faced lady. I didn't meet her for years; she was not a singer. I found her to be a most gracious hostess, though, mainly doing kitchen duty for the annual singings at the Jackson home church of Union Grove Missionary Baptist, where surely no one ever left a session hungry.

My first contact with Mrs. Jackson was a brief and endearing phone conversation. Passing through Ozark once with a couple of singing friends, I had called to see if I could take them over to the Jackson residence to meet the son of Judge Jackson, this much admired figure in his own right. I placed my call, in those pre-cell phone days, from a phone booth. A soft-voiced woman answered. No, Mr. Jackson was not there at the moment, but she was expecting him in a little while. I explained that I was going to be in town only briefly, and had hoped to be able to see or at least speak with her husband before we had to leave.

"What time is it there," she asked?

I looked at my watch and gave her the time.

"Well," she said, as if with mild surprise, "it's the *same time here*. . . ."

I found a charmingly symbolic resonance in that line - something about commonality across distances. . . .

In later years, and more than once, Japheth told me what would become one of my favorite stories: how he met his wife-to-be.

"My daddy was teaching a singing school," he would begin. "A community about ten miles southwest of Ozark. He told me he wanted me to be there on Friday to sing bass."

Japheth and his brother were sitting in a truck near the church on that Friday, he said, when a pretty young girl walked by.

"I saw her, and I said to Shem, 'There goes my wife!'"

"You don't even know her!" Shem said.

"No, but I'm goin' to. I'm gonna marry her."

He lit out after young Miss Gussie Matthews and caught up with her.

"Where do you live?" he asked.

"Why do you want to know where I live?"

"'Cause I want to come see you. I want to marry you!"

"You can't come to see me!"

"Why not?!"

"Because my momma don't let boys come to see me."

"Why?"

"Because I'm too young."

She was 15 at the time, and he was 20.

"I'll wait," he said.

"I knew she was too young," he told me the second time he recounted this story, "and I knew I wasn't ready."

Along the way in that early, exploratory conversation, Gussie had asked Japheth's name. He gave her "Henry," his first and more formal name. She laughed and said, "We got a mule named Henry!"

But Henry Japheth was not deterred. And he waited. He told me young Gussie had afterwards told her momma that she had met a crazy young man at the singing school – a man so crazy he'd told her he wanted to marry her the first time he ever saw her!

Three years later they were married – in 1939, on the first day of the year.

Theirs seemed an especially close union. Twice or more, Japheth told me about how, early in their marriage, Mrs. Jackson had stayed his hand when he had intended a forceful physical discipline of one of their older sons. That story seemed framed in an almost biblical aura, and it was impossible not to see the lifelong significance it carried for him, the strong and tender pride he had come to feel in the rightness of her intervention, the forthrightness of her compassion.

A final image I have of Gussie Matthews Jackson is from the day of her husband's funeral, when, as the family slowly filed out of the auditorium, with two of her sons holding her up, her knees buckled, as if under the palpable weight of such a loss.

The Sisters

In the years I visited the singings at Ozark, I found myself in the company of two or more of Japheth's siblings. In the early years, I was greeted by brothers Shem and J.C. (John), and over time I got to know three of the sisters: Dovie Reese, Pauline Griggs and Ruth Johnson. Dovie, a treble, and Pauline, an alto, had been members of the performance groups that accompanied Dewey Williams to D.C. and Montreal: Pauline to D.C. and Dovie to both.

Pauline Jackson Griggs: "I am a black woman that loves Sacred Harp singing!" (Photo by Kim McRae, 1990)

Pauline in 2005 told a reporter from the *Dothan Eagle* about one of her earliest Sacred Harp memories: listening to her father and older brothers and sisters singing together. In that recollection, Judge Jackson and everyone else in the family had been recovering from the flu. He had stopped singing long enough, Pauline said, to tell her to take some corn out to feed the livestock. She could still recall singing along on the song she heard from inside as she walked out to feed the animals. She and younger sister Ruth had in their youth spent many happy hours singing together on the porch of their home. In old age, they sat side by side on the alto bench at the singings at Union Grove. Later victims of Alzheimer's, both died in 2012, one week apart: Pauline at 97 and Ruth at 89.

In greetings with individual singers, Pauline was often expressive, but in front of a group, always seemed meek, had little to say. Whenever she was called to lead, she would simply stand or, in later years, sit in the chair placed before her, call out the number for her song, lead it and then return to her seat. One exception was memorable to me. From time to time, one or more of the Ozark singers would be inspired to stand and "testify." At some point between songs on this occasion at the Jackson Memorial Sing, Pauline, maybe then in her late 80s, abruptly stood, with body attitude indicating she had something to say. Whether joy, great pride or exhilaration, something had welled up inside her and now had to be freed. With no preface to the statement at all, but bearing down on the words, she proclaimed, "I am a *black woman* that *loves* Sacred Harp singing!" It was as pure and unadorned and forceful a declaration of self-identity as I could imagine – and it made for a riveting moment.

In what seemed almost stream of consciousness, then, she blurted out a few more remarks before, amid general laughter, making clear an intent to continue lording her age over the three younger siblings there – Shem, Japheth and Ruth. "I tell them what to do," she said with the biggest grin, "and they *do* it, too!" The years of her having so little to say in public had, for me, all been worth the wait for that single, explosive declamatory paragraph.

Ruth Jackson Johnson, 2002 National. Per her daughter Jackie: "Showed out!" (Photo by Steve Grauberger, courtesy of the Alabama Center for Traditional Culture)

Ruth, from south Florida, became another favorite, though I didn't come to know her until the later years. A great affection for Sacred Harp was deeply ingrained in her, too. For several years she and her daughter, Jackie, attended the National Convention. On those occasions she led either WARRENTON, 145 top, or HARMONY, 172. The choice of the latter song, one of the old fuging tunes, surprised me the first time she called it – it would not have been one the class at Ozark could have rendered at that point. But she knew it well from her childhood and loved it, and I was pleased that she had this opportunity to hear it once more in full vigor. At the 2006 National, just after she and her small group arrived, I slipped her a note saying that although she could of course lead anything she chose, my feelings wouldn't be hurt if she led 172! I watched her read the note and then slump forward with a laugh. Shortly, when summoned before the group, she announced "172!" and led a stirring rendition, with marching steps ("Showed out!" Jackie, filming it, later said).

In April of 2011 when I called Ruth at her home, asking to start with if I had interrupted her dinner, she mentioned that she had already eaten, but, as typically, had eaten "very little" – which then reminded her of something her father used to say. "My daddy told my husband, 'She likes dresses and skirts and blouses, but that's the *nibblinest* girl I've got!'. . . He was always tellin' men, 'She won't hardly eat anything!'" A man of humor within the family, Judge Jackson had insisted on a barnyard nickname for this his youngest. "He always called me Rooster," she said. "He'd say, 'Hey, *Rooster!*' I'd say, "My name is *Ruth!*'" He was, though, a "wonderful man," she said. And the two of us then spent a few minutes reflecting on the challenges he, as a black man in the rural South, must have gone through in the era in which he and his wife had brought up their large, close-knit family.

The Jackson five: John, Shem, Japheth, Dovie and Pauline. Union Grove Baptist Church, Ozark, Ala., 1995. (Photo by Steve Grauberger, courtesy of the Alabama Center for Traditional Culture)

One of my favorite scenes from the visits to Union Grove – and one I'll use to bring this chapter to a close – involved neither Japheth nor his sisters as principal figures. Pauline and Ruth, on alto, were in the background. Japheth was off to the side, front row of the bass, listening to and nodding along with remarks to the gathering by his brother John.

J.C. Jackson was a short man, a fiery, rough-voiced speaker. When he led a song, electricity seemed to course through his body. It was sermon time now, though, in this break between the morning and afternoon singing sessions, and he was hurling his words at the small church's congregation. After each volley, he would step back, smiling, to assess the impact. Each time, the congregation would answer back perfect agreement.

"Jesus said He would R-I-S-E on the third day – *and He did!*

"That's right," the congregation rejoined.

"He said He would, and He did!"

"Yes, that's right!"

"You women saw Him first," he said, after so brief a pause, looking from one side of the church to the other. "If I remember it right . . . it was *women* who saw Him first. . . ."

It was a complimentary gesture, from the men who preach the lessons, and the women smiled broadly. "Mm-hmm, that's right."

"Y'all must have been up *early* that day!"

"That's right."

"You must have been *busy!*"

"Yes."

Hattie Mae McKenzie, a short, wide woman with a bright blue dress and a big white hat, sat on the front row.

"That's right," she said, nodding her head. "*Still* busy."

12

Buford McGraw

Thomas Buford McGraw (1911-1982)

Buford McGraw, son of Sacred Harp patriarch H.N. "Bud" McGraw, was a tall, gaunt man, a machinist and then a retiree when I knew him, from Mt. Zion, Ga., a small community near Carrollton. He had begun in 1929 a lifetime marriage with Gladys Wallace, from another area singing family. They had six children, four of whom they could count as regular and accomplished singers. Along with his other projects, Buford kept a garden – and bees, though I didn't know that until years into our friendship.

I doubt that anyone who knew him would say Buford was a complicated man. I never detected in him a trace of vanity, pretense or meanness. He was purely what he was, purely what you saw.

His handshake was firm and quick, with emphasis on the shake. The warmth one felt for him was likely not reciprocal response for any warmth of personality in *him* but a simple appreciation for his genuineness, for what he quietly, solidly contributed. He was no jokester, but when something struck him as funny, he would laugh aloud, often with a smoker's cough trailing just behind.

Guarding over a cherished event: Buford at Holly Springs, 1970s. (Photos by Betty Oliver)

At a singing, if Buford were anchoring your treble, you were already off to a good start for a class. On the first or second row, and often in first-chair position (closest to the tenor bench), he sat upright as he sang and typically cupped his hand over his left ear (a not-uncommon practice for steadying one's own pitch amid the din). He was good for every song and for a full day of singing. I have no memory of him ever complaining in public, or in private conversations off to the side.

In a modern-turning world, Buford was something of a primitive. At Holly Springs Church, early in my visits there, someone once asked Buford, as chairman of the day's singing, about bringing in a tape recorder to capture some of the music-making. Buford himself had participated in the studio recordings of the Sacred Harp Publishing Company, and no one would have thought the singing at the church there as being more worthy of preservation than he. But now without the counsel of the senior McGraws, father Bud and uncle Tom, he stood in the square and ruled out the request. I don't recall the exact words but got his sense that the act of recording might somehow tarnish a spiritual act that, for him in that place, had always awaited a natural kindling. Mechanical equipment crossing the threshold of that 1880s-vintage woodwork might represent a violation of sorts. (His decree seemed a bit forced even then, as his words fell out on the floor. And of course it didn't hold for long, shortly to be submerged in a wave of increasing informality and innovation in the singing tradition at Holly Springs, as everywhere.)

In the square, it would be fair to say Buford almost barked his words. He didn't know or speak the King's English. And didn't, in fact, speak much at all. When he did, it was often in exclamation. When we rode together for long distances, usually as passengers in Hugh McGraw's car, he generally looked out the window, listened and let others do the talking. It was from Buford McGraw, though, that I heard two of the more memorable utterances of my Sacred Harp experience.

The first had its setting in the last night of a singing school Hugh had been teaching out from Tallapoosa, Ga. As was often the custom, this final evening was in the format of a regular singing, with singers from the surrounding area attending to give support and round out the parts. And with enough seasoned singers there to add substance and consistency to the sound, this particular session was going extremely well.

Close to the end, Buford was called to lead. Awash in the glow of a splendid evening – young people off to a handsome start in their singing and old friends gathered close by to help – he rose and called out his song selection: 346, THE AMERICAN STAR.

This was not, to say the least, a promising choice. THE AMERICAN STAR belongs to that small group of quaint old songs (WAR DEPARTMENT and THE BRIDE'S FAREWELL come also to mind) that were almost never put up at singings. Tricky stair-steps of pitch, a high range in the lead part, syncopation, compound time, an upbeat tempo – and all to a weighty and unfamiliar text. None of the young singers there would ever have heard the song before, and none at that point would have been capable of it. Dimming prospects further still, the experienced singers in the group were spread out across the large room, on back benches for the most part, so that their individual voices were isolated and unsupported.

Undeterred by any of that, Buford started the song – and we lurched forward.

In a word, it was a disaster. When the few of us who had managed to continue singing throughout had finished – when the thing at last came crashing down – Buford clasped his book under his arm and began to pace slowly up and down the leader's space. A tense quiet fell over the room like a heavy blanket. No one uttered a word. Buford, bent forward, strode awkwardly and frowned, as if in deep study. His eyes raked the floor. We seemed on the cusp of something momentous – but what?

Head down, he turned back one more time – then suddenly glanced up, with a look of challenge on his face.

"I've heared it worse!"

The room exploded in laughter. Peal after peal, and loud and long, the laughing seemed to rattle the house. Buford, though, was immune to the hilarity all about him. His sincerity in the midst of all this, the absence of any trace of irony in his tone or on his face, crowned the comedic effect. And if shorn perhaps of his in-the-moment adventurousness, he stepped back from the square, his store of innocence intact.

The other memorable statement came as a little fragment of backseat conversation as Buford and I and two others again rode with Hugh on some singing expedition. At some point, a mention was made of bees and of Buford's hobby of bee-keeping. I hadn't known about the bees, so this mention was a surprise. The two of us then exchanged just a couple of sentences on the topic, with my rounding it off by saying something probably as bland as "Well, they're really something, aren't they?"

Buford turned to me with that quick motion of his head – a head jerk like we might have seen from one of the chickens he raised – and declared with an almost defiant pride: *"They's give out to be the curiousest and most peculiarest creature they is!"*

The moments that followed were doubtless not remarkable for the others in the car, if any of them had even been tuned in to our conversation. I, on the other hand, felt as close as I could remember being to an out-of-body awareness. And the grin on my face, if anyone had been watching, would probably have seemed to extend almost all the way around to the back.

As we rode on, mile after mile, there was a continuing murmur of conversation. But in my mind I sat suspended above it, hovering somewhere between wonder and delight, aware that I had just received one of the most astonishingly colorful phrasings I would ever be privileged to hear. I did the mental equivalent of pinching myself to see if I had really heard what I had just heard. . . .

And here I must stress: It's one thing to hear those words, in imitation, sounded from one's own mouth or to pick them up, from flat-lying on a page, and soundlessly run them through. It's quite another to have heard them propelled fresh from that raspy throat in their full vernacular – like suddenly, in the woods, coming upon some outlandishly bespeckled, one-of-a-kind creature, not peering out from snapshot or glossy picture-book but wriggling there across one's very path. . . .

Fast and as surely as I could, I attempted the preservation. Over and over again, in inner voice, I repeated to myself the phrasing, the inflection – bearing down on it, etching it into memory: *They's . . . give out to be . . . the curiousest . . . and most peculiarest . . . creature . . . they is. . . .*

Mixed in with it all was Buford's awe and his pride in the bee, in the bee's industry, the mystery of the bee. . . . The vibrant gift of his speech – archaic, rule-fracturing – leaves me still in wonder.

Buford McGraw: son and father of Sacred Harp singers, fearless tune-leader, stalwart tribble, stoic traveling companion and bee-keeper. An American original.

13

In Search of the Lost Tribe of Sacred Harp

Ever since the '60s and my first involvement in Sacred Harp, I had the notion that there must be isolated groups of singers unknown to the rest of us. Great stretches of the Deep South had been awash with the tradition in the 19th and early 20th centuries. As the tradition ebbed over the decades, it must have left pockets here and there, small communities of singers who had lost touch with any larger network. The research for my book in the '70s had already turned up a good many sessions not generally known; there must be others, I thought. For almost 30 years I kept eyes and ears open, hoping to discover such a group.

I didn't just sit waiting, either. On weekends, I often drove many miles through unfamiliar countryside to singings or to visit with family and friends. A ring of cars about a little brick or white, wood-framed church building on any Sunday morning would have likely confirmed regular church services there. But on Saturdays? Cresting a hill on some country road, I would catch, ahead, the glint of car hoods through the trees. Expectation would then vault up: an undiscovered singing in some unfamiliar site, a place where I might walk in and hear that familiar sound, weaker than in other settings maybe, but familiar still. . . . As I drew closer, with the trees opening up to a clearing, I would then see a car-and-truck graveyard – and drive on, chastened once more.

So finding the Lees of South Georgia – or rather having them find us – was a dream come true: a large family, centered in Hoboken, Ga., whose Sacred Harp roots apparently went back at least to the 1860s. In isolation, this community of singers – mostly family but some church friends as well – had evolved, or just as likely kept alive, a way of singing distinct from that of other Sacred Harp groups. Beautifully ornamented, it rolled itself out slower than almost any other version I had heard. It had its own characteristic group and individual intonation, even a slightly different pronunciation of both shape syllables and many common words.

I first got word of the family, I believe, from a report about a member of the clan showing up at a singing at Holly Springs Church near Bremen. The representative who appeared there, as a scout it seemed, was reported to be from a community deep down in southeastern Georgia, almost at the edge of the Okefenokee. My first contact with any of the Lees then came a few months later, following a letter from a singing friend (now Alice Bejnar) from Tallahassee, Fla., who had become acquainted with several members of the family. David Lee and his wife Kathy, Alice wrote, planned to attend, for their first Denson-book singing, the Georgia State Convention, at the DeKalb County Courthouse in Decatur in just a few weeks (March of 1995). If I showed up there, she promised an introduction to them.

I entered the handsome, marble-appointed courtroom on the targeted date after the morning session was underway. As I scanned the large class, which included a good many singers unknown to me, my eyes fell on a tall, dark-haired, young-to-middle-aged man in first-chair position on bass. "If he is in this house," I said to myself, "then that is David Lee." And sure enough. At the break, he and I made our way to each other for what became an emotional first meeting. "Your book," he said, "opened a whole new world to me." And then quickly the words poured out: "Sacred Harp has been my life – the words, the music, the worship . . . ."

A cousin, the one who had taken the scouting trip to Holly Springs, had found out about my book, had ordered it and had told David about it. Skeptical at first, David asked him to bring it to him. He had read it, he told me, with excitement, as he looked forward to the inevitable section on the Lees. "Then I realized," he said with a big grin, "we weren't even a blip on the screen."

I would soon follow up with a trip to Hoboken to sing with the family and their local community at a Saturday night sing, as they called it. I stayed with David and Kathy – much enjoying, the next morning, Kathy's hand-patted biscuits with sorghum – and visited with David's father and mother, Johnny and Delorese; cousin Clarke Lee and his wife, Julie; cousin Tollie Lee and others. I brought with me a recording of the Wootten family, whose singing I thought they would most appreciate.

I had heard from David already, and heard more now from David and Clarke and others, that they had come, over time, to see themselves as *the last of the Sacred Harp singers*. . . . It was an impossibly romantic notion, I guess we could say, one held on to with some persistence within their community – but also one of late amusement for David and Clarke: "I mean, where did we think these *books* were coming from?!" There might still be a few people out there singing Sacred Harp, maybe the thinking was, but were they *true* Sacred Harp singers? Insularity had made them protective of their tradition and, for some in their number, suspicious of others who might try to inject a different style, different values. "You may encounter some ice tonight," Clarke said to me just before we left for the singing at the schoolhouse – and he wasn't talking about the weather.

In the 19th century, the Lees and their friends had sung from the B.F. White editions. After 1911, they sang from the J.L. White book. In time, a few of the 1936 Denson books appeared in their area, but local singers were never able to obtain enough copies for an entire class. In the 1940s, they got copies of the Cooper book, which then became the main songbook for them. When some members had the Cooper and others the Denson – and when a particular song appeared on different pages in the two books – Silas Lee, the longtime "sing leader" for the area, would call out one number for one book and one for the other. And so they proceeded, awkwardly, two-bookedly, over the years, with gradually diminishing numbers of singers and a discouraging loss of momentum.

When Alice was looking for people in the general area of Tallahassee to invite to an upcoming singing, someone mentioned that, well, there *were* these folks over in Hoboken, Ga., who kept ordering books. . . . With the name of a Hoboken contact, Alice had then written Clarke Lee, inviting him and other members of his group to join them. Clarke had shared the invitation with David. After hearing the report about the Holly Springs singing and after reading about this much wider Sacred Harp community, David at last found curiosity too strong to resist. He and Clarke and Julie and another cousin set out for Tallahassee.

It was an interesting, a mind-opening experience, they said. But the singers they found there, including several from southeastern Alabama, then wanted to repay the visit in kind. Uh-oh. Did the Lees really *want* outsiders within their fortressed tradition? David later recalled the dilemma: They weren't eager for the meeting but didn't want to seem inhospitable. Might as well let the visitors come, they decided – and, as David laughingly said, "We could always talk about 'em after they were gone."

The Test: RELIGION IS A FORTUNE

Maybe more than the others, Tollie Lee, Silas Lee's son, was wary. As he considered the impending visit from people he had never met and whose singing he had never heard, he set his mind on a shibboleth, and shared it with Clarke and David. RELIGION IS A FORTUNE, one of the great old mid-19th-century songs of the camp-meeting spiritual type – probably not in the Lees', or any other major group's, Top 40 – would prove a worthy test. Would these visitors know, could they readily sing it? Or would tripping over it expose their superficiality?

The group of visiting singers from hours away – Bill Aplin, Stanley Smith, Tommie Spurlock, Don Clark and a few others – appeared, received a cordial greeting and got down to singing. Early on, Tollie called for 319. Without missing a beat, the visitors sang it, notes and words – and sang it as heartily, maybe as heartfully, as any of the other tunes called. The two groups had thus found a common language. And though they might not have realized it at the time, the singers from Alabama had passed a crucial test – and paved the way for all who would later come.

With Tollie Lee – and with no shibboleth needed. Mount Pisgah Singing Society, Stroud, Ala., 1999. (Photo by Laura Densmore)

As David said, the Lee family members were aware that, in taking these early steps, things would be changed for them forever. There was no going back. He wrote me in an early letter that the whole prospect seemed like the transformation a chaste bride might ponder. Once married, she could never return to her virginal state. All, for better or worse, would now be different, the passage irrevocable.

In short order, "the Lees" became a Sacred Harp sensation, over the years visiting distant places and receiving in turn eager delegations from across the Sacred Harp world. Assimilation inevitably ensued, and with it a not-unexpected exchange: the loss of some of the contours of a beautifully blended, a *familial* singing style for the gaining of a countrywide, even global, community and a more powerful way of singing – along with, I suppose, a growing tolerance for hearing cherished songs rendered much faster than they had ever expected to hear them. For the Lees in general, I think it's safe to say that, while they must probably always have nostalgia for the unity and closeness of singing through tight local family and church bonds, they had gained joys in singing and relationships in newly discovered countrymen and even other-countrymen far beyond what they had imagined.

In my first visit to Hoboken, I had written in David's copy of my book: "I was always looking for the Lost Tribe. But you found me." Johnny Lee, in a follow-up note from that visit, wrote, "Perhaps we were lost; perhaps you found us." However it came to be: "How distressing the thought that this meeting may have never happened. . . . It is this type of enrichment that many of us have long dreamed and cherished in our imagination." Years afterwards, and still enjoying their emergence, Johnny shared with me what I knew to be a well-considered view: "Our greatest enemy was our exclusivity."

Another Tribe: the Calvary Convention

Discovering the Lees fulfilled a longtime personal quest. I didn't then expect to find, in the spring of 1997, another such unknown community of singers almost right under my nose. From Jim Carnes, who in turn had heard from Birmingham resident Joyce Cauthen, I heard about a group of African American Sacred Harp singers from Camp Hill, Ala., who were said to have a cut on a CD featuring rural Alabama song traditions. Camp Hill, which had been just off my path on many trips to and from Auburn over the years, is in the east-central part of the state and well north of the Wiregrass area, where African Americans sang from the Cooper book. This group, listed as "Sacred Harp singers of Camp Hill," was singing the song ANTIOCH, mentioned as being from the 1971 edition of the Denson book. Black Sacred Harp singers from Alabama using the Denson book meant a new variant discovered!

In the years that followed, I could find no one in the wider Sacred Harp community who seemed to know about this group of singers – or the more than century-old tradition they had emerged from. Segregation as a way of life in our region over the decades would account for much of the invisibility of a separate tradition running alongside the mainstream one. Still, it's remarkable that this one could have held forth to virtually the end of the 20th century without the rest of us knowing of its existence.

The recording listed no individual names, and it took me a while to track down a contact person. Ultimately I was able to speak by phone with the lead singer, Samuel Holloway of LaFayette (a short distance from Camp Hill), who told me that he was 67, that he had been singing Sacred Harp since he was nine and that the tradition in his community went back to the 1800s. "We have a class of about 25 or 30," he said. "Class" – the indispensable term sounded. I knew I was on the right track.

At my suggestion, some days or weeks later, on the fourth Saturday in May, Mr. Holloway came by the Cooper-book singing at Mount Pisgah in the Stroud community, within 30 miles of his home, so that we could meet. He had to attend a funeral, though, and couldn't stay for the singing. I shook his hand, and was pleased that the next two hands he shook were those of David and Clark Lee – a greeting between emissaries of these two distinct tribes once lost to the rest of us and now found.

I followed Mr. Holloway out to his car to see the 1971 songbook he had brought. He gave me the names and phone numbers of six other singers in his group. And he shared with me a couple of printed programs from the 112th and 113th (1993 and 1994) sessions of the

"Calvary Sacred Harp Singing Convention" at two different churches in the Camp Hill area.

There were 14 classes in this branch of the tradition, he told me, with singing groups in LaFayette, Alexander City, Wadley, Wetumpka and a few other towns and communities in that section of the state. They were named for their local churches: Poplar Springs, White Hall, Enterprise, Centerview, Macedonia, Hopewell, Pine Grove, Ozias, Murray Chapel and so forth. Giving the expected news, he said the singing was not nearly so strong as it had been in earlier years. In a familiar refrain, he expressed concern that "the young folks" were not picking up the tradition. Members of his local group used to go over to Atlanta to sing a good many years ago, I was surprised to hear, but for some years had just been singing in their own sphere. I was later to get confirmation from other members who indeed remembered riding with parents or older folk to sing both Sacred Harp and seven-shape music at African American churches in Atlanta, Cedartown, Ga., and Chattanooga, Tenn. (With the demise of the older generation, the names and locations of the churches where those singings had been held were now lost.)

Samuel Holloway was a congenial man and a young-looking 67, open and apparently eager to make connections with the broader community. He had a conflict during the upcoming National Convention in June but thought that others might be interested in coming. "Maybe we can learn something," he said. And I offered that I and others had something to learn as well. Inside the cover of his book were inked-in song numbers: 277, 53, 62, 85, 77 . . . familiar and reassuring figures. But my guess was that these numbers might represent only a narrow pool of songs commonly used. That supposition would turn out to be correct.

Notes I kept from attending the next two annual sessions of the Calvary Convention are listed below.

OCT. 26, 1997, THE 116TH ANNUAL SESSION

Inside the Pine Grove Baptist Church just out from Dadeville, I felt like the bride in that quaint farewell song (p. 359): "Griefs and hopes my bosom swell." I had looked forward to this day for months, but was immediately saddened to see how much of the glory of this apparently once-strong tradition, and sound, had faded. I had missed the long Saturday session, which reportedly lasted into the evening, but was there for the Sunday session (12:30 to 2:30), which followed a regular church service.

The sound and style of singing were close to what I had heard over the years from the Wiregrass singers, and I wondered whether the two groups might have forked from a common tradition.

There were about 40 in attendance, maybe 25 of whom sang, or sang somewhat. Most sang tenor, and mostly from memory. There was harmony in the room, but it was fairly free-flowing. One elderly woman sat alone in the traditional place for treble. No one sat in the traditional bass or alto sections – well, three of the four officers sat where we would normally expect the altos, facing the tenors. A couple of singers had dilapidated books from the '30s; the 1971 edition was the latest anyone had until the seven new books I had brought with me were purchased and distributed. I failed to find out when any other singings in their territory occurred. They had no printed minutes beyond those of the convention session itself; their local singings must have been small indeed.

In evidence there were all the signs I've seen over the years from singing traditions grown weak. The number of songs they could sing had become quite limited over time. They sang very slowly and had trouble getting a song started. They didn't strictly observe time markings at cadence points; their rests were often either significantly longer or shorter than what was written. Pitching was low.

They sang THE OLD SHIP OF ZION (twice), RETURN AGAIN, VICTORIA, THE PARTING HAND, THE MORNING TRUMPET, THE TRAVELER. They called on me to lead, and I asked for a song I felt would fit with that grouping:

SWEET RIVERS. There was polite hesitation, as it seemed they did not sing this any more. But the recording secretary, Fatha ("Faitha") Mae Carlisle, a delightful lady, said, "My father used to sing that song!" Should I lead it or not? Yes, they encouraged me to go ahead, some of them wanting to hear the song again (though, I'm sure, not wanting to embarrass me by a poor effort). And so we sang it – Fatha Mae was with me every step of the way – and they approved the choice. "A beautiful song!"

They called for their visitor to lead several more times. I led JOURNEY HOME, and then was asked to lead a couple of requests. The first one, COWPER, surprised me, because it was a fuging song (the only one we did), requiring that we get a couple of basses to take their places on my right. But we did fine, and they seemed pleased to be able to resurrect this choice. AMAZING GRACE surprised me even more. I couldn't imagine their having lost easy entry to this one, but that seemed the case. All they needed, though, was someone with a carrying voice who could lead with confidence. And so we made good music.

Like the Wiregrass conventions I had attended decades before, the session had kept many of the formal trappings of conventions of old, including printed programs. Ribbon-badges were sold (50 cents each), and there were a number of collections and financial reports. As the old conventions used to do, the program agenda included a time for representatives from each of the constituent classes to lead a lesson, even though most did not send, or no longer had, representation. Macedonia, Centerview, Ozias, White Hall, Pine Grove, Enterprise, Hopewell, Poplar Springs, Murray Chapel – and "Seven Shapes" (though no shapes but our four were sung during the day). Several of the songs rendered were gospel tunes – THIS WORLD IS IN A BAD CONDITION, I'VE HAD MY SHARE OF UPS AND DOWNS, SOMEWHERE AROUND GOD'S THRONE. There were several solos, with general class accompaniment.

Saddened as I was overall to see how relatively feeble the group and the singing were, I was touched by the beauty of much of what I heard and by the clear love these folk had for the songs and the tradition. They seemed to take heart from my visit and from what must have seemed to them a promise to help. I wished I could have provided more.

I told them I brought greetings from the larger Sacred Harp community now spread across the country. Most had not heard that there were now Sacred Harp groups in Chicago, Boston, L.A. and so forth, and they were cheered by this news. When I invited them to the National Convention in Birmingham the following June, a number seemed genuinely interested (I ended up with 11 names and addresses on a sign-up sheet I left for flyer invitations). Convention president Holloway and others said that they would like to be able to sing better, would welcome opportunities to brush up on their singing.

Several followed me out to my car afterwards to hear a little of the National recording I had brought along. I played ANTIOCH, a song I knew to be familiar to them, and they expressed surprise and pleasure at hearing "so many *young* voices!" And: "They do sing faster!"

⁂

OCT. 24, 1998, THE 117TH ANNUAL SESSION

Sardis Baptist Church, out from Camp Hill, down Highway 280 from Birmingham, past Childersburg, Sylacauga and Alexander City, should not have been so difficult to get to. I had two sets of directions, which differed on key points, and when neither got me there (I later learned I was only a couple of miles away at one point), I retraced my steps and asked a series of seemingly well-intentioned folks for help – and got as many different directions.

Before I turned off 280, though, I had stopped at a little store and asked an elderly black woman on her way inside if she knew where Sardis Church was. She looked me over good (ordinarily I would have said skeptically) and said, "You must be going to a singin' convention."

That was sweet to hear from a stranger in a strange place, and it reminded me that Sacred Harp has not yet altogether sunk out of sight
in these communities.

But back on my way, I raced up and down country roads, trying this one and then another before piecing together the bits of the
puzzle. (Part of the problem was that there really were that many ways
to get there! Most of the roads intersected with each other so many
times. . . .) Still, I arrived about noon, only an hour late.

Once again, I had the glass-half-full-or-half-empty reaction. Moved
that these people remained faithful stewards of a cherished tradition,
but disheartened that they had let lapse so much of the discipline that
makes the whole thing work.

There were only about 15 or 16 there when I arrived, but the
number swelled into the 30s before I left (at 4:00). They were set to go
well into the evening and expected several more to join them.

The printed programs listed the seven classes who are called on,
in turn, for a lesson. They are dutiful to their format. Even when no
one attends from a particular class, someone is asked (as I was this
year and last) to come up and sing for the missing group.

They sing the notes, but don't really sing in parts. A man and
a woman sat in what would normally be the treble section, but I
couldn't make out any treble coming from them. No alto bench and
no alto sound that I could hear. And no bass bench – just one, two
or three bass voices on the few bass entrances. Some harmony, but
indistinct and free-flowing. They don't beat time, and consequently
begin and end phrases the way people might who are sitting around
in a leaderless group singing carols a cappella and very slowly. The
singing has beauty – but on its own terms.

Steve Grauberger, from the Alabama Center for Traditional
Culture, and I were the only whites in attendance. We were cordially
welcomed.

Again the number of songs used was quite small. The 1997 printed program had listed the songs called at the previous year's session:
a total of 41 and only 22 different ones. "Been used" is not a phrase

you would hear in this assembly. In that 1996 session, RETURN AGAIN was listed as having been sung five times over the two days. Especially surprising was this pattern: one person might get up to lead THE OLD SHIP OF ZION or THE MORNING TRUMPET, and the next person up would call for the same song!

We had already sung THE TRAVELER (108, bottom), and after a number of other songs were sung, someone got up and called 108. Steve, sitting in front of me, said with obvious hope in this voice, "Top?" "Bottom" was the spoilsporting reply.

When I was asked to lead, I took the opportunity to lobby a bit. If you don't use it, you lose it, I told them – and received affirming words and nods. These old songs, I said: if we don't occasionally shake them out, they will become lost to us! They knew where I was going and urged me on. I told them I would like to use for my lesson songs they might not have heard in a while but would now like to hear. 406 (NEW HARMONY) and 288 (WHITE) were called out, and so we sang those.

This is a poignant thing to see and to participate in. They know what is happening, they see it slipping away. But they don't quite have the whatever to turn it around. So a number of them sit and sing without a book, not because they know all the songs, but because they know all the songs they will need to sing. "We need to find a way to get the young people singing," convention president Holloway said, in a refrain as familiar as that of RETURN AGAIN.

One of the promising things about the day was that Steve had brought with him Barney Roberson and another gentleman from the black Cooper-book singing tradition from further south. The Calvary folk seemed greatly pleased and grateful at this infusion, and the Wiregrass visitors also seemed to relish the day. Though most of the singers from both areas are elderly and though the traveling distance is a formidable obstacle, maybe, I hoped, these two faltering traditions could help support each other.

From my invitation at the previous year's convention, four members of the group had attended one day of the National Convention the following June and led RETURN AGAIN to a class mesmerized by the pace and pitch (slow and low). Lee Kyles and his wife had been two of the four, and on this day he stood and spoke glowingly about that experience. "I was tired when I got there, but once I got there, I wasn't tired anymore for the rest of the day. If you go once, you'll go again!" Over lunch I told him I was sure he had heard songs sung much faster in Birmingham than he was used to hearing and many songs he hadn't heard in a while. "Yes," he laughingly said, "y'all sing all those songs we've been avoiding!" A number of the group talked about renting a bus or a van or two and attending the next year's National. The prospect of walking into a singing where each of the parts numbers in double digits was clearly exciting to them. (And several of them did attend over the next few years.)

Members of the Calvary Convention at the 1998 National: Lee and Margaret Kyles, Velma Walker. (Photo by Ginnie Ely)

A final note on one of the highlights of the day for me and surely for the rest as well: An elderly woman, slight and stooped, with a fur-rimmed hat on, was called to represent the "Seven Shapes" class. (Other seven-shapers would arrive later and lead us in gospel standards like HOLD TO GOD'S UNCHANGING HAND and I'LL FLY AWAY.) She brought one of those little paperback gospel books, and Steve helped her pass out copies of the song she would lead, JOHN KNOWS. Singing the seven-shape rendition by herself before leading us in the words, she enunciated each syllable with an almost stealthily whispered staccato – Mi, mi, mi, mi, do, do – and just about brought the class to its feet.

'Our Classes Emeritus'

I may have missed the 1999 session but attended in the years 2000-2003. In 2001, the obituary report included a total of ten singers or supporters from four of the community classes, Lee Kyles among them. At some point around that time, the annual Sunday session was discontinued, and I was usually unable to attend on Saturday.

The 122nd session in 2003, at Greater Poplar Springs Baptist Church, out from LaFayette, was the last I attended. Hugh McGraw and Bobby Jackson from Georgia were notable visitors that day. For "participating classes," the program listed only White Hall, Enterprise, Poplar Springs and Seven Shapes. On the back was this note:

** In Appreciation **

The Calvary Sacred Harp Singing Convention wishes to acknowledge and give sincere appreciation to those classes that have served this Convention over the years. These classes shall be our classes Emeritus: Hopewell, Ozias, Centerview, Pine Grove and Murray Chapel.

God has blessed us with some great Sacred Harp note singers, whose voices were anointed by God to sing His praises. We shall forever remember them.

It was, I could see, a gradual letting go. In early 2012 I spoke again with Alfred Jennings, a regular convention participant and a visitor once or twice to the National as well. He had left the area as a young man when he joined the military and had then lived in other states before returning to Alabama in 1967. His father, he told me, had been a great singer: "He was a whiz at it." But when Alfred came back, he found that the singing "was almost fizzling out then – I got in on the end of it." He and his sister had given great effort to support the singing since, but, past a point, realized that their effort was futile. At the 2011 session, he told me, there were "only five singers there," none of them strong leaders and not all of whom could even "sing the notes." About ten to 15 observers filtered in as well, he said, but the convention was now only the faintest shadow of its former self.

It was a fiercely proud institution that had endured for more than a century and a quarter. At its peak, the Calvary Convention must have seemed self-sustaining, so pleasurable were its central events, so obviously worthy its proceedings. And then, over the many years, the timbers began to weaken, the whole structure to sag. The power of tradition, beautiful in its way (when not frightening!), inspires awe. What I found so remarkable was the dedication of the convention's last-quarter-century participants, their strong impulse to prop the singing up for as long as they could, to carry out its format, perform its rituals, lift up once more the songs their parents and grandparents, the great classes of the past, had shouted to the heavens.

14

George M., Remembering and Remembered

George M. Mattox (1891-1987)

His middle initial stood for nothing but itself and traveled with almost equal status wherever his first name went. He was, to everyone, "George-Em." And in the years that I knew him – the late '60s and '70s – Mr. George M. seemed the granddaddy of Sacred Harp singing in Tennessee.

Sly-humored, sweet-mannered, he was an irresistible personality – and surely as flavorful a talker as the Sacred Harp world has produced. He seems now, in my recollection, to have squinted somewhat when he stood to speak or lead at singings, a sort of friendly grimace playing on his face. When he called for Heavenly Dove, one of his "sugar sticks," he would turn and charge the altos to "let me hear those white *Sol's!*" the sustained high C's (whole notes and dotted halves with their open noteheads) that strung an appealing tension and proved the mettle of a good alto class.

His wonderfully textured speech, the cadences of his voice, reminded me of my own grandfather, who was almost exactly his age and who traveled many of the same back roads in north Alabama and in Lawrence County, Tenn., following new-book singing, while George M. plied the old book.

George M. and his Emma, 1914. (Courtesy of their daughter, Jeanette Dewberry)

Born in Cullman in 1891, the sixth of nine children (eight of whom lived to adulthood), he was – like my grandfather – raised in neighboring Winston County, in hardscrabble farming life. His mother, Phronie, was from a musical family, the Daniels. His first cousin, from Alabama's Sand Mountain area, was the organizer and key member of the John Daniel Quartet, one of the most popular gospel groups of the 1940s.

In his mid-20s, with his beloved Emma ("Emmer," as he and the others said it), he struck out for Tennessee, settling in Lawrence County in a wooded section just north of Lawrenceburg, where he would be a pioneering farmer and raiser of livestock, a carpenter and, in time, an operator of heavy outdoor equipment for the county. Together he and Emma whipped their 40 acres of countryside into shape and forged a life for themselves and their children that made them proud. They both lived to be 95.

A lightly faded photo from 1914 gives us a portrait of Emma Jane Parker and George M. before their marriage. Sitting, and casually cross-legged at that, with his sprightly-looking chosen one standing beside, a hatted George M. seems to be seriously eyeing the camera, daring it to capture his essence. No hiked-up smile there, but no apparent shyness, either. And not to make too much of it, but the photo has the look of someone who knows that his life, with its great opportunities, is all before him.

I shook hands and briefly conversed with George M. at the Cullman courthouse, at Holly Springs and at a few other locations for a decade or so as our singing circuits overlapped. But to my later regret, other than a brief quote or two, I didn't capture details of those conversations. (One set of words from an appearance at Holly springs, his lively invitation to a session close to his Tennessee neighborhood, did make it into my book: "We may not have much to eat, but we'll have plenty of Hardshell coffee[24]. We'll treat you so many different ways, you're bound to like some of 'em.")

Over the years, though, his words about his early life and upbringing and about what Sacred Harp meant to him were forwarded to me.

The first source was a cassette recording of a tantalizing conversation with him from 1974: a gift to me from a relative of the two interviewers, a mother and daughter who had visited with him following a singing they had attended but who otherwise seemed generally unfamiliar with Sacred Harp. More recently, his family shared with me copies of newspaper articles from 1971 and 1985 that featured extensive quotes from the man himself. More than any photo can, his rich and ambling language, even from his old age, brings Mr. George M. back in all his charm and caginess.

The first piece, his "Letter to the Editor" (constructed from an interview with him by the now defunct town newspaper), a regular feature for those entering the *Democrat-Union*'s "Over-Eighty Club," is initially fairly straightforward, as in this passage:

> I was carried to Winston County, Ala., when I was three months old. My father bought 160 acres of land in the woods for $9.00. The first job I had for pay was chopping cotton for 35 cents a day. Not eight hours a day but from sunup to sundown. I worked for my dad until I was 21 years old. I have broke three steers in my life to plow. I have plowed many a day in new ground with a steer and barefooted. That was a slow way to make a living. The next public job I had for pay was driving a three-yoke cow wagon with eight wheels hauling logs for $1.75 a day. When I was 21 years old, I told my daddy that I had worked for him till that age and now I'm going to work for myself. He sold me 40 acres of land which he had cultivated when I was a baby for $150.00 on credit. I made this crop before I married. In 1915 I married Emma Parker.

And then he begins to be more playful:

> I reckon me and my old gal have done a pretty good old job. We got 30 cents in money we haven't spent. We bought land in Lawrence County with the little we had. We cleared this

land and made a farm of it. We have been living together for 56 years. We have never argued in our lives, but sometimes you could hear us reasoning things for a quarter of a mile.

I am in excellent health and could work all day. I have the majority of my farm sowed down and black angus walking all over it.

Along the way, the reader will come to a curve or two in the road: "I learned ten or twelve years ago that I could take it easy and live off the interest I owed."

The 1985 article from the *Lawrence County Advocate*, when George M. was 93 – and on oxygen (and still frequently on tobacco juice) – is more expansive. And I credit the reporter for taking his words down just as she heard them.[25] Observing that the couple had celebrated their 70th wedding anniversary a couple of months before, the writer notes that George M. and Emma had known each other all their lives. The story picks up there:

"I said to Emmer one Sunday evening. I said, Emmer you've got the chance to marry a boy who lacks about 50 cents being a millionaire. I don't want you to answer too quick, you've not thought about it," Mattox recalled.

"I had three dollars the day we married and I owed $80. I told Emmer lots of times I thought she used very little judgment in taking me. But I reckon she thought I was going far.

"I've provided a pretty good living for her. We both worked hard in Alabama just a farming, but we worked extra hard when we came to Tennessee."

George M. and Emma at a family reunion. (Courtesy of Jeanette Dewberry)

"Me and Emmer walked every where we went that first year we was married, then I bought a one-horse wagon. We was prouder of that $75 wagon than we've ever been of the $5,000 pickup out there.

"And Emmer, she never, never asked me for a dollar that I wouldn't give it to her, but millions of times she knowed I didn't have it and she didn't ask me for it."

Hearing about land for sale in Lawrence County, they had moved, by mules and wagon, to Lawrenceburg in the early spring of 1920 when their second son was just six months old. The four of them had slept on the ground along the way. About the same time as he and Emma did, all of George M.'s siblings, except for brother Joe (who ultimately came), moved there as well with their young families and purchased adjoining land. George M. and his brothers cut a road to and through their little community, which naturally became known as Mattoxtown. Over time, George M. and Emma bought additional land from one or more of the siblings and ended up with 87 acres for themselves and their children.

"When I bought this 40 acres, I went in debt $1,200," George M. told the *Advocate* reporter, "and if I'd had to showed you a dime of money or died, I'd had to died.

"We thought we sure were in the back woods out here, but one day when the wind was out of the northwest, the 10 o'clock local left Ethridge [town just north of Lawrenceburg] and it blowed for miles across and down the road a little ways. You'd a thought it was gonna come right through the back door. I said to myself, my Lord, I ain't in the back woods atoll."

"For a while after we moved up here, Emmer wasn't satisfied, but I didn't know it," he continued. "She didn't know I wasn't satisfied. If we'd let each other knowed it, we'd went back to Winston, and it would've been the awfulest move we ever could've made.

"But we worked hard, cleared the land, built a two-room house, and made a living for six children – three boys and three girls."

The Depression years were the most trying. But George M.

pushed on. His daughter Jeanette Dewberry (born in 1922) recalled that her dad loved to go to the annual Mule Day in Columbia, roughly 30 miles to the northeast, and hitchhiked there for several years during that period. From one of those trips, he came back to announce, "I've just bought the prettiest pair of iron-gray mules you ever saw!" Clearly a sentimentalist, he pronounced them "Emmer and Dora." (A photo taken for a 1933 publicity release by Purina Mills, and published in the *Democrat-Union* more than 40 years later, shows George M. with Emmer and Dora – the mules looking peart and pretty and he, in overalls and rolled-up shirt sleeves, holding a straw hat in one hand, looking sober as a drought-hardened field.)

Jeanette remembered that in the worst of those times, with supplies seemingly scarce everywhere, she overhead her daddy saying to her momma, "I don't know how we're gonna make it. . . . If we had ten cents to spend, I don't what we'd buy with it."

"Times were hard then and you couldn't get ahold of money for anything," George M. said in the 1985 article. "When we just had to have a sack of flour, to keep from spending what little money we had, Emmer and me would go out to the corn crib, shell and shuck five bushels of corn. I would take it to town and get a dollar – 20 cents a bushel, for it. That would buy me a sack of flour and I'd have a quarter left over. That wasn't much, no sir."

The contrast in his capabilities between those long-ago days and the present was striking to George M., as he pointed out to the reporter: "You know, girl, I can't even sign a check now-a-days. I'm so shakey I can't get the pencil to stop atoll; so I don't even try to sign a check. I might write out a check for a million dollars before I knowed it."

The reporter rounded out this warmly personal article with a quote from George M. that characteristically resolved itself in simple economics and simple morality: "We made a good crop and paid every dollar we owed."

The Bull Calf

Emmer and Dora and the other mules the Mattoxes kept were critical to the family's livelihood in those early years, but equipment eventually replaced them. Cattle, and black Angus in particular, became George M.'s focus in later years. And about those cattle, his grandson, Jerry Dewberry, remembered what a canny operator his grandpa was.

"Grandpa was a very good judge of black Angus," Jerry told me. "When he was driving, he would see a pasture sometimes and he'd slow down and just look. He could see an Angus cow or bull in a strange pasture and almost tell the blood line.

"Back in the late '70s, he had this registered cow he'd bred to a certain bull to make the blood line the best it could be. I was there one day when the cow was about ready to deliver, and this gentleman drove up in a new Cadillac and said, 'Mr. George M., I'll give you [? – Jerry couldn't remember the exact amount, only that it was hefty indeed] for that calf when it hits the ground – if it's a bull – and put it in my back seat.' Well, Grandpa said he would call him."

What Jerry and the prospective buyer didn't know at the time, though, was that George M. would have an ace in hiding.

"Well, I was back there in about two weeks," Jerry continued, "and the man was there in his new Cadillac. He gave Grandpa the cash for the bull calf just like he said he would, and sure enough he put it in the back seat. After he left, I said to Grandpa, 'I cannot believe you sold that bull calf.'"

"Grandpa said, 'Son, come with me, I'm gonna teach you somethin'.

"We started out to the barn, and on the way there he gave me a great lesson in economics. When we got there – there in a stable was the *twin* to the one he had just sold.'"

But while Jerry keenly remembered his grandpa's business acumen, he and other descendants also recall George M. as an admired citizen and neighbor, a carpenter who not only built his own house and those of his children but through the years donated his labor in helping build a number of area churches. "He always taught us to help our neighbor, to treat the other fellow like you'd like to be treated," Jeanette said. He and Emma were just "that kind of people."

Harmony Primitive Baptist Church, about four miles from Mattoxtown, was where the family did much of their singing: at their regular church service the first Saturday and Sunday of each month and at the annual singing the third Sunday in May. The church, on a hill with a spring below it, was already there when the Mattoxes moved to the area. After joining his siblings in Lawrence County, brother Joe served as the church's pastor. Ultimately, George M. and his youngest brother bought the land on which the church sat, and as the old building continued to deteriorate, the two of them bought materials and built a new church structure in 1957.

Jeanette remembered going to singings in the area from childhood on. And then, around 1938 when George M. bought his first car, an old Model A – "We thought we were really uptown then," she said – she and other family members rode with their dad to singings in Decatur, Cullman, Jasper, Hamilton and other Alabama towns.

George M. sang bass, his mother and sister Viola sang treble, and the rest of the siblings, another sister and five brothers, all sang tenor – though George M. was far and away the most active participant. There were no altos in the original bunch, Jeanette said, so that's why she surmised her dad directed his daughters to sing alto (two of them, she and Janie, did and loved it).

In the recording of the 1974 interview, one can best picture George M. in his singing environment. In it, he talks only about singing, answering questions that fortunately assumed almost nothing as background and thus proved probing. For me, hearing that conversation for the first time was like discovering a little cache of gold, his words so alive and beckoning, drawing one in to scenes 70, 80 and more than 100 years ago. What follows is my transcription of those words, as faithful as I could render it, with some filling-in-the-blanks along the way.

On the Hearth Rock

"How come me, Sister, to learn this music?" George M. says, reframing the interviewer's question.

"My mother, 'fore she was financially able to buy her children a book, way before I was born even – and I'm 82 – she drew those notes on the hearth rock of the old fireplace [with a piece of coal, according to Jeanette], and she taught the two older boys the notes. And she finally bought a B.F. White book, as printed by Major B.F. White – he owned the plates then – but it just had three parts to it then. And then of course the older boys learned *me*, don't you see. Just naturally, I took it up and went to singing."

His mother, he said, had "learned it in Georgia." "Folks moved off and died out. . . ." And even though "there's a great bunch of us Mattox boys," he indicates that the succeeding generations had not kept pace in the pursuit of Sacred Harp.

"So how often," comes the question, "would you say that maybe you sing with the Sacred Harp singers?"

"Oh, most every Sunday, somewhere. Yes sir, yes sir, most every Sunday somewhere."

And what about when he was young?

"Well, those days, you know, it was mules and wagons and buggies. . . . But I've started the day before the singing . . . and spend the night somewheres with a neighbor and then go on to the singing, don't you see.

"And those days . . . they sung 20 minutes to the director. And then sometimes you'd have to double back on some of 'em to sing all day. And I've heard all my life, ever since I could recollect, that the old Sacred Harp would soon die out. . . .

"There's some very old songs in that book. And I tell folks, if I didn't know I could buy another book, I wouldn't take a thousand dollars for that book, I sure wouldn't."

One question we will have heard before: "Why do you enjoy it so much, what makes you keep on going back?"

"Well, now, there's quite a few songs in that book – I can't sing alto on the high pitch like a lady can – but there's quite a few songs in the book that I can sing either part of it, don't you see. And you get five or six good tribble singers sittin' over there singin' tribble, and 30 or 40 back there singin' sopraner [tenor or lead], and 10 or 12 good bass singers, and six or eight good alto singers back there – *and it's just something fine for me!* [You can hear the smile in his voice as he contemplates a self-evident good.] Yes, it's just something *fine* for me."

Mr. George M. was not shy about answering a question, even if the only response that came to him was to bend the question back on itself. At one point on the tape he mentions that there are "more singers, *good* singers, in Alabama than any state in the Union."

"Why?" the interviewer asks.

"Well, there's just more singers, that's all, in Alabama than there is in Georgia or Florida or Mississippi or Tennessee either one."

And so we have it. But if the *why* of a question sometimes eluded him, he seemed keenly ready to cover the what, when and where of his Sacred Harp experience.

Old Uncle Vaughan

I'm glad the interviewer asked him one more question toward the end, because, as it turns out, it was one Mr. George M. was almost uniquely qualified to answer – one that involved a surprising admission from the camp of the enemy.

"The Vaughan music people, were they interested in this kind of music?"

I'll interrupt here to say that the question is a reference to Lawrenceburg's most famous citizen, James D. Vaughan (or Vaughn,

1864-1941), sometimes called "the father of Southern gospel music" and creator of a gospel music empire centered in that very town. Vaughan was founder of the Vaughan Publishing Company, credited with selling more than a million seven-shape gospel songbooks in the early 20th century. He was creator of the Vaughan School of Music, which drew students from across the country; sponsor of many traveling gospel quartets (including, for a time, the Vaughan-Daniel Quartet, with the Mattox cousins John and Troy Daniel); owner of Tennessee's first radio station, WOAN, which, from 1922, specialized in playing gospel music to an audience reportedly stretching up to Canada; and, through his Vaughan Phonograph Company, producer of the first gospel record albums.

I used the word enemy above, and that is of course a bit strong. Rivals they were, the old book and the many proliferating new ones, vying for the affection of the folk at that pivotal time in shape-note history.

The Sacred Harp had the appeal of decades-long tradition, a cappella voices, time-tested melodies and harmony, the lofty texts of Isaac Watts and often an emotional wellspring that defied explanation.

The new music had instrumentation and piano flourishes, harmonic progressions and textual metaphors (My Non-Stop Flight to Glory) more in keeping with modern life, it must have seemed to its adherents. It had polished quartets, linkages to the popular secular music of the time, everywhere the scent of newness and somehow inherently the very notion of progress.

Not least, the newer music had a considerable commercial enterprise behind it, an industry of song-writing, publishing and performing. The Sacred Harp, by contrast – with maybe one edition per generation – had about as much industry appeal as a light bulb guaranteed to burn for 30 years. (Willodean Barton of Jasper, Ala., a niece of O.A. Parris – prodigious writer of gospel songs and composer of The Better Land and several other favored entries in the Denson and Cooper books – remembers him once telling her that the Sacred

Harp would always be his real love, but that he "couldn't make money" writing for it, as he could and did by churning out gospel music.)

If I say more here, though, I will have gotten in the way of George M. and his story-as-answer. Here it is, then, in his words.

"Well now, I tell you . . . old Uncle Jim Vaughan was a very good friend of mine. And I don't know . . . when I'd be in town, if I just had my *overalls* on, why, if I didn't go in to see him, he'd knock on his winder and motion for me. . . .

"But way back, he said *that* [the *Sacred Harp*] couldn't be played on an instrument. And we got a lady from Georgia to come here once in the county convention and play it [the piano]. And old Uncle Vaughan bought him a book.

"Well, one day I's in town, and he knocked on his winder and motioned for me to come in. And he said, 'George M., are you mad at me?' I said, 'No, Uncle Jim, I ain't mad at you – and ain't a-gonna be!'

"'Well,' he said, 'sit down and let's talk a little bit.' And he wanted to talk to me about the two books – his book and this'n – billing [a singing] in the auditorium back of his printin' office, and have it for the general public – but have it understood that there wouldn't nothing interfere with *that* book's singing, nor *his* book's singing.

"And I said, 'Well, Uncle Jim, I haven't got no money – but I'll do as many days' work on it as anybody else will.'

"'Well,' he said, 'we need that just as bad as we do money, George M. But,' he said, 'I'm gonna tell you something.' He said, 'I'm in the music business for the *money* I make out of it,' and said, 'you're in the music business for the *pleasure* you get out of it.' And said, 'You know, when you and me's boys, and we needed a few boards of lumber, we'd cut a log and put it on the wagon and carry it to the saw mill, and the man would run four lines, then go to sawin' boards . . . .'

"I said, 'Yes . . . .'

"'Well, now,' he said, 'I've got the *slabs* off that log, and you've got the *heart* of it' – said, 'That ole Sacred Harp will never die!' That's what he told me."

Before the tape runs out, Mr. George M., now like Uncle Vaughan long gone from us, adds the one more line:

"And I believe there'll be somebody singin' it as long as time lasts."

A not-exactly-clear snapshot of Ed Thomas, who never had trouble making clear to a class what he wanted out of his lesson; about 1968. (Photo courtesy of Jan Nesbitt)

15

Ed Thomas and Willie Mae

Henry Edward Thomas (1897-1985)
Willie Mae Thomas Latham Moon (1915-2010)

Ed Thomas was a farmer and house painter for most of his life, a man of scant education but rich life experiences. He hailed from the countryside near Blountsville, a small town some 50 miles northeast of Birmingham.

A stout fellow of normal height, Ed had stubby fingers – two with nub ends, the result of a refinery accident long before I knew him. With red-rimmed eyes that bulged a bit, he was not really what you would call a good-looking man, but made up for lackluster looks with personality. To use a term he probably would have been proud to own, he was a pistol! When he greeted you, he wore a big grin that could have been taken for a leer. He wasn't effusive; he simply drew you toward him. "Come here to me!" he would say, and take a hug or, up close, a tight handshake. At singings he was unrelentingly cheerful, grinning throughout.

He loved singing – *loved* it. A tenor and another one of those leaders who led without a book, he often sang with a pencil or a fan in his hand, and led with it, too. In one memory I have of him, at a singing in the

Birmingham area, he stepped into the square calling "455!" (Soar Away), sidled up to the front bench of the treble, waited till he had everyone's attention, and said, not just to them but to the class at large, "I want you to sing this like you's hungry!" He took the pitch, tossed his arms up, and we were off. I'm sure we satisfied his bidding; when Ed entered the square, the excitement meter always went up at least a couple of notches.

One memory of Ed Thomas rises above the others for me, though: a scene at one April's session of the most gentrified singing I attended in the 1970s, the one at Harpeth Presbyterian Church, just west of Nashville. Figuring prominently in that singing for years were Dr. William J. Reynolds, then head of the church music department of the Baptist Sunday School Board, and Dr. Emory S. Bucke, long-time book editor for the United Methodist Church: two great fans of Sacred Harp and major influencers in the infusion of shape-note melodies into the mainstream hymnody of that era.

At the lunch hour, from an adjacent spot, I watched Ed pull a chair up to the table across from those two luminaries – in Ed's sphere, the Sacred Harp world in which he traveled and sang (he was in this case more than three hours from home), he was the equal of anybody else. Once seated, with his wife then joining him, he took out his teeth and laid them at the side of his plate as casually as a field hand at lunch might doff his cap before digging in to the vittles. (Dentures, at that point in his life, must have been solely a matter of cosmetics; he had evidently learned to eat well without them.)

Together these acquaintances seemed to have a hearty conversation, chuckling and enjoying their food. When he had finished his meal, Ed reached into his mouth with one of those stubby fingers, rimmed his gums to dislodge any remains and picked up and reset his teeth. He was ready now to go sing again.

The beauty of that act to me – the marker for a great memory – was not in the physical detail, crude as that will appear, but in Ed Thomas' naturalness, his lack of intimidation by the occasion or by figures the world might hold to be his natural superiors. At the host's table, he used the same manners he found practical at his own. In Ed

Thomas' world, it was all good and down-home – good singin', good eatin', and pleasant talkin' with old and new-made friends.

Willie Mae Latham Moon, Ed's daughter, was a character in her own right – a quipster and, like her daddy, a fairly salty sort. She was a pretty woman who remained trim and upright throughout her long life. She had a ready eye for the world around her, for the peculiarities of people measured up against the societies they moved in. She was plainspoken and pithy, and, as her preacher once said, "If you didn't want to hear the answer from her, you'd better not ask the question."

"If you didn't want to hear the answer from her, you'd better not ask the question": Willie Mae at the 1998 National. (Photo by Joel Cohen)

After she had married in young life, she and her husband moved from Blount County to the Birmingham area. It was 17 years until their own daughter came along, and in the interim the Lathams boarded four young ladies with them for more than a dozen years. Early on, Willie Mae clerked at a grocery story and then for a long time at a hardware store. In later years, she was a cafeteria worker in a local school system, retiring twice there – the second time at age 84.

After her first husband died, Willie Mae had a brief second marriage. Married again later, she then again became a widow. She lived to be almost 95 and, until her mind slipped in those last years, she was a faithful supporter and generous cook for singings throughout our territory.

She began to make her mark on the singing scene when she was still a young woman. In 1934, when she was not yet 19 and at a time when many more men than women were called to lead, the minutes printed in the local Cullman paper show that "Miss Willie Mae Thomas" offered a lesson after dinner on the Sunday session of the courthouse singing there. She began her singing career as an alto but, when that became hard on her voice, switched to treble. She and another alto, Mae Howton Seymour of Bessemer, were dear friends – "Mutt and Jeff," her daughter put it – and they traveled thousands of miles together to singings. (At Mae's funeral in 1998, Willie Mae stood with Mae's brother Bickett and led GREENLAND, her friend's signature song.)

Willie Mae once shared with me a view of child labor as she experienced it in the 1920s in the Alabama countryside, under a pitiless sun. "We's poor, and we had to pick cotton," she told me. "Picked a bale a day – when the other kids was in school. That's when I lost my religion! [For what it's worth, she did get it back over time.] I only finished the eighth grade, 'cause we had to work." Times were hard then, and her dad, she said, hired her and her siblings out to pick cotton for others after they had picked their own. "I hated that ole man," Willie Mae said – and said it with the kind of affection that only flowers, it seems, well past a troubled time.

At singings, when I didn't get a chance to talk with her during the session itself, I could perhaps catch up with her around the pots and pans after a well-supplied dinner-on-the-grounds, the clean-up duty she was quick to undertake. There, repackaging a food basket with leftovers or scraping off a big platter, she was available for the wry and pointed observations I always found entertaining.

Once during the noon-hour break at the Alabama State Convention, on the grounds of Mt. Pleasant Home Church in north Birmingham, when she was probably in her early 80s, we were standing together and talking when some nearby action caught our eye. A mother of a nearly school-age son was overseeing his vigorous play with a number of other kids. Displaying nifty footwork, she was dancing sideways, back and forth, trying to hem the boy up and keep him from heading down the long sloping lawn and into the roadway below.

Willie Mae took in the mother's antic, half-frantic steps with a steady gaze – and with child-rearing perspective left over from a time when a single command should have been enough to tether a frisky youngster. Turning back to me, she gave the little event a plain but earnest epitaph. "I'd rather be in jail," she said.

A singer with attitude, a kick and a voice like a horn. (Photo by Steve Grauberger, Ozark, Ala., 1996, courtesy of the Alabama Center for Traditional Culture)

16

Aunt Jewel

Annie Jewel Casey Boyd (1915-2006)

Personality discernment, but especially being able to peg someone in terms of likability, is something I've always thought I was good at - at least as good as the next fellow or two. In a few cases over the years, though, I've found my confident early impressions so spectacularly wrong as to have pushed me off any pride of place on the matter.

And no one, from starting point, ever advanced a greater distance along my appreciation gauge than Annie Jewel Casey Boyd, one of the African American singers from Ozark. Aunt "Jearl," as she was sometimes called by friends and family, started in negative territory, as far as I was concerned, but ended up being one of the most irresistible figures of my acquaintance.

I had seen Jewel at singings in and around Ozark for a good many years, probably as far back as 1967, but didn't know her then. We were not in each other's close company, and for some time may not even have exchanged a word of greeting. At a short distance, she was an intimidating presence, and seemed not particularly welcoming to a visitor from another community. She had a voice like a horn, and on the floor, leading, she could stomp with the best of them. She sat always on the front row of the tenor, usually catty-cornered to her brother-in-law, Dewey Williams (she called him "Pappy"), who, along with Japheth Jackson and others, held down the front row of the bass. When she was not smiling broadly, she carried herself with what was, as I later came to see, a mock-sullen, scolding demeanor – the outer crust. When others picked at her with affection, she beamed, and always fired back in kind.

Mutual respect across the singing square ultimately drew us closer. "That tribblin' man" I would hear her speak of me, in reference to the singing I did in the usually small section off to her right. Once the ice was broken between us and I got to know her, I found a person of immense likability.

Jewel was easily the most physical leader I ever saw in the square. Imagine a child exaggeratedly stepping off a parade march to loud music, or cutting big samurai strokes with a make-do sword. In the square, Jewel showed that same childlike quality, in movements that could best be described as . . . well, as *martial*. The scowl on her face when she led wasn't a reflection of mood but simply the parade mask she wore.

Before old age left her unsteady, she typically *kicked* each beat when she led – a hard, shaking kick as if she were thrusting off a snake loosely coiled round her ankle. And she would fling her fisted arm out as strongly as if she were trying to knock a passerby off his feet. All of this seemed to me an act as unselfconscious as it was unexampled, unheard of, really. Not that she didn't know what she was doing, but that – I'm confident – it was not calculated for any effect on others. Over the years she must have worked her way into a ritual of receiving the music, in the middle of the square, that grew more and more vigorous and trance-like. She seemed to lose herself completely in the moment. When the singing was good, it shot through her, pulsed in her limbs, and she danced not so much to or with it as *against* it. She pushed and thrust and kicked against the beat, against the music she got thrillingly from her companions – and could get only from them. If some new singer were to pull up and try such a stunt, we would likely look away in embarrassment. With Jewel, you had to see in the act prancing pleasure, pure exultation.

Gradually, over time, the years began to take their toll, to rein in those bold and fearless feet. Jewel was in her early 80s in 1997 when I attended the Jackson Memorial Sing just out from Ozark. I watched as, beneath a wide straw hat, she stepped off the music in pink-patterned bedroom slippers. Toned down a bit overall, she was still able to fling her feet out with the beat.

At the 1998 National: "I almost cried I wanted to go back so bad." (Photo by Joel Cohen)

She had never attended the National Convention, but as I described the event to her in invitation that day, she seemed ready to try it. "They'll sing a lot of the songs faster," I told her, trying to manage expectations. "That's all right," she said. "I like 'em fast. I've *always* liked 'em fast." She beamed, as though she were sharing a choice secret with me.

She went on to attend the National in June of that year and the next as well, joining Japheth Jackson and a few others for the long drive up from Ozark. No one in either instance could have failed to note her presence. At the 1998 session, she arrived slumped over, after suffering what we would discover was a diabetic swoon – and needed an hour or so, in a wheel chair in the church library, to sleep it off. After reviving and being called to lead, she slowly bumped her walker forward to the square. Then, cutting loose her moorings, she stepped from behind the walker and amazed the class and onlookers with a stirring version of LIBERTY.

No more beneath th'oppressive hand
Of tyranny we groan.
Behold the smiling, happy land
That freedom calls her own.

When I saw her the next spring, she mentioned that Friday appearance and then said, "I almost cried I wanted to go back so bad on Saturday!"

That was Jewel. I'm glad that I made and then posted lengthy notes from two singing-day visits with her over the next two years, among the last times I would see her. They help to bring her back to me, and I hope to others, in something of her crusty cantankerousness, her unsurrendering faceoff with old age and infirmity.

AUNT JEWEL

March 1999, the Dewey P. Williams Day singing, Ozark

I was pleased to see Aunt Jewel again, just months before her 84th birthday. I found her not in the peak of health but intent on savoring the day. Joel Cohen had taken some great photos at the previous year's National and had sent me copies. I gave Jewel and three others the photos of themselves I had brought along from that collection. At first she didn't recognize herself in a robin's-egg-blue dress and a red hat with black band, but later laughed at the photo: "I didn't know I had my hat on backwards, look at that!" she said. (I couldn't tell the difference.) "Don't you tell nobody." But I didn't promise.

"I didn't know I had my hat on backwards! Don't you tell nobody." (Photo by Ginnie Ely)

At the lunch hour, we maneuvered her walker through a maze of chairs in the sanctuary and through slow, old-folks traffic, then down a number of steps to the basement fellowship hall. After she had been steered through the serving line – she wanted to check the food out herself and not just have someone bring her a plateful – she sat down to eat. A minute or so later, she leaned to me and said, "I'm 83 years old, and this doesn't taste like any ham I've ever eaten in my life!"

We had to admit that what was earlier presented as ham, in a bit of confusion at the serving table, was in fact rotisserie turkey.

"That's what I thought," she said. "Well, I'm not going to eat any more of it. I don't eat turkey."

The tea was not sweet enough for her and the food not salty enough. But food was not what brought Aunt Jewel here; it was the singing. And after the food was put away, she was ready to make her path back up those impossible stairs.

On our way down the main aisle, an old friend, Estelle Snell, reached out to catch her. She drew back, a pretend pugilist. "Don't you start up with me!" she said, tossing her head back and forth. "I've got somebody here to take *care* of you!" and quick-nodded at me, a suddenly sheepish accomplice. Estelle, a sweet-looking woman, said, "Oh, I know not to mess with you – you've *always* been trouble!" They laughed and clasped hands, closing out another installment in longstanding shenanigans. Then Jewel bumped her walker on along to the front row.

Loneliness is her great enemy, she confided a short while later. She now lives alone, and the days and nights pass, she said, with long hours. "I sing to myself all the time, but I want somebody *else* to sing with!" She is proud of the red-backed book she received last June in Birmingham, but is frustrated she's not able to sing many of the songs that are new to her. "I know I could sing 'em if I just had somebody to key it for me," she said.

A last remembrance from that day: She didn't have her usual "kick" when she led LET US SING (461 in the Cooper Book) in the morning. But when she sat down, I heard her say to Barney Roberson sitting next to her, "I didn't mean to sing that! I wanted to sing 450 [LEANING ON JESUS' BREAST]!" In the afternoon, when that number was called out by someone – and with no leader on the floor – she suddenly pulled herself up to the walker and moved into the square. With the walker, she began to step it off. And as the song got better and better, she began to kick the beat, kicking with her medium-heel shoes. One kick for every beat. Amazing. When the singing was over, she told me, "I'll be singin' all night long tonight."

APRIL 2000, THE JACKSON MEMORIAL SING, OZARK

When I pulled up to the church, I saw Aunt Jewel, aided by a younger relative, struggling with her walker at the church door. Within two or three songs after she got seated, she was called to lead. "108," she said, "top." Though she required help getting out of her chair, she led a strong version of WEEPING SINNERS.

Sometime before the midday break for lunch, Jewel suddenly summoned the strength to get up again, found her walker and started to the back of the church. A couple of relatives rallied and caught up with her there. They went out the back together and then returned shortly afterwards. When she was seated again, a man was dispatched on an errand – and returned with the elixir, a plastic cup of water that I knew would be thickened with sugar [to address her sugar imbalance]. She drank it and carried on.

At some point during the day, we sang a song she has said before to be her favorite (because it was the favorite of her mother, Nancy Casey, a noted treble singer from that community), LEANING ON JESUS' BREAST: ". . . and breathe, and breathe, and breathe my life out sweetly there." She took it all in heartily, singing some and listening some and smiling deeply.

Now consigned to (imprisoned in, would be her version of it) a local nursing home, Jewel fears that her days traveling to singings are over. It's a rarity when she can be allowed out of the home. I think I'm right in saying that this singing and the funeral of her sister Alice Williams last month represented the only times it's been possible for her to leave in the better part of a year.

She is 85 now, and she remembers that another sister who used to live with her was 85 and in a nursing home when she died. She mentions that her vision is getting bad. "I'm gettin' to where I can't see *anything*."

The loneliness in her room must be nearly overwhelming – and the inability to join her old buddies, an ongoing frustration. "A lot of times at night, though, I have my own singing," she told me, in a hint of the passageways the mind provides. And smiling: "Sometimes it'll last nearly all night long."

It wouldn't do for the nursing home to ask Jewel for a recommendation – certainly not any time soon. "This is the *awfullest* place I've ever been at in my *life!* I'm telling you the truth." That was her summation of things back in March, following the Dewey Williams Day singing, when I had gone by to see her at the home.

The nursing home was again on her mind when she sat down now to eat in a little alcove area above the church kitchen. She didn't want to eat in the dining room, another set of stairs below.

I asked if the food at the home hadn't improved. "Honey," she said, "they don't know how to cook *nothin'!* You ought to see their pancakes." She grimaced. "Not a drop of grease on 'em!"

"They're about *this* big," she said scornfully, and raised her hand up eye-level to show just the slightest separation between her extended thumb and index finger.

"They put a little *hickey* of syrup with it about like *this*. . . ." She widened the space between thumb and finger by a smidgen.

"And not a *drop* of salt in 'em!" Contempt was all over her face – but maybe also, I thought, the satisfaction that comes from doling out, when justified, the severest possible verdict.

She ate slowly and enjoyed the meal. The dressing and the cake in particular drew her compliments. When she was close to finishing, she had an idea. "Tell somebody to fix me a plate for my supper. I want them to see some *real* cookin'! I'm going to take it and just let 'em *see* it."

I started off to fulfill the request. "And no beans," she said.

Once up from the table, she got her walker in gear. Japheth

Jackson pulled himself up the stairs below by the railing, and they met – walker to walker. The two of them must have been singing together virtually all their lives. He reached across and took her hand. "Jewel, I was so glad to see you come in. . . ." He knew.

With and without the walker, we got her from the alcove, down the small stairs and back into the sanctuary, back to the gathering class.

As always, the afternoon of the singing brought a more rousing session. When Jewel was called to lead, Japheth said, "You know what I want you to lead . . . 137." LIBERTY is the name of the song, and what else could be more appropriate for her to sing?

She obliged the request, and this time was a more animated figure in the square. At the chorus entrance, she was turned just slightly off from the tenor toward the treble (clock-face-wise, about 10:30) and, without pivoting, thrust her right hand back strongly to the bass for their entrance – a no-look pass. She stepped off the music as she sang and even made the walker walk. On the final chord, she extended her arms wide, soaking up the sound. And then she popped her palms together the way you'd pop a naughty youngster's bottom – well, at least the way that would have been done in her generation.

On in the afternoon, I would occasionally see her sway with the music. When it got particularly good, she would stop singing and close her eyes and smile big and extend both hands out in front in a frozen gesture as if she were measuring a wide span. And when the song got too good – *too* good – she would shake her body, fists clenched at her sides in a boxing stance, as if she were sassin' an umpire big-time.

Jewel is a born fighter, and she's not about to take her nursing home sentence – or the indignities regularly visited upon her there – lying down. "Sometimes I do hateful things to 'em," she had told me back in March. "I do." She sounded a little guilty about it, but unrepentant in the main. "They" won't fight back, though – not at least on her terms, not the way she would want them to. Their responses, I take it, are bland or saccharine – as irksome in their own way as that tasteless little platter of a pancake meal they send around on her tray once a week.

When the singing was over and others were exchanging farewells, Jewel was already thinking ahead. "Go get that plate out of the refrigerator and put it in the car for me," she said. "I want them to see some *real* cookin'."

She had not yet seen what was under the foil wrapper – surely the paper plate had no beans on it – but whatever it was, it would be comfort food. Comfort food for eating at leisure later on in the afternoon or evening. But first and foremost, the comfort of revealing to those nursing home minions what she felt they could hardly imagine – and, given their mean abilities, could never replicate.

And then she could begin the singing in her mind, reliving by the hour the events of that day and calling up tunes led and un-led, with a class, now enlarged, of present-day singers and those beyond the vale.

17

Lonnie Rogers

Lonnie Lee Rogers (1916-2012)

To get to Lonnie Rogers' home in Ephesus, Ga., you drove in on Lonnie Lee Rogers Highway, the roughly 20-mile stretch of Georgia Highway 100 in Heard County dedicated in 1994 to this thoroughly good and thoughtful man. A strongly built figure with kindly face – who could have seemed like everyone's favorite uncle – Lonnie was as much revered in his home area and across the broad Sacred Harp community as anyone I ever knew.

The Rogers home, built in 1923 by Lonnie's father, George Franklin (Frank) Rogers, was one of those big, comfortable-looking, white, wood-framed country houses, sitting back from the highway, with wide porches on the front and back and a total of nine doors opening out to them. I was in that home only once. When I visited Lonnie there in August of 2011, six months before he died, he was frail and confined to his bedroom. My other conversations with him, over a period of four and a half decades, had almost always been at singings – at a few of which, in the late '60s, I had exchanged greetings with Frank Rogers, then in his 80s.

Lonnie told me that August day that, at age 95, he had reached

Lonnie, who seemed like everyone's favorite uncle. (Photo courtesy of Karen Rogers Rollins)

the greatest life span of any of his family, at least as far back as the Civil War. Frank and Tessie Word Rogers had raised nine sons and five daughters, and Lonnie had outlived all but his younger sister Opal. In the earlier generation, Tessie's parents had produced nine boys and five girls as well, and Frank's, nine boys and four girls.

In his history of the Chattahoochee Musical Convention, Earl Thurman wrote that, "for a number of years, the G.F. Rogers family has been the leading Sacred Harp group in Heard [County]," and added, "Many say that Frank Rogers has been the life spark of Sacred Harp singing in Heard for a long number of years." Mr. Rogers was known to be a good singer, a good keyer of music, a stalwart of the tradition.

A strong song-leader himself, he had valued genuineness in other leaders, Lonnie told me: "He didn't like a put-on." He also didn't favor one practice often seen at singings in that era: putting a child up on a table to lead, with the congregation applauding at the end of the song – "popping their hands together." "He didn't like that," Lonnie said. "You were there to praise the Lord, and he didn't think that was appropriate." He didn't like the slower pace that some took in their leading back in those days either, Lonnie remembered: "Some of 'em would just drag it out. . . . He sang like he worked; he'd pick up and go with it!"

Frank Rogers had owned a sawmill, and Lonnie had worked with him there, gaining knowledge about the lumber trade, but also learning much about human nature and dealing with the public. In time, Lonnie, along with his son, Denney, would form his own construction and lumber business, L.L. Rogers and Son.

There's a reason, aside from the strong family resemblance, that those who knew Frank and Lonnie Rogers could have seen the two figures as being almost interchangeable. "Lonnie modeled his life after his daddy," Lonnie's adoring sister Opal told me a few weeks after his death. "Lonnie was a little slower moving than Daddy was," she said. "He didn't just *spin* all the time like Daddy. What I'd say is, he was steady – his love was steady, his energy was steady, his progress in life was steady." Lonnie, she said, "was a peacemaker. He was easy-going. I never in my life saw him really angry. I've seen him hurt, but never seen him really angry."

Frank and Tessie Rogers, 1954. (Photo courtesy of Karen Rogers Rollins)

Another difference between father and son, a slight one, occurred to her as well. When I mentioned the difficulty in understanding Lonnie's speech toward the end of his life, she pointed out that, unlike his father, Lonnie was never a very forceful speaker. "We'd be riding to a singing over in Alabama, across those red hills," she remembered. "Daddy and Lonnie would have on their white shirts and ties. Of course, it would be hot and you'd have to ride with the windows down – and when a car passed you, there'd be a roar and that red dust would settle in on their shirts. . . . Lonnie would be mumbling about something, and Daddy would cock his head to one side and say, 'Lonnie, *speak up!*'"

When Lonnie spoke, though, people listened. When it came his time to lead at a singing, especially as his voice became weaker with age, I, like others, would find myself leaning forward as he spoke. You didn't want to miss a word – of commentary, of self-deprecating humor, of wisdom sifted out from his many decades of experience.

The Best Satisfied . . .

It was from Lonnie, and ultimately from his father, that I heard one of my favorite characterizations of Sacred Harp singing. The anecdote I had Lonnie repeat to me more than once centered on an old black man, born a slave, who had worked for the Rogers family. This longtime member of the Ephesus community had heard of Sacred Harp singing and its reputed attractions but apparently had never experienced either, so at some point Frank Rogers took him along to one of the singings. On the way back, Frank was curious about what effect the event had wrought on his affable old retainer, who until that point had kept mum. "Now John," he said, "tell me sho' nuff what you think about our singin'." If the old fellow was not immediately forthcoming, he did, when pressed, come back with a memorable line: "Well now, I tell you. . . . You folks'll travel the *farthest* and hear the *least* and be the *best satisfied* of anybody I ever saw. . . ."

Lonnie's memory, keen until the end, could reach back easily to Sacred Harp singing in the early decades of the previous century, as well as to family singing around the fireplace in Frank and Tessie's home. In those times, before tables were built outside the country churches, singers or church-goers would place a sheet or table cloth on the ground to spread their food on at the noon-hour recess. It was not just "dinner on the grounds," then, but, literally, dinner on the ground, or, as Lonnie remembered an old fellow's phrase for it, "chicken on the dirt."

Lonnie was also one of the surviving few who could remember the presence of Uncle Tom Denson. Lonnie had attended the legendary teacher's last singing school, just months before Uncle Tom's death in 1935. "He made it easy to lead," Lonnie told me. "He'd be sitting there in front of you, and he'd say, 'Watch me'" [with open-hands gesture to demonstrate the proper beating of time]. "That's like my daddy told me when I first started singing. He'd say, 'Son, keep your time straight and you'll be successful, you'll stay together.'"

Mike Hinton once asked Lonnie to tell him about that singing school and about Mike's grandfather. "Mr. Lonnie said there were three older boys in the class and they were giving Uncle Tom a hard time during one morning session," Mike reported. "Mr. Lonnie said at the first break he followed the boys a little ways from the church and told them, 'To get to Mr. Denson you are going to have to go through me!' Mr. Lonnie smiled and said 'That stopped the problem and the singing school went on without any more trouble.'"

Though all of Frank Rogers' children grew up singing, as Opal would tell me later, Lonnie was the only one who fully dedicated himself to Sacred Harp. His eldest daughter, Karen Rollins, in the eulogy she gave for her father in February of 2012, spoke about how singing had been an inescapable part of her youth and that of her brother and three sisters. "I guess we couldn't avoid it," she said, "since Sacred Harp goes back as far as we can trace in both sides of our family." She could especially remember the family singing together in the car as they rode one place and another. "Dad would have his arm out the window beating time. And in those days of hand signals, other drivers must have wondered where we were going. . . ."

When Lonnie married Vivian Denney in 1939, their union brought together two of the notable Sacred Harp families in western Georgia. Vivian was the daughter of Newman and Willie Myrt Shadinger Denney. Newman, the longtime secretary of the Chattahoochee Musical Convention, was one of the most gracious Southern gentlemen I ever knew. Lonnie and Vivian had, by all accounts, a wonderful marriage. Vivian died in 2002, but Alzheimer's had stolen her away some years before. (It had already claimed her mother, her grandfather and several aunts and would take three of her brothers as well.)

Lonnie as a young man. (Photo courtesy of Karen Rogers Rollins)

As we conversed on that August afternoon, Lonnie's mind drifted to the memorial lesson at singings, one of the themes he circled back to again and again in the last year or so of his life – and then to thoughts of one of Vivian's kin of an earlier generation. Did I ever know or see Uncle Charlie Denney? No, I told him, he must have been gone before I came over into that area. He was, Lonnie went on to tell me, a somewhat misshapen man – "bowlegged, crippled, with one leg about two inches shorter than the other, hump-shouldered and bony-faced, kind of poor-faced" – but a man of extraordinary effect when he led a song. "He liked to sing AMAZING GRACE," Lonnie said. "But instead of 'When we've been there ten thousand years,' he wanted us to sing 'ten million years,' because 'it's *eternity!*' Tears would just drop off his chin as he led. People from out in the yard would come to the doors and windows just to see him lead – a crippled man, joltin' up and down like that. . . . If you had *any* feeling about you, you *had* to be touched."

A Man and His Pig

Something in our continuing conversation reminded Lonnie of an old fable, a story about a man and his pet. It clearly pleased him to tell me this story I'd never heard before. A man had a little pig that he was especially proud of, the tale began. And one day he carried his prized pig with him to town in a sack, intending to show it off. While he was otherwise busying himself, several fellows got the sack and exchanged the pig for a cat. Surprised as he was a short time later when he reached into the sack and found a cat, the old gentleman couldn't help being impressed by what a fine cat it was – and so remarked on it. Before he left, the pranksters got the sack again and made the switch back; so this time when he opened the sack, it was the pig he found inside. He took it out and addressed it thus: "It doesn't make all that much difference to me whether you're a cat or a pig. But *whatever* you are, I want you to *be that.*"

Lonnie's gentle laugh burst through the end of the story, a testament to the charm he found in its simple but salient point. "But whatever you are, I want you to be that." To be sure, no one ever had to wish such about Lonnie Rogers. Constancy and integrity were hallmarks of his character.

Constancy of spirit, maybe, but not of body, Lonnie might have pled. Great frailty was now his circumstance. At the singing at nearby Hopewell Primitive Baptist Church the previous June, Lonnie, who led a song from his wheelchair, had said that he might as an infant have been taken to that singing in diapers, but this was certainly the first time he had shown up there in his pajamas!

Karen later told me that Lonnie believed he may never have missed a session of that annual singing at Hopewell. "I do know that he attended the day I was born," she said, "and just went home at lunch to see if I had arrived yet. His first child! And he left mom with the doctor and went to sing awhile. . . ." He had possibly even attended 63 years before his last appearance by getting a weekend pass from the hospital in Rome, Ga., where he was confined for 16 months with the tuberculosis that almost robbed him of his life. That hospitalization, when he was 31 – and with a wife and three young daughters at home – was particularly trying. At first he had refused to be hospitalized, Karen said, but the doctor told him that if he didn't, he would likely die. Lonnie had had an older brother die at a week short of 15 when he was seven, and that loss had left a strong impression: "He didn't want to be the next to go. He had a lot of time to think in that hospital, and his life afterwards was guided by the lessons he learned there."

Another shaping experience for Lonnie's character and outlook, as for so many others of his generation, was living through the Depression years of the '30s. Like most others around them, the Rogers family had to work especially hard to make ends meet. Lonnie, Karen said, told of working at home from sun-up until the bell rang for school, then resuming chores when the bell rang again to dismiss classes – a practice, she smilingly pointed out, he had instituted with his own children as well.

Opal later told me a story from the time of her father's youth that well depicts the kind of deprivation that farming families often had to face in any of those decades. The Rogers family at that time, Opal said, lived in a dogtrot house – that Southern rural structure that features a breezeway or open hall between the kitchen and dining area on one side and bedrooms on the other. Besides providing natural air-conditioning, a dogtrot house offered the advantage of separating sleeping quarters from the always fire-risky kitchen. Boll weevils had just about destroyed the Rogers' cotton crop that year, and at one point the family had little between themselves and starvation, Opal said. Mainly, they had biscuits to eat – and syrup, from two large kegs her grandmother kept in the kitchen. When a fire broke out in the kitchen, quickly engulfing the whole house and threatening the loss of their food for the season, young Frank had to help pick up the big kegs and run with them. "At a time like that," she remembered him telling his children, "you'll have strength you never knew you had." (I wondered later if the memory of that fire led Frank Rogers to put outside doorways in each of the nine rooms bordered by the big porches in the house he built.)

In her eulogy, Karen mentioned a telling incident about the death of a man in the Ephesus community during the Depression years. The man's family couldn't afford to take him to Alabama for burial, and so, she said, "Dad helped to build a casket and hauled it on an open-body log truck to the cemetery in Alabama. That experience really gave him a heart to help others."

The principles that Lonnie exemplified, the moral scaffolding that framed his life, were, as he might have put it, *old-school*. They likely differed little from those of his father or *his* father before him. In many conversations we had over the years, Lonnie expressed disappointment at what he increasingly observed: everywhere a loosening of standards in conduct, in social interactions. With the passing of that earlier way of life, something essential had been lost to the community, to families and to the common good. A neighborliness, along with moral rigor, had, except for pockets here and there, gradually seemed to evaporate, leaving a social landscape as foreign and perplexing to him as the waves of new technology that threatened to swamp the whole.

And *his* neighborliness? It never left him. In December of his 95th year, just two months before his death, Lonnie, bedridden by then, dictated notes to Karen, as he had done in previous years, to include in a Christmas letter to be sent to friends. After taking notes,

Karen would write up the draft, and Lonnie would look it over and make minor changes. "He also sent many cards during the year and would write statements in them after I addressed them," Karen said. (I remembered being moved by a thank-you note Lonnie had sent following my visit in August.) "He kept thinking of names for his Christmas cards . . . and would have me check to be sure we sent a card to someone. That went on for days. I think he sent slightly more than 100 cards this past holiday – less than the previous years because we lost part of his list."

Lonnie and Vivian: "He loved that girl!" (Photo courtesy of Karen Rogers Rollins)

When I had seen Lonnie at the annual memorial singing for Frank and Tessie Rogers back in March of 2011, he had again been wheeled into the meeting hall. His knees were brought close together, a blanket covering them. As we shook hands, I asked how he was doing. "My knees, Buell . . . ," he said, and said it with the down-sloping intonation we use for things sorrowful. But then that familiar grin broke across his face. "These knees – they tell me to *sit down* and *shut up.*" "That's what my daddy used to tell me," he added, his grin widening further as he remembered with apparent pride a father's instruction to the young and brash: "Sit down and shut up. Just sit down and shut up."

Lonnie with children, about 2004. From left: Karen Rogers Rollins, Karleen Rogers Williams, Denney Rogers, Paige Rogers Harrod, Sherry Rogers Lovvorn. (Photo by Susan Lovvorn Rice)

'And Part Are Crossing Now . . .'

Lonnie died at home, with his family close around. The death was not a surprise, as he had begun to drift away a few weeks before. The funeral day was, to me, inevitably sad but somehow magnificent, inspiring. A large crowd of singers had joined an impressive turnout from the general community to remember a cherished spirit.

We sang more than two dozen songs for Lonnie, most of them

just before the main service and a few more during it. His nine adult grandchildren stood in one long line stretching across in front of the pulpit and, synchronously beating that three-quarter time as he would have taught them, led the congregation in AMAZING GRACE. Later, reflecting on the songs he had chosen to be sung, I realized that not a one was a minor tune. And as I thought back on it, the songs associated with Lonnie over the years, the ones he tended to lead, were all in fact major-key songs: REYNOLDS, PROVIDENCE, PRESENT JOYS, FREDERICKSBURG, FLEETING DAYS . . . .

When I later mentioned that observation to Karen, she recalled her dad occasionally pointing out that one or another singer "likes to lead minor music" - a distinction he obviously found noteworthy - sometimes followed by a comment that such choices were "too sad" for him. "He told me that he sang 'to praise God,'" Karen said, "but I would think that one could do that in minor music as well." That remark brought to mind a story of an old shape-note singer known for a strong preference for minor music that I had used in my book and that I then relayed to Karen. A friend, the story went, was needling the old gent one day about whether he thought there would be "any minor music in heaven." "I guess not," the man had conceded, "but it'll sure help you get there!"

We heard a number of revelations about Lonnie that day, though none that would disturb the generally held image. "You may not know that, although dad reached out to others everywhere he went, he was really a timid man at heart," Karen told us in her remarks. "Mom said that he was the most timid man she ever dated. He did not start dating until he was 20 because he was so timid."

This man who was such a leader in his community - over time having held a dozen or more local and area civic positions, and once being named Agri-Business Leader of the Year for the 23-county metro-Atlanta area - timid! And more: "He told me that he never lost his fear of leading a song. After going to singing school with Uncle Tom Denson for 20 days, he finally managed to keep his pants leg from noticeably shaking."

A crisp, deeply pulsed leading style. (Photo by Martha Beverly, 2005)

My longtime admiration of Lonnie's song-leading must have mirrored that of countless others. The image in my mind, crystallized through many repetitions over the years, captures a crisp, deeply pulsed leading style: Lonnie knifing his arm through the air, stabbing into the heart of every beat, and, as the group of voices converged on the final chord, giving his arm, now thrust above his head, a little lariat whirl to finish the song off. And to think that that heartfelt act, seemingly the very core of confidence, belied or overcame a natural fear. . . .

And another revelation: Lonnie as "very romantic." "He could tell you the first time he saw Mom at a singing the third Sunday in May in 1935," Karen said. "And he could tell you many details about the pink-checked dress she was wearing. He could also tell you the date and details of the time he first spoke to her, and he could describe the manicure set that was his first Christmas gift to her when they started dating. [It was said elsewhere in the eulogies that Lonnie had asked one of his sisters to recommend a gift for that occasion that would be "personal – but not *too* personal."] He loved giving Mom gifts, and we have spent many hours shopping for her at his insistence."

And at the end, a little lariat whirl. (Photo by Laura Densmore, 1990)

"He loved that girl!" Opal told me later. And in her remarks at the funeral service, she gave us a view of that attraction. "Daddy had a truck for his business, and a car," she said, "and with all those boys, that car wasn't available much of the time." But occasionally Frank Rogers would send Lonnie to town in the car, to pick up small supplies. The Denney home, as Opal said, was on the way, just off Highway 27, and invariably Lonnie would manage to stop by and invite Vivian for a ride. When Frank and Lonnie were driving to town together one time, Frank had said, "Lonnie, every time I go from Roopville to Carrollton and I get close to Newman Denney's house, this car starts pullin' to the left. . . ."

Denney Rogers had affectionate remarks about his father in his eulogy, too, further reminding us that the man whose life we had come to honor was not some marble icon but a warts-and-all human being - a person, like the rest of us, with his own idiosyncrasies. Having worked so closely with him over the years, Denney wanted to tell us a little about "the Lonnie you probably didn't know." His dad, Denney said, drank a Coke every day of his adult life: "Pour me a Coke," he would say each morning as he came in to the office - but only a Coke from a bottle, never from a can. (A Coke machine was kept at the office to accommodate this request.) From there, the list of eating *Don'ts* grew imposing: Lonnie didn't, wouldn't, eat pizza, lasagna, a hamburger or a sandwich. "Made it kind of hard for us to keep him fed," Denny said. Lonnie had also made a stand against eating chili - which seemed a shame, since Denney's wife, he said, made "great chili." "But Dad wouldn't eat it. We did finally get him to eat some of her 'white bean soup,' though, and he liked that - but it was really chili."

I had to smile at the thought of this soup-and-chili switch there at our great friend's dinner table. Surely Lonnie himself would have appreciated the application my whimsy led me to: "But *whatever* you are, I want you to *be that*."

18

An Endearing Prickliness

I liked Charles Creel – could even say that, in a way and at some distance, I loved him. This affection took hold despite the fact that, though I'd observed Charles over a good many years (our singing territories closely overlapping), our total time in conversation probably amounted to little more than an hour or two. And I liked or loved him not really in spite of his storied and spirited contrariness, but in part because of it!

Mild-mannered as I've thought myself (what is, I might guess, a generally held view), I admit to a perverse streak of vicarious enjoyment in hijinks and light-handed trouble-making. Fortunately, when, in my college years, this impulse flowered into a few solitary, big-time, campus-wide dirty tricks, I managed to escape capture and censure. From that point on, mine has mainly been mischief by proxy. So seeing Charles Creel in occasional wrongheaded combativeness goosed this less honorable side of my nature. Whenever I glimpsed an opportunity to catch him in action or, in conversation, get to hear him air his irritation with others or with the current social scene, I would feel a near-giddiness in advance of the fun. I was rarely disappointed.

I should say that what I often saw in Charles, this figure some 20 years my senior, seemed an almost congenital rather than an intentional orneriness. Charles, who knew and taught the Scriptures, surely regarded his occasional outbursts as the stuff of righteous indignation. To give him his due, he seemed to make his way through life with, in Kipling's phrase, a Levitical scrupulosity.

The first episode that led me to this appreciation took place during a session of the Cullman County courthouse convention when I was still a young man. I had come back inside late from a break and was standing at the back of the large room as Charles was about to lead his selection. PETERSBURG was a song rarely called in those days, and, from my point of view, deservedly so. I was thus content to hang back for a bit and let others carry the load on it. A couple of measures into the song, Charles waved his arms for a halt and lashed out at the class for not having followed his lead. The problem, it seemed to me, was instantly clear: though I can no longer recall which it was, his hand beats had indicated a tempo either twice as fast or twice as slow as the tune his voice was carrying. The front bench, as it's taught to do, had started out by following his hand movements and so had given him something other than what he intended. But far be it from anyone there to tell him so. . . .

The pitch-giver and main man in the middle of the front bench that day was Preston Crider, mainstay for the singings in the Cullman area and a direct descendant of B.F. White. Generally honored for being a good, meek and affable soldier in the Sacred Harp cause, Preston, in front-bench duty, was nonetheless known to slump low in his chair or bench as he sang, one knee across the other, all the while peering deeply into the book in his lap instead of watching the leader. Careful observers might therefore have noticed a tendency on his part, surely unintentional, to override the leader's tempo with the default tempo, the one he was used to singing. I can't imagine, though, that even Preston Crider that day was not looking up at the face and the hands of Charles Creel, who carried with him, as he went about the singing world, a reputation for testiness.

Charles, it seemed to me, was clearly in the wrong that day, but, bathed in right, he stormed forth. The song was started up again, with the same mixed messages and the same abortive result. This time, though, the class was made to feel the full brunt of his ire. I don't recall ever witnessing a more heated dressing down of a group of singers (I had missed Paine Denson and, in his prime, Marcus Cagle). In Charles' view, the front bench had run roughshod over the most basic precept of proper class behavior: Always follow the leader. At the root of it all seemed to be the presumption that, if something is going wrong here, it must be *their* fault. . . .

No one tried to explain or question; they simply sat through the brief verbal beating. The third time, on super-alert, the front bench prudently ignored the hand beats and followed the voice. And so at the song's end, having had his patience thus sorely tested, Charles could return to his seat gratified, having performed a useful and necessary service.

Charles, who spent most of his career as a service writer for automobile dealerships in the Birmingham area, was from a large, talented singing family: the Creels and the Reids. He was the grandson of a seminal singing figure from the area: James Harris Reid or "Singin' Jim Reid," as he had been called (or even occasionally "ole man Jim Reid," though he was only 47 when he died in 1919). Reid was a singing-school teacher from the area around Reid's Gap, near Blount Springs in north-central Alabama. It was said that he could sing all the parts, even sing alto "like a woman." Charles' sister Marie proudly told me a story one time that put Jim Reid's reputation in perspective. As a young girl, she had found herself sitting on alto next to the great Whitt Denson, famous for singing the part on the high pitch. At one of the breaks, Denson, impressed with young Miss Creel's singing ability, asked who she was. She gave him her name, adding that she was Jim Reid's granddaughter. "Well, no wonder you can sing!" Denson had replied.

One report about Jim Reid's life and death seemed especially graphic to me. Probably as he neared the end, he was said to have left instructions for his body not to be carried to the cemetery at Reid's Gap because he hated the thought of his bones being jostled across the big rocks in the dirt roadways between their home and the cemetery. He and his wife were buried at Old County Line Church instead. (That story has left me to muse about ROCKY ROAD, one of our songbook's inescapable numbers. The cycling words "It's a mighty rocky road, / I'm almost done traveling" could seem quaint to most today, but for many rural singers who grew up in the early part of the last century, that central metaphor was surely more than sufficient for conveying in brief the arduousness of life.)

Before I knew Charles and several of his siblings, I regularly saw at singings their aunts and uncles, the sisters Mamie and Mattie Reid Creel (daughters of Jim Reid) and their husbands, the twin brothers Chester and Hester Creel (distant cousins to Charles and the others on their father's side). Annie Reid Creel, Charles' mother and Jim Reid's oldest daughter, and her husband, Charlie Creel, oldest of 11 in his family, were singers of impact in the area (who had first met at a Sacred Harp gathering), but they were gone before I had the chance to know them.

As mentioned, the Creel-Reids represented a musically accomplished family, one its members could take pride in. And they did. They wore that pride like a rich brooch. Linked with the pride somehow seemed to be an almost institutional responsibility for enlightening or correcting others. Now, a person intent on catching mispronunciations in Sacred Harp singing could have an easy enough afternoon at just about any country church in the territory. But in the recurring phrase "I'm a long time trav'ling," from the song WHITE (in the original and in all versions since but those of the Cooper book), the senior Creel siblings had long ago noticed a tricky little fact about the contraction "trav'ling": though applied to a three-note run, "trav'ling" presented but two syllables of text. And so if a singer at elbow's length from any of the senior Creels happened to be lured into singing "trav-el-ling" instead of "tra-av-ling," this error in performance would be quickly pointed out. Knowing this potential impediment in the music and being able to instruct others in it so generously could be seen to affirm the rightness of their place, the gift of their example.

Of the members of that generation of the family, maybe the

best-known and most-admired was Marie Creel Ryan – Marie Aldridge, after her first husband's death and her remarriage. Marie was as accomplished and graceful a leader as I saw in all my years. Late in her life, she led a lesson at the 1997 Midwest Convention in Chicago – rendering one of her standard choices, the long and complicated song MORGAN – and I remember then thinking that, in it, after a lifetime of honing and polishing, she had achieved perfection of motion in Sacred Harp leading. It's often said by those who follow professional basketball that this or that player has "the quickest step to the basket." Well, Marie had the quickest step from the treble to the alto. In the rotation of entering parts, that meant a whirl around to the alto from the treble by sweeping back past the tenor, or tenor-bass, benches, a 270° instead of the easier 90° pivot (excellence, in old-time Sacred Harp leading, being demonstrated in part by never turning one's back on the tenor class). Her feet, her close, cupped-hand movements without the book were speedy instruments in the flurry of interlocking parts in MORGAN and the other fuging songs she excelled at presenting.

As I savor that memory, another scene of Marie's mastery of motion tugs at me. I once attended a party at the home of Marie's and Charles' sister Edith Tate in celebration of a significant wedding anniversary of brother Harrison and his wife, Flarce. At some point I stopped at the dessert table to have a piece of a towering coconut cake. A number of family members were around, but Marie hovered closest. As I started to reach for the cake knife, she said, "Would you like me to cut that for you?" Ordinarily I would have put up a fussy show of self-sufficiency – "Oh, no, thanks, I can get it!" – and blundered into the operation. Something made me stop this time, though, and I said in essence, "Well, yes, please. . . ."

Now, I probably knew then that Marie had worked as a server in a school cafeteria, but whether I did or not, I was thereby treated to a sight of sheer artistry. The knife sank into the frosty mound and began, with practiced ease, to saw back and forth in a steady dance, advancing and then retreating. The blade seemed to cauterize what it touched, so that every crumb adhered to the side it was meant for.

The large, perfect slab then fell away entirely intact against Marie's steadying hand, and she laid it onto the plate. It was a scrumptious piece of cake, as I recall, but the image of its high-skilled delivery has lasted many years past my consumption of it.

I never had the chance to know Charles' and Marie's sister Lucille Tolbert, but only to hear about her voice that could climb the heights. (Billy Williams, a reliable observer of singers in his area, told me more than once that Lucille was the best treble he ever heard.) Brother Hadyn I occasionally exchanged greetings with near his usual place on the tenor bench at singings, but I didn't know him beyond those brief encounters. The other siblings - sisters Pauline Childers and Edith Tate and brother Harrison - rounded out the rest of this formidable group.

Harrison, many times blessed as father and grandfather of good singers, seemed easily the mildest of his set, the least likely to take or give offense. He amused me always by employing a little set piece of greeting chatter. When, at the handshake, he would ask someone, "How ya doin'?" and then would have to answer the toss-back question, he would invariably pause as if it were a new or unexpected query. Following what seemed the briefest self-assessment, he would reply, with emphasis and face turned serious, "... *fair* ... just *fair* ..." For the sake of accuracy, it was important to steer clear of "fine" or any similarly sanguine phrase. In his usual place on front bench, first chair, Harrison was better than a fair bass singer, though, and was perennially a class favorite.

Edith, generous and loving - and every inch and ounce a Creel - was the one I was closest to over the years. We often sat together at singings, and from time to time talked by phone. Only once did I run afoul of her, but that one episode left me stranded in bafflement. In 1998 I had driven over into Georgia for a singing at Holly Springs Church. Arriving late, I took up a position somewhat back from the main class. Edith, over from the Birmingham area as well, was seated a few rows in front of me. At the first break, I saw her turn and then found myself caught in her gaze. She leveled a stern index finger in my direction and, with what seemed a frosty half-smile, said, "I've got a *bone* to pick with you!" What? What could I possibly have done to her or to any family member to elicit such a threatening greeting?! Frantically rummaging through my store of guilt, I came up empty-handed – and then she was right in front of me.

"I *saw* that article you wrote."

The tone was triumphantly accusatory, as if she had caught me in the act of trying to steal a chicken from the coop and had just slammed a heavy implement down on my thieving hands. . . . It turned out that she was referring to a reminiscence I had posted online a few months earlier upon the death of her aunt Mamie. I had intended in that post a heartfelt tribute to Mamie and Mattie Creel and their husbands, Chester and Hester, all by then deceased, and I could have imagined nothing in my comments that would be offensive to family members or anyone else. (The post, my short testimonial to the lives and quiet example of that quartet of yeoman folk, is included in the next-to-last chapter here.)

And then she laid it on me: "I want you to know, my momma and daddy did *a lot more* for Sacred Harp than Mamie and Mattie . . . ."

Startled as I was by the accusation itself, I was bowled over by the rationale behind it. . . . I had, after all, checked with Edith to verify information about Mamie and the others before I had posted my reminiscence. And she, like the rest of the family, had always seemed to revere Mamie, who had survived, through great travail, into her upper 90s.

"But Edith, I didn't know your mother and father . . . ," I tried to protest.

"Well, they did *a lot more* for Sacred Harp . . . ."

Falling precipitously off my bearings, I managed to glimpse a ledge of logic and grabbed hold: "Well, B.F. White did more than all of them put together, but I didn't know him, so . . . ."

It was not an argument to be won, and I suppose it ended in stalemate – but with Edith maintaining, in a trailing comment, "Well, my momma and daddy did more for Sacred Harp than Mamie and Mattie and Chester and Hester ever thought about. . . ."

The central issue there – my sin, I guess, of omission – was never mentioned between us again, and, happily, I stayed clear of further trouble with Edith.

Older sister Pauline, who always sang tenor, was as sharp-tongued as any of the bunch. A scene of some little amusement to me serves up the point: At one of our gatherings, I was sitting close by a tight little group of the family – Pauline, her sister-in-law Flarce Creel and another family member – and overheard a snatch of Pauline's under-breath fussing about someone's singing. (It may have been me she was grousing about; I was after all at that point singing another part within the fringe of the tenor section.) Probably aware that Pauline's indiscretion was rippling out beyond them, Flarce – a Creel by marriage and not by birth and upbringing – put a stop to it with a forceful whisper: "Oh, *hush!*"

With or without a minder in tow, Pauline was ever outspoken, a frequent dispenser of zingers. She was always ready to laugh, though, and to make others chuckle as well. I greatly enjoyed her company and managed to avoid cross words with her, experiencing only one moment of awkwardness between us. At the 1998 session of the Midwest Convention, I was stepping from the square after leading a resounding rendition of a song from the mid-19th century often today considered a period piece: THE DYING BOY. For me, when sung well (and it was, surpassingly, that day), this song can achieve a power that transcends its sentimental text and somewhat wooden musical framework. And a supreme class of singers, pouring out their voices in a great acoustical setting like that of Ida Noyes Hall, can be mood-transforming. Like many other leaders leaving the square, having just experienced the best two minutes of the day (their moment in the center of that focused maelstrom of sound), I felt transported. As I passed her on the outer edges of the tenor, I saw and felt Pauline lightly catch my arm with her hand and noticed what seemed a look of sad reproach, which I could interpret only as an expression of surrender to the beauty of the moment. At the break, we passed each other again, and Pauline held me up just long enough to say, "My son died [?] years ago today, and I told them this morning, 'I *hope* nobody leads THE DYING BOY. . . .'"

About such offenses as mine, even unintentional ones: be sure your sins would be pointed out. . . . As best I can understand it, reaching out to stamp the other person with guilt was, for Pauline and Edith and Charles, an act of cleansing. It was like the brandishing of a holy sword, with any resulting violence just the inevitable consequence of order being restored. In that irrepressible inclination, no wound was to be left unvisited, no bone left unpicked.

Unlike Edith, Pauline or others in the family, though, Charles seemed to have assigned himself an almost daily duty of bending a recalcitrant world back into shape, even if at times he wearied of the Sisyphean task. Some ten years or so before I would see him for the last time, I had a chance to talk with him at a wake we were attending. In our conversation, he bore down on the wickedness all around us, around the world in general. The signs were all there, he felt: the end must surely be near. "I think the Lord will come before I'm in the ground," he said. "I'm pretty sure of it – I think the end will come before I'm in the ground!" I couldn't help but find some amusement, as always, in Charles' view of things, this time in the satisfied sureness of his position. When I shared this anecdote a few years later, a friend had joked, "Well, he's not wrong yet, Buell!"

"He's my brother and I love him," Edith once said to me about Charles, "but he's wrong." She wasn't talking about his end-of-world prognostications, but about some matter of contention. Charles was, from time to time, at odds with members of the family in general – and, for a few years, remained estranged from most of them, failing to join them at Old County Line Church, their common family meeting place for all of their lives.

It was thus a surprise in 2009 to see him show up at Old County Line for the annual Reid Memorial Singing the third Sunday in October. Arriving late from his home in Jacksonville, Ala., maybe a couple of hours away, he was ushered up toward the center of the class. You could almost feel an exhalation from family and friends throughout the room, a palpable sense of the healing this appearance promised.

Just before the noon hour, Charles was called to lead. He asked for number 216, DELIGHT. Propping himself with a cane, he spoke briefly, occasionally freeing his right hand for rhetorical flourishes. "I can't sing much because of coughing," he said. "And I don't have much breath, because my blood pressure goes up and down like a window shade."

It was a flawless job of leading, nonetheless. At the sequenced entrance of the parts in the chorus, he remained in place but turned toward each part in rotation, each time delicately opening his fist at the top of the downbeat, like dropping a coin in each of four stations: fa mi *la* la sol . . . .

"I was at this singing 84 years ago, my momma told me," he said, after finishing the song. And then, pausing for breath: "Now I want to sing the first song I remember leading at this singing, 77 years ago. 80 on top. SHOUTING SONG."

At lunch I was able to sit by him, and we talked about his difficult health conditions, the frailties of old age, and about the old days of singing, about Reid's Gap and about the Creel and Reid families.

He had been, I knew, first a good and then, for the bulk of his life, an excellent singer. When he was young, he said, "Daddy cleared a spot for me on tenor," and he pointed to a place on the front bench just to right of center. "When Harrison [two years his junior, and by then ready to assume his place around the square] came along, he moved him over to bass." The implication was clear: He had been given the favored spot, and he had kept it.

I had been seated behind him on tenor in the morning session, but in the afternoon I joined him for a while on the front row of the bass. He coughed a good bit and occasionally sang the tenor notes when he had not memorized the bass line. But at the soft part in PLEYEL'S HYMN, I leaned my head in toward his and could hear his voice clearly. His bass tones were perfect, and it was a pleasure to try to blend my voice with his.

He was shortly called again into the center of the square. Slowly hoisting himself up on troubled knees, he made his way forward with the help of his cane. He wanted to address the class before he began singing and so had not called out a number.

"Several people have told me how much it meant to them to see me here today," he said. "Well, let me tell you, it means even more to *this boy* to be here!" It was a poignant moment.

He then said that he wanted to lead "131 on bottom," a song his mother had led at this place several times many years before. He pointed to first-chair position on the front row of treble. "And I can just see her over there singing tribble on it, too."

INVOCATION has been one of my favorite songs since I first heard a captivating version when J.L. Edge of Rome, Ga., led it at Holly Springs many years ago. I was glad now to have this connection to add to my already warm associations with it.

The point has been articulated in many ways, but I don't know of a more succinct version than that by Anaïs Nin: "We don't see things as they are, we see them as we are." The biases we lead with in life tend to be self-sustaining, self-reinforcing. They see authentication in so much that they survey. I was reminded of this as Charles proceeded into his lesson.

He appeared to have concluded his prefatory remarks, and we were getting ready to start the song. A pitch had been given, and sounded by several. It was a brisk day, and Charles had on what looked like a heavy sport coat. As he lifted his left elbow awkwardly to free himself of it a little and to shift the cane from left to right hand, all the while balancing his book atop his hands, a couple of young singers on the front bench to his left mistook this action for the start of the song. Eager to assist, they jumped in for the first two or three notes.

How could they know they had fallen into a trap of their own making?

From a sharply singular point of view, the class had once again shown itself unruly, mutinous. And needful as ever of reproach. Charles Creel – feeble now and with a weaker voice than he had had to use in similar skirmishes in the past – was ready. No sooner did the unfortunate notes fall out than he shot back. "*Wait a minute, now!*" he barked, looking not in the direction of the lead offenders but out across the insurrectionist class in general. His tone was arched, but it was overall a milder rebuke than family and others had heard from him before.

"When *I'm* off the floor, y'all can sing like you *want* to! . . . [and preaching now] Uncle Tom Denson taught that when *you're* on the floor, you're in *charge!*"

Evidently satisfied that he had wrested back control – that everyone now knew who was in charge – he started the song. The pace was deliberate and good, the accent strong. Perfect execution. And another memorable lesson from the now elder member of the Creel and Reid family.

Back from that scene a good ways, I ask myself a fanciful question: Should we reserve a place in the peaceable kingdom for the hedgehog? Accommodate, if not encourage, prickliness?

Oh, absolutely. The mornings and early afternoons of my years of singing were not otherwise dull. But they were always enlivened by the presence of members of that redoubtable clan, the senior members of which someone once used the term Velcro to describe.

I would be remiss if I failed to say it: no family provided more support for singings in our territory. In van or caravan, they sped across the miles – north, south, east and west – and, at singing venues big and small, unloaded onto the four parts. Many a communal meal was bolstered if not made possible by their cooking. And just the spirit and personality they brought to the mix!

Charles Emory Creel died in 2012 at the age of 87. He had outlasted all six of his siblings. Over the years, he had lost his first wife and three of his four children. He had persevered to the end. True to his vision, he saw the world, he might have said, with the only eyes he'd been given.

If in description I have roughed him up a bit here – him and the others – I still do intend a nostalgic, a most affectionate send-off. I miss the hiss and burr, the bristling pride, the joy in mischief. And I chafe in thinking it: We won't see their like here again.

19

Stories from the Civil War

When director Anthony Minghella used the shape-note song IDUMEA as the soaring backdrop to the Battle of the Crater scene in "Cold Mountain," he drew from what was popular musical fare in the rural South of the 1860s. *The Sacred Harp* was more than two decades old by the time the Civil War drew to its convulsive close, and the songbook and the tribal singing practices surrounding it had by then put down extensive roots in upland areas across the southernmost states.

Anyone who feels the power of Sacred Harp today would probably expect the songbook to have played a special role in a place and time of such travail. A letter I referred to in my 1978 book would help to answer that expectation. From his post in Richmond, Va., in 1863, Confederate Sergeant-Major William Jefferson Mosely had written his family in Macon, Ga., and assured them that his non-fighting hours were not wasted in playing cards and gambling. "I have been in the war for two years and I do not know one card from another," he wrote, "but I do know my notes and we have some of the best singings around the camp fire I have ever heard. Ma, you and the girls get out the old Sacred Harp songbook, turn to the old song Invocation, sing it and think of me." And in an early 1864 letter to the family, he made a request of "Sister Emma": "I want you to sing Invocation in the Sacred Harp and think of me, for I think it is so pretty, I sing it every day, that is nearly all the amusement I have is singing."

That "old song Invocation" – with words penned in the 18th century and a melody affixed to them less than 30 years before the date of Mosely's letter – had references to mourning and sorrow and the flight to heaven. But other songs, like the stirring CONFIDENCE (p. 270), made Christian metaphor available for topical use in that harrowing time:

> No, in the strength of Jesus, no!
> I never will give up my shield.

Douglas Rodgers, a friend from our college days, once recounted to me a conversation he'd had with an elderly woman at a Sacred Harp singing at a country church in Pike County, Ala., in the 1960s. The woman had relayed to him that day a story about her grandfather's return from the conflict to loved ones long wondering whether he had survived. After the war had ended, a family member had looked out at one point, she said, and had seen the young man "comin' across the field – and he was a-singin' CONFY-DENCE!"

Another Civil War story I was to hear later drew the Sacred Harp connection tighter still. For a good many years I attended the Doss Memorial Singing at Sardis Baptist Church in the Morris community in northern Jefferson County. There one year, as chair of the singing, Dick Nail, great-grandson of Seaborn Denson and grandson of Whitt Denson, was about to open the session after the noon hour and had decided to lead number 277, ANTIOCH. Most of the class, though, was not yet in from the break. As I was sitting right by him, Dick, with a few minutes to kill, shared with me what was on his mind. He began by asking if I had ever known Frank Miller, from the Empire area in nearby Walker County, who he said used to rebind the songbooks for area singers and who had been dead maybe 15 or so years. I told him no.

Frank Miller, he then went ahead to tell me, had asked him once if he had ever known Uncle Ben Miller. No, he was dead before Dick came along, "but I've heard stories about him," Dick had said. Frank had the songbook in his lap at the time, turned to page 277 and said, "You know why I always sing this song? . . . You'll not see a Miller sit through a singing without somebody singing this song."

Dick then began to tell me the story Frank Miller had told him, although, as he said, "I've got to be really detached to get through it. . . . I'm right on the verge, anyway. . ." The story proceeded as follows:

Ben Miller was 14 when the war began. He begged to enlist but was refused. He slipped off from home anyway and followed the Alabama 19th until at last they took him in.

He was struck down at Shiloh, and the family received word that he had perished. Several men of the community who had seen him fall wrote home to relay the news. But though none of his fellows or family knew it, young Ben Miller had survived. He was taken up off the field by the Union troops, and when the war was concluded over three years later, he found his way home.

When he turned onto the little road leading to his home place, he could make out the figure of his father on the front porch and, moments later, saw his father lean forward, straining to discern who was walking toward him up the roadway.

As Ben drew closer, he saw his father suddenly "go like this," Dick said, broadly waving his arm up and down. The elder Miller, that is, had begun striding from one side of the porch to the other – and was beating time.

When Ben got close enough, it was ANTIOCH he could hear his father loudly singing:

Shout on, pray on, we're gaining ground,
Glory, hallelujah!
The dead's alive, and the lost is found,
Glory, hallelujah!

This is what grabs me still. In that moment of unimaginable joy, Mr. Miller's impulse was not first to run out and throw his arms about his son, but instead to rise to this sacramental act: to *sing*, with those words that he knew so well but that surely had never spoken to him so intimately as they did now – in this story that would live on to inspire generations of his family and Dickie Nail . . . and me, in turn, to share with others.

Dangling-from-the-ceiling room only? Cullman courthouse, July 1943. "Youthful Mary Kitchens Gardner" leading, possibly with a frequent choice, ALABAMA. Consider that the chamber's ringed balcony would have been packed as well. (From the George Pullen Jackson collection, courtesy of the Jackson family)

20

Cullman and the Courthouse Singings

It is no longer – as it may once have been – the biggest and best convention in all the land. But well into the 21ˢᵗ century, it carries a distinction nonetheless: it's the last of its kind. An annual courthouse singing – and one dating back over a hundred years.

The start-up date for the Cullman County Sacred Harp Convention has been difficult to nail down. Various sources say 1880s, 1891, 1898, 1900, 1901. . . . At some point, the printed minutes failed to record what was so evident, and so the train of time was lost.

The convention wasn't, to start with, that remarkable. County seats up and down the state sported such a courthouse event: Huntsville, Russellville, Moulton, Decatur, Jasper, Double Springs, Vernon, Guntersville, Ft. Payne, Talladega, Ashville, Ashland, Alexander City, Andalusia, Greenville, Elba, Dothan and more (in total, as many as 28 of Alabama's 67 counties). Other Southern states boasted a courthouse singing here or there for some period, but nothing like the flourishing in Alabama, the state which, for the 20ᵗʰ century and beyond, has represented the heartland of Sacred Harp singing. Even an urban center like Birmingham, seat of Jefferson County, held an annual courthouse singing as late as the 1950s.

When Sacred Harpers could take over the local courthouse for a one-, two- or three-day sit-in, sing-in, pray-and-eat-in, you had to know that four-shaped music still ruled! Country-dwelling tenor, bass, treble and alto seemed to settle into those uptown surroundings as assumptively as a summer robin flouncing about in a courtyard birdbath. Over time, though, every other annual courthouse singing disappeared, as in each case the broader community that bolstered it lost interest and the class of local singers slimmed down or withered entirely.

In its heyday, the Cullman Convention, always the second Sunday in July and Saturday before, drew wonder – and hot and thirsty crowds. Longtime convention-goer Velton Chafin once told a story that brought specificity to the picture. At the courthouse event some years before, he said, he had come out of the singing chamber during one of the session's breaks and nodded to an older gentleman seated on a bench in the hallway. "Having a good singing, aren't we?" "Yeah," the old fellow had grudged, "but it's not like it used to be. . . ."

That line might be every old-timer's refrain, but Velton, tarrying there for a bit, was repaid with a neat little narrative from someone who had first experienced the convention decades before.

It was in the '30s, the old gentleman said, and he was driving from Tennessee to Birmingham down U.S. 31. Cullman was a spot along that journey. Approaching the township, he said, he came upon "a traffic jam." Velton later surmised that this was not so much automobile traffic – though some of that, for sure – but mainly crowds of people, maybe some wagons, a few horses and mules, crossing the roadway. As the man drew closer, he saw a policeman directing the traffic. Edging forward to the intersection, he asked the officer what in the world was going on. . . .

"Oh, there's a fasola singin' at the courthouse." The terminology piqued the traveler's curiosity. He was soon able to park and make his way over to the big building.

"You couldn't get in the courtroom at all," the old fellow told Velton. Even the hallways were jammed. Outside pulsed this great throng of people – country folk come to town for the biggest two days of the year. And out the open windows, soaring sounds that captured the Tennessean's imagination.

A *Cullman Tribune* report of one year's singing from that decade confirms the hubbub: it estimated the 1937 crowd at 5,000.

Five thousand. Well might the food committee from any of today's conventions read that figure and gulp. There likely wouldn't have been a food committee at all in that era, though – nor any responsibility for feeding the multitude. Families and individuals generally provided their own repast, although a commonly heard line might have been something like, "Come over here and eat with us – I've got ham, cornbread and a mess of turnip greens. . . ."

Nor, of course, would all those folk have been singers – or even intentional listeners. Some doubtless would have been there out of mere crowd-envy, or to puncture a mid-summer boredom. Many more would have come to mix with either town or country friends and relatives they rarely got to see, to swap farming stories or speculation about prospects for rain. But singing was the core and cause of it all. And there likely wouldn't have been anyone there – including now a late passer-through from Tennessee, or Birmingham, Montgomery or Mobile – who wouldn't have understood that.

For several years in the '30s, a blaring full-page *Tribune* ad greeted the event: "Cullman Hangs Out the Welcome Sign to the Annual Court House Singers." The ad's 21 listed merchant-sponsors "look forward," it said, "to the great crowds that will fill our streets on these two great days."

The lead article on the front page of the *Tribune* the week following the 1935 convention mentioned the "record breaking attendance" both days. "The weather was ideal except the heat," the article stated, "and the farmers being well up with farm work gave an excellent opportunity for all who wished to visit Cullman, take part in the singing and listen to the old songs so dearly loved by thousands of old and young people." And in possible reference to the traffic jams the convention often created: "So far as we have been able to learn not a single accident occurred to mar the pleasure of any one."

Among the "beloved leaders" there for the event, the article stated, was "Hon. Thomas Denson of Jasper, and one of his brothers from Winston County who organized the Cullman court house singing years ago." Tom Denson would die two months to the day from the convention's closing session, and his brother Seaborn would die two months before the following year's session. The mid- to late-'30s, though, would have been an exciting time in the central Sacred Harp world with the publication of the Denson brothers' 1936 revision of the *Sacred Harp*, especially in this area where Tom and Seab had taught so many hundreds to sing. Songbooks, probably for the first time in years, would have been plentiful – and highly prized. It must have been a joyful time, even in the Great Depression era, to sing or listen to singing.

Although the new book would not be off the press until late August, the '36 convention should have been abuzz about the prospects. But it was not to be. A week before the convention, a huge front-page headline in the *Tribune* warned, "Sacred Harp Singing Called Off." An outbreak of polio in the state – infantile paralysis it was called at the time – had resulted in the Board of Health urging that all gatherings be suspended until the epidemic passed.

Two songs in the new revision sure to have been celebrated in those years were additions, and eventual classics, Soar Away and Sacred Mount by A.M. (Marcus) Cagle, who had grown up in western Cullman County and who lived in the area until 1937. A tall, handsome figure and dynamic (and volatile) personality, Cagle may have been the territory's preeminent singer, leader and keyer of music – though he would be better known today for having contributed, over a period of five decades, 11 tunes to the songbook's several editions, more than the total number of pieces by all but a handful of other composers.

For three years in the 1960s I attended the Cullman convention when Marcus Cagle was present, and each time got to see him lead a lesson of two songs, as was the custom then – though not in either case one of his own compositions. In 1968, five months before his death at 84, he and I sat together on the long front bench of the tenor. That scene, as best I can summon it now, represents to me one of Sacred Harp's finest features: a bringing together of people from different generations, different backgrounds, different ways of life. There we were, sitting side by side, blending voices and chatting, the young man and the much older man – he in fact three and a half times my age – a newbie with one of the great Sacred Harp composers of the songbook's two centuries. Looking back now from a vantage point well within the 21st century, I realize I was singing that day with someone who had composed the durable tunes PRESENT JOYS, NEW HOPE and JORDAN in 1908! He in his turn had sung with men and women who had sung with B.F. White. Thus do the generations overlap in this tradition, which so casually, gracefully fosters such a sharing.

Other names in Sacred Harp lore passed through the Cullman courthouse chamber in those years. Among the most popular of the 1936 book's new "class songs" was ODEM, whose lead-off phrase in the chorus, "Give me the roses while I live," would become one of the favorite sentiments in the book. That song by Tom Denson was named for a legendary figure from the era: Lonnie P. Odem (1887-1978), the financial sponsor of the book and the estate owner of Odem's Chapel, the convention-worthy structure built near his home in St. Joseph, Tenn., primarily as a host site for Sacred Harp singing, though it was also made available for "the singing of modern church songs," according to a long article about Odem and the chapel in an August 1948 issue of the Lawrenceburg, Tenn., *Democrat-Union*. Odem built the "$12,000 rock chapel," the newspaper reported, in 1945. For a number of years, he hosted there a *ten-day* Sacred Harp convention (annually from the Friday before the second Sunday in August through the following Sunday). On the day the *Democrat-Union* reporter attended during the 1948 event, the convention register listed participants from "28 states, Canada, Spain, Brazil and Germany," with Odem estimating (with some exaggeration?) full attendance at 5,000.

Odem's interest in Sacred Harp, the article stated, began in 1900 "when he made all such singings around his home and in north Alabama. Since then he has been all over the nation singing and hunting others to sing with him. He admits the Sacred Harp songbook is his magnificent obsession and that, hand in hand with the Bible, it is next to his family in his affections." The hospitality he provided as host of his home convention may be without parallel. Three free meals a day were served from the chapel's basement, "a huge and fully-equipped kitchen and dining hall," beginning with breakfast at 6:30 each morning, by a battery of local "kitchen helpers." And Odem and his wife, Comella, hosted visitors, including Marcus Cagle, in their "nearly 16-room" house, with "sleeping quarters for 30-odd people in his upstairs rooms alone."

In happier times, company at Lon Odem's house: Ruth Denson Edwards, front, far left; Comella Odem, to Ruth's immediate left; Odem, back, second from left; Marcus Cagle, back center. (From the collection of the grandchildren of T.J. and Lola Akers Denson, used with permission)

Sacred Harp singers through the decades, though surely not poor of spirit, could generally not boast of wealth. Odem, however, positioned himself well outside the norm, and the *Democrat-Union* reporter recounts in brief his impressive achievement. With his new wife, Odem had driven "a yoke of oxen 40 years ago from his Alabama home to [their] 223-acre farm which they bought for $280 on credit here, and plowed the steers for the first four years after arriving. By honest hard toil his farming, stock trading, and real estate interests have brought him remarkable success" – success that included owning at that point "35,000 acres of land in several states" and having once owned "a 1000-acre Texas onion farm and a 5000-acre Colorado sheep farm." "Friends say no neighbor is ever in need if Odem can supply him," the article concluded.

It would not just be neighbors who would turn to him for help. Odem was cited in the new Denson book's first pages, under his photograph (though his name was spelled there as Odom), as "a good singer, the Sacred Harp's best friend and the man who made this book possible. His love for T.J. Denson has known no bounds." Those words were surely written by Tom's daughter Ruth, with whom Odem clearly had a close relationship.

An extraordinary letter from Odem to Ruth in January of 1936 brings perspective to that transitional time. The letter, in pencil on yellowed, small-tablet writing paper, was only recently discovered among family papers by Ruth's nephew Richard Mauldin. For ease of reading, I transcribe parts of it here by regularizing the spelling (typically eccentric for that country generation) and adding punctuation (of which there was not a dot). Though the letter begins simply with "Dear old Pal," with no name affixed, the identity of the recipient cannot be in doubt. The weather had been cold in St. Joseph, producing a prodigious six-inch snow. And along with some friskiness at the start – "I sure wish you was here and would snow ball you and have a big time" – Odem couldn't help but crow a bit (as he was often said to do with respect to his financial dealings) about his success that day in mule-trafficking. "Don't you think I am some salesman," he wrote; undoubtedly he was, having just returned from Memphis the previous night with a load of mules and having already sold "32 head." He then got down to business, addressing the songbook's prospects and his part in them:

Odem's Chapel, 1940s. Notable figures: Ruth Denson Edwards, to left on front row, book in hand; Marcus Cagle, in white, just to right of center. (Photo courtesy of Jeanette Dewberry)

The class at Odem's Chapel, including Lon Odem, against the wall, far left; George M. Mattox, fourth from left on the wall; Ruth Denson Edwards, seated, far right. (Photo courtesy of Jeanette Dewberry)

Front and center amid a multigenerational crowd in the basement of Odem's Chapel: George M. Mattox (kneeling, with young Jimmie Lou McGough and companion), Tom Harper (seated, immediate left) and Lon Odem (immediate right, with suspenders), about 1948.

Girl, you don't know how I appreciate how you feel toward me. You are the only one that has shown your appreciation for what I have done for the book. [Is chief book editor and general commander Paine Denson a telling omission there?] But Girl, you know I told you the book would be finished. I told Uncle Tom that I would stay with him till it finished and he knew I would do it. He did not doubt it, and that was the reason he always said we will have the best book ever was offered to the public. He knew he could get the max to do it with, and you know what I told you when you was here. We was going to carry out what he had started to do. Girl, I can't tell you how I love you and I never will forget those words and letters which you have written. Girl, forgive my mistakes and for not writing. Girl, write me every time you can and come to see us and at any time I can be of any help, call on me as ever. Your friend, LP Odem

By the 1960s, the Odem-and-Denson-family relationship had strained, with Odem losing a legal struggle with the then-stewards of the publishing company over ownership of the songbook rights, which he had gradually tried to assert. Ruth sat in the opposing party when the judge delivered his ruling, and then joined the little group of company loyalists as the judge summoned them to his quarters. "Now let me hear one of those tunes," the magistrate urged. They complied with a celebratory version of RAGAN: "I belong to this band, hallelujah."

Sitting in the Cullman courthouse in 1967, I heard the arranging committee summon "Lon Odem." Out of the class then emerged this short, slightly pear-shaped (by then) 80-year-old figure, who called for and led WORLD UNKNOWN and SWEET MORNING, both without the aid of a book. If I could relive that day, I would certainly swap what was probably idle chatter with others for a meeting and conversation with this (for me) mysterious figure, this mule merchant and much more, who could have told so much about one of the most bustling periods in Sacred Harp history – about a heartfelt commitment to "Uncle Tom" and then about the disheartening denouement.

And Other Courthouses

Elder J.L. Hopper of Eva, Ala., a third-generation singer, remembers attending, as a boy, courthouse singings in nearby Guntersville, Decatur and Huntsville and, as a young man, a few times in Cullman. But it was at a convention singing in the Oneonta courthouse, in Blount County just to the south, that he stumbled upon what would become a Sacred Harp historical footnote oddity.

Some background for that story, first: The Warrior River Convention (named for the area around the Little Warrior River running through Blount County) was one of the old singing conventions, dating from 1875 and continuing until 2003. This once-robust convention may have gotten by with little controversy in its early days, but the period around 1911 had brought it to crisis. Members were then confronted with the choice of adopting the new Sacred Harp revision called the "James book," the overwhelming pick of other singing conventions in central and northern Alabama, or continuing to use the last B.F. White edition (of 1870). It's impossible now to know the full set of issues leading to the juncture, but one supposes many of the traditionalists in the ranks simply preferred the old book as they had always known it – with most of the songs in three parts rather than four. As well as offering many new songs by the Denson brothers, Marcus Cagle and others, the James book added an alto part to virtually every formerly three-part song.

Unable to resolve the issue, the convention split: there would now be *two* Warrior River Conventions, in the same county, meeting the first Sunday in August and Friday and Saturday before. By 1950 that pattern had held fast for nearly four decades. J.L. Hopper was 17 at the time and at that point was working, cutting pulpwood, in the Oneonta area. On the first Saturday of that August weekend, he happened to ride into town with a cousin. When the two of them got close to the courthouse, they were surprised to hear singing – that familiarly irresistible shape-note singing – from inside. In short order, J.L. was himself in the midst of the treble, looking on someone else's book and singing, for the first time, song after song in three-part format.

The next day, as planned, he would join his father at the *other* Warrior River Convention, then held at a site called the Tabernacle or Wilson's Chapel, with singing from the Denson book, which had succeeded the James book a decade and a half before. "Boy, where were you yesterday?" the senior Hopper inquired and, when told, replied, "You better not tell that here – they'll tar and feather you and run you off!" All would have been forgiven shortly as it turned out, though, because during the day a hats-in-hand delegation appeared from the rival convention at the courthouse. The die-hards had for decades been unable to get more books, and their surviving copies were now worn almost beyond use. Doubtless spurred on by would-be altos in their midst, they had come to ask for, and were then granted, reunification. And thus did J.L. Hopper become probably the only person to attend, not as delegate but as full-scale participant, *both* Warrior River Conventions in the last year of that stubbornly forked existence.

Jewel Alexander Wootten, who grew up in the Hopewell community out from Oneonta, attended, along with her parents and siblings, the courthouse singing there in the years of her youth, the 1930s. The 1889 minutes of the Warrior River Convention had listed her grandfather, J.A. Alexander, among its leaders, and all the family since had been Sacred Harp singers as well. About those convention events, Jewel remembered in particular a feature of the dinner-on-the-grounds: her mother's famous chicken pie, a version of chicken and dumplings, which Mrs. Alexander made in a big dishpan used for nothing else but that recipe. One year, Jewel said, "a bunch of boys came up from down in town" to the courthouse, drawn there not by the singing but by the dinner to be spread. It was their intent, she said, to "hog the table." When they jumped up in the family's wagon to help themselves to the chicken pie, her daddy, John Alexander, scattered them. "He could get 'em gone, I'll tell you!" Jewel said. "They got run off of that hill!"

Jewel also attended the Cullman and Birmingham courthouse singings with her parents in those years. "It was the thrill of my life to go to the big Cullman singing," she remembered. And to a country girl, the Birmingham singing was thrilling, too, because it offered an elevator to ride up and down in.

It was the lack of an elevator that in the late 1950s brought the Fayette courthouse singing to its demise, according to Linton Ballinger, who grew up in the countryside out from Fayette in northwestern Alabama. The Fayette convention had been important to Linton from early in his life, because, as he said, "When I was young, it was often the only time I got to go to town all year long." Originally called the Old Folks Singing Association and then the Old Book Singing Association before becoming the Fayette County Court House Sacred Harp Singing Association, the convention had been founded in 1909 by Judge Hobart M. Bell, remembered by at least one Sacred Harp oldster as the state's last "hanging judge." Over the decades the set of stairs up to the courtroom had become more and more of an obstacle for the predominantly elderly class that supported the singing, and so at last the convention opted for housing that would be easier on the knees.

Linton and other members of the Ballinger family attended courthouse singings in surrounding counties, too. The Fayette and Tuscaloosa singings especially made an impact on Linton because the courtrooms in both cases were across the street from the county jail. "As a little fellow," he said, "I remember those who were jailed standing up to their cell windows listening to the singing" – the bright chords of Sacred Harp, in those instances, raining down on the just and the unjust alike.

Linton has earned a reputation as a magisterial arranging committeeperson, and I've relished an anecdote he once shared with me about the power of that position. In the Fayette courtroom, the committee sat behind the judge's big desk and called the song leaders from there. The arranging on the day of Linton's story was being handled by his father, Hamilton Ballinger, and Edward Black, who kept a pocket watch. This was back in the day when only the best leaders were called, each being given a segment of time to direct the class for multiple songs: the half-hour for a lesson in the 19th century had typically been reduced over the decades to a quarter-hour in the early- to mid-20th. During this session, Linton said, Benjamin Cunningham, a sometime Baptist preacher who arranged the song HAPPY CHRISTIAN, was called to lead for his 15-minute lesson. He began talking, which soon morphed into preaching of a sort. We won't know whether, during those ruminations or exhortations, others began to look out the window, leaf through their songbooks or settle into a doze, but we will know that Edward Black was eyeing his pocket watch. When at last Cunningham finished his lengthy preamble and announced his song number, Black called time on him and summoned the next leader.

That tuneless lesson must have made the rounds of convention talk back in those years. A few courtroom interjections have survived the decades as well. Runie Heath Glover of Ozark was one of the great characters of my experience. Tall, willowy and rough-talking, Runie was a strong-voiced alto, and when she would go up for a high note, she would often let it fall off precipitously, like paint thrown up against the wall. She had a keen, country sense of humor, and talking as well as singing was her game. People in attendance at one session of the courthouse singing in Ozark from years back remember Runie abruptly rising to full height just before the noon hour. "That's not my collards y'all smell. . . ," she loudly advised. "That's the cotton gin up the street!"[26]

Estes Jackson of Hamilton remembers, from decades back, an indiscreetly sounded remark that broke up a singing he had traveled to in the courthouse at Dadeville in Tallapoosa County in the east-central section of the state. Daphene Causey of Alabaster wasn't in attendance that day, but she had heard the story about it and could pinpoint not only the song that was the locus of the outburst but the exact spot in it where the damage had occurred. By Estes' and

Daphene's reports, a couple of women – non-singers evidently, though maybe, for the event, collard- or other-vegetable-cookers – were talking away in the back of the class. With all the singing noise around them, they found it necessary to raise their voices so they could hear one another. Page 268 had been called: William Billings' famous rendering of David's grief at the death of his son Absalom. Just at the spot where the singers rang out David's cry, "O my son!" closing it off with a full-measure rest, the two talkers were caught unaware. As the echo of the last chord did a quick fade, "*I fried mine in butter. . .*" came out of nowhere to tower over the moment. Such a roar of laughter and commotion then ensued that the song was abandoned and David's lamentation, that day, went unfinished.

These are remembered moments that, bubbling up as narrative, bring personality and character to an institutional scene now almost folded away. The trappings, for some, still linger in the mind. Bruce Johnson, originally from north of Cullman, came to Sacred Harp in the '50s and recalls going to the old Cullman courthouse for the singing: going up the big steps to the central chamber, which later reminded him, he said, of the courtroom scenes in the movie "To Kill a Mockingbird." Maycomb, the fictional town of the novel and film, was based on author Harper Lee's hometown of Monroeville, seat of Monroe County in the deep southwestern part of the state. And the "Mockingbird" movie set is said to have been built as a replica of the Monroeville courtroom. Monroeville, coincidentally, was one of the last Sacred Harp courthouse settings to go, with annual sessions there up into the '80s and two subsequent sessions in '94 and '95.

By the 1950s, most of the courthouse singings were already gone. Bud Oliver once told me a story about the Etowah County Convention in Gadsden that showed how the edges of support for that and other conventions were noticeably fraying by the time of his youth. On the convention weekend in what was probably the 1940s, he had gone with family to stay over for the two-day event. A leading member of one of the prominent singing families from a nearby area got drunk that first night and put in jail, Bud said – and added, "They had to get him out so he could key the music the next day!"

Only a handful of the courthouse singings were left by the 1970s, and one by one they fell away. Along with Cullman County, Marion County, by the Mississippi border in the northwestern section of the state, had the only other of Alabama's courthouse singings to glimpse the new century. In 2000, citing a lack of community support, the Marion County Convention officers brought to an end this event that had been held in the county seat of Hamilton for 86 years.

As with almost all the other county conventions, the Marion County singing was held in the courtroom itself, that upper hall where on weekdays justice was dispensed, where both the aggrieved and the advantaged sat awaiting a pronouncement meant to restore a proper equilibrium. I could think of that one year while watching Hollis Godsey, leading without a book and dispensing the chorus entrances, throw a soft, underhanded pitch to the altos, that voice part famously both aggrieved and advantaged. The Hamilton courtroom offered what were surely among the singing world's most comfortable environs. The wide, handsome wooden chairs we sat in bore arms. And the room itself was splendidly resonant. On a song like DULL CARE – with the class observing each prominent rest – the last sounded chord would go ringing down the oblong chamber.

Attending that convention in the 1980s and '90s, I found numerous parallels with Cullman's slightly older singing. Carlos Williams, a non-singer, once shared with me his recollections of showing up for the Hamilton singing in the 1930s. He remembered paying ten cents for a truck ride to town. With any money left over, he would "buy a Co-Cola." "They had a cement wall around the courthouse square," he told me, "and people would sit on it to hear the music. You couldn't walk through the yard there'd be so many there." Local businessmen would sell lemonade all day out of No. 2 washtubs. That and an artesian well at one corner of the square helped to keep the crowd hydrated.

Chairman Estes Jackson and Vice-Chair Elmer Conwill also told of going to the convention in the '30s. Originally held the fourth weekend in June and later changed to the same weekend in July, the Hamilton singing was, Estes said, "the biggest day in the county." People would sit in the windows, stand along the walls. There was a balcony where singers at recess could go to cool off. Speakers were hung out the windows to carry the sound to the crowd below. Carlos Williams was pleased that in more recent times he could easily find a seat, listen in air-conditioned comfort. He wondered, though, where all the crowds had gone. . . .

Elder Gerald Hand, a Primitive Baptist minister originally from northeastern Alabama who lived most of his 94 years in New Mexico, was left to ponder a rather opposite question when in 1919, at the age of five, he attended his first convention singing. (His daughter Carol Selleck remembers hearing that the site of this event was the courthouse in Heflin in Cleburne County, though it's possible it was across the state in Russellville, the seat of Franklin County, instead.) Hand's mother, Exer Sheppard (aunt of Jeff Sheppard), came from a family of Sacred Harp singers in Cleburne County, and, small-world-happening, in the mid-'20s the Sheppards lived on a farm neighboring that of good friend Tom Denson. Riding in a horse-drawn wagon on the way to the big singing, young Gerald had learned from his mother the song CUBA ("Go, preachers, and tell it to the world. . . ," words he would put into practice in a few years). When, late in his life, Carol asked her father about his recollections of the event, he reflected that "the courthouse was overflowing, that it was surrounded by horses tied to hitching posts and that buggies and wagons covered the court-house grounds." When she asked for his most vivid memory of the day, his reply was from the remembered perspective of a wide-eyed country boy: "Where did all those horses come from? . . ."

Singer, "country lawyer" and bon vivant John Merritt, a friend and contemporary, once told me about attending the courthouse singing in LaFayette, seat of Chambers County, in 1947. Like Elder Hand, John was only five at his first courthouse appearance, but old enough to be aware that day that "Big Jim" Folsom was in the room. Folsom, the famously populist governor of the state, was, John told me, a big fan of Sacred Harp, having grown up around it in Coffee County, a couple of hours' drive south. For John, the memory of that day was secured by what had happened after he led a song – his first time ever in front of a class, and, of course, in front of a governor. Following the lad's successful rendering of THE GOLDEN HARP, Granddaddy Merritt had reached into a front pocket, pulled out a deep wallet, the kind that snapped to open and close, and presented John with a dollar bill.

Although Big Jim Folsom actually lived most of his adult life in Cullman, I never knew of any connection between him and the courthouse singing there. Connections between humbler folks and the convention, though, were always popping up. Once hearing someone in my family mention Sacred Harp, a woman who occasionally worked for us when I was a young man spoke up and said that her mother, who had lived some miles out in the country, used to walk all the way in to town to the courthouse every year on that second Saturday in July. Agnes' mother must have joined hundreds of others who made a similarly long trek over the years. For many in that generation, the courthouse singing was an event one just didn't miss.

Thinking of such a long, hot walk to town to hear fasola singing reminds me of another country resident from my years in Carrollton, Ga., back in the '70s: a short, stocky farmer I had met at a local-area singing. This fairly elderly fellow, who didn't own a vehicle, had told me he regularly walked in to town from miles out whenever there was a singing there. Not a singer himself, he said Sacred Harp was as close as he could imagine to "what it must sound like in Heaven!" For a couple of years, I sometimes stopped by his place in the country and picked him up to ride with me to singings further out. I noticed on those occasions a slightly ripe smell about him, as if he had disdained one or several mornings' or evenings' baths. He always, though, wore clean and starched work clothes. One bit of his conversation was attention-getting, a mentioned remedy I took note of but never put to use. Whenever he experienced stomach trouble, he told me, he would first swallow the contents of a whole bottle of cod liver oil and then follow that up a while later with a second bottle. "I call it washin' and rinsin',"he would say with a proud smile, his pronunciation nearing what I imagined the experience must have felt like: "washin' and wrenchin'." Compared to me and my city-dwelling bunch, he and others of his countryside generation were just built of sturdier stock. Along with his fearless self-medicating, his walking in to town from miles out in the country just to listen to others sing Sacred Harp was evidence of that.

The connection between the Carrollton and Cullman areas in that era was a well-traveled one. As land or opportunity played out, many families from west-central Georgia over the decades had moved to Cullman County and settled in. There was a good bit of traffic, and some relocation, back and forth between the two similar areas. So when the McGraw brothers, Bud and Tom, and their son/nephew Buford and cousin Hugh drove over to the Cullman courthouse, they could reunite with individuals or families who had originally sung with them in Carrollton, Bremen and surrounding communities.

I would of course have loved to hear what the McGraws and other across-state visitors in those years heard in Cullman from surely one of the largest, most capable classes of singers in the territory. For now, I'm left with the recollections of my own time, and largely those from the new rather than the old courthouse. My porous memories are patched up a bit by notes I took at two convention sessions in the 1990s, reproduced below.

July 12-13, 1997

Since I first started attending this convention in the mid '60s, I may have missed a session or two, but no more than that, and may have as many as 34 sessions built up in a blurred amalgam of memory.

The crowds have dwindled now. But this year's session was again in the courtroom itself (the first time, if I have it right, since 1965) – a large space and one not unfriendly to Sacred Harp sound.

At the end of the day on Saturday, Billy Williams, the arranging committeeperson, reported that he had led 42 leaders – less than half of what he had called in some years (he referred to 87 as being the most in his tenure). But it was a comfortable day, a good day overall. Sunday was better, I thought, and Henry Guthery, the chair for the past few years, agreed.

On Saturday, I ended up during the noon hour speaking with an older gentleman who had not been at this singing for many years, he said, and who had now come in late, asking when we were to start up again. He thought he had attended the convention first in 1931. He'd left the area in 1939 to join the service and had not returned until 1972. Expecting the answer, I asked him about the crowds in those earlier years: "I'll bet they pretty well filled the balcony. . . ." "Filled that and about everything else," he replied.

"My best friend killed himself one year when I was here at the singing," he said, speaking of the years before he left. "Shot himself. I found out about it when I got home." When I suggested he stay and have lunch with us, he said, "I've already eat." And so he left. But I noticed later that he had returned and was sitting in one of the long pews.

When Arrie Chandler, son of noted singer Walter Chandler, stepped into the middle of the square, he said, "Today's my birthday. I'm 79. Now I'll be looking 80 in the face!" He was immediately then greeted with the birthday song. Before he led the group in the song of his own choice, though, he added, "On this day in 1918 my mother was home giving birth to me, but my daddy was at the Cullman courthouse for the singing."

When called to lead both days, Reedie Denson Powell Evans, a slight woman of advanced years and dignified bearing, with hair twisted and netted on top of her head, rose, steadied herself with the railing in front of her (the wooden railing that on weekdays separates court observers from the main parties) and then edged her way slightly sideways to the center of the square – apparently to accommodate a tricky hip. On Sunday she led WESTFORD and then BEAR CREEK.

She is a granddaughter of Seaborn Denson. Her father was Evan ("E-vin"), who died young. "They said he had the best voice of all of them," she once told me, and said he sang bass. (I remember thinking: Better than Whitt? A better bass than Whitt Denson, who specialized in alto on the high pitch, but who, on recordings I'd heard, could reach down for a low bass note with richness and power?)

After lunch, Willodean Barton, a longtime singing buddy closer to my parents' generation, was called to lead. She asked for 418, REESE, the song that Edmund Dumas wrote in honor of J.P. Reese around 1859. "My momma woke me up at night one time singing this song," she said to the group. "I laid awake listening to it all the way through." She grinned, and then we hoisted up the song.

> I long to see my friends again,
> and hear them sweetly say,
> Come, weary dove, Here is thy home,
> Then fold thy wings and stay.

Sweet stuff, and, to my ears, well sung. As we were doing the *fa-sol-la's*, I looked out into the back of the class, where an elderly couple I didn't remember seeing before had come in and sat down. The woman was a robust figure with plain, short-cropped white hair and no discernible make-up. A band-aid crossed her nose, and later I noticed that she dabbed her eyes with a handkerchief from time to time. She didn't appear to have a book, and was looking straight into the square – and singing the notes.

This is one of the things I love about attending these sessions: knowing that many hundreds of singers have come through the halls of three successive courthouses here; seeing, as I have, the many different faces over the years; and yet still being surprised by new ones, older faces but new to me, each one a story if we just had access to it and time. . . .

On another song or so I looked back out at the couple and the woman would again be singing – not all the time, but now and again. The man just sat and watched the square, occasionally keeping time with a hand that he rested over the end of the pew. At one point the woman put her head on his shoulder for just a moment and softly laughed.

I happened to look out as Harrison Creel led, by request, THE SPIRIT SHALL RETURN, a song that Elmer Kitchens, from nearby Jasper, had written in 1959, a full century after Edmund Dumas' song was written, and one called frequently in this area in the subsequent decades. The woman in the back sat passively, not a flicker of recognition on her face. O.K., I thought, I know what it is: to her, this must be one of the "new songs"!

Harrison was about to sit down when Henry Guthery said, "You'd might as well sing THE OLD-FASHIONED BIBLE." Only a mild protest from the leader ensued, and we were shortly in the swing of it at a rapid pace. I looked back out at the woman, and she was fasola-ing. A song (by L.P. Breedlove, 1850) that her momma and daddy likely sang. At the clip we were going – though I couldn't see beneath the pews in the back – I could imagine her feet doing a little jig.

When someone led WELLS ("And while the lamp holds out to burn, / The vilest sinner may return."), I would have otherwise thought that she and another woman now sitting close by her on the other side were conspiring to laugh as they leaned their heads toward one another. But the other woman's face was red, and tears were streaming down her cheeks. The white-haired woman now dabbed at her eyes more vigorously.

At the end, when Henry stood to close the session, someone spoke up from the back to ask how long this convention had been running. Henry answered that he had researched that a few years back, and thought it was now around 99 years. A short gentleman toward the back, a Mr. Parker, who looked as if he might have more years on him than anybody else in the place, spoke up. "Ruth Edwards, Tom Denson's girl, told me her daddy organized this singing in 1900. . . She said he organized it in 1900!" A satisfying answer, bringing, as it did, a certain roundness to the issue. For the crowd (and for me, for the moment), that settled the matter. [Other sources would later put that date in doubt.[27]]

When we dispersed, I met up with the couple in the back on my way out. Cleghorns they said they were. The man reached out a big hand to me. "Sure did enjoy watching you sing." I asked if they were from the area. "We're from Nesmith, over in Winston County," the woman said.

A few minutes later, as I went out to the car to fetch a minutes book, I saw her again and asked when she had first come to this court-house singing. The answer was indeterminate. But then she said, "I was a Denson, and when they started saying something about the Densons, I . . . ." At that point I lost the rest. "You were a *Denson*? What part of the family?"

"Seaborn was my grandfather. Tom was my great-uncle." "Who was your father or mother?" I asked. "Evan." Reedie's sister, it dawned on me. "My daddy was 38 when he died. He left my mother with nine children at home, from three months up."

Those startling statistics – nine children at home, from three months up – have stayed with me, as I've tried to imagine the early life of Iva Denson Cleghorn, Reedie Denson Powell Evans, their siblings and their mother. The suffocating grief, the rallying warmth and goodness of neighbors and extended family, and then just the hardness of a life stretching out years in front. But Iva and Reedie survived it all, and sang again on this summer day. And I have added another set of memories to that blurred stack that warms and stirs when the second weekend in July rolls around.

July 11, 1999

The singing was again this year in the courtroom on the third floor, and Mark Davis, from Mississippi, and I heard the familiar strains as we climbed the stairs together just before ten o'clock. Familiar especially for me (rarely one to get there before the singing starts): the same sound in the same stairwell for the better part of 35 years.

The convention this time had several notable out-of-region visitors, but my focus was on a few longtime Alabama singers. E.E. Kilgo, who sang new-book music with my grandfather decades ago, I had seen most recently at the singing at Little Vine, the day after the National Convention. He's 87, a short man with personality that draws you to him and as good a spirit as you can find. A look at his stiff, gnarled hands tells you that arthritis has him firmly in its grasp. When you see him toddle, penguin-like, as he gets about, you know that his body must be bristling with pain. "This arthritis makes me miserable," he had told me at Little Vine, "but it don't keep me from being happy!"

He seemed happy again today, pronouncing "Sweet harmony!" and "Good lesson!" now and again, as leaders stepped from the square.

Pauline Creel Childers was called to lead. "Don't let me step on that stick," she said, in a joking reference to the cane poking out from under Mr. Kilgo's chair. The cane was twisted at the top end and, when his dark fingers folded over it, it looked as if a serpent extended out from his arm. "Hit him over the head with it!" a buddy offered. "No, don't do that," he said, "it's crooked enough already!"

Mr. Kilgo had with him for the occasion a spry old acquaintance, Otis Gulledge, from Robertsdale, at the lower end of the state. When Mr. Gulledge's name was called, he stood up and stated that he had been a seven-shaper most of his life, but that he had wanted to hear again the fasola singing he'd heard in the old Cullman courthouse back in 1932, when he lived in a nearby community. "I've longed for years to hear singing like this again," he said. "I drove 300 miles to get to hear it again." He then led rousing renditions of HOLY MANNA and PROSPECT.

"He's stayin' with me tonight," Mr. Kilgo said, when his friend finished the lesson. "He did so well I'm gonna take him home and feed him some cornbread and buttermilk!"

Marie Creel Aldridge led a fine rendition of BALLSTOWN just before noon. At the break I asked when she had first attended the courthouse convention. "I was two and a half or three," she said, "and that was 80 years ago. I'll tell you the reason I remember it if you won't tell anybody." I promised, but then once I heard the story, immediately asked – and was granted – permission to tell.

"I remember it so well," she said, "because there at the old courthouse was the first time I'd ever seen a flushing toilet. Momma tried to put me on it, and I was scared to death of it!"

A great little story, I thought, but it proved an omen for the afternoon. We hadn't been singing long after lunch when Billy Williams came in to announce that a commode in the women's restroom had overflowed badly and would we please now use the restrooms on the first and second floors instead. So much for modern conveniences at old-time singings.

A latecomer among Alabama cities, Cullman was founded in 1873 by Bavarian-born Colonel John G. Cullmann, who then welcomed waves of fellow German immigrants. In 1877 Cullman became the seat of a new county, as portions of three counties surrounding the city were pieced together to make a new whole. The following year a local businessman of German descent donated a site on the corner of 4th Street and 2nd Avenue West for the building of a courthouse.

The resulting structure, said to be one of the finest in North Alabama, was completed in 1879. Over the following century and some decades, fire and strong winds would put the test to that building and its two successors.

In 1894 a fire that swept the entire block badly damaged the original building. In 1912 another fire gutted the main stairwell and probate judge's office, with most of the structure sustaining water damage. Later that year the cornerstone was laid for a new courthouse, the building in which I would hear my first sampling of Sacred Harp singing. The current courthouse was built in 1964 and dedicated the following year. The minutes from the 1965 convention session refer to a county official giving the assembled group a "hearty welcome to use the new courthouse for their singing."

COURT HOUSE, CULLMAN, ALA.

Original Cullman County courthouse, destroyed in 1912. (Photo courtesy of Cullman County Museum)

Cullman's "old courthouse," 1913-1964.

In a dispiriting come-down for the event, a loss of political support over a three-year period in the mid-'70s resulted in the convention being bounced to East Elementary School. There in the school's auditorium, the singers' space looked awkward and offered woeful acoustics. In 1977 things were righted, and the convention came home again. For now, the county's commitment to one of its oldest traditions still holds.

In April of 2011, a furious tornado tore off part of the courthouse roof and caused significant damage to much of the rest of the building, which then required major renovation. In the old days – I can muse – the singing itself provided fiery stuff and threatened to raise the roof!

I always enjoyed the sessions I attended, the earliest ones especially. But I confess to feeling a greater draw, an altogether unfair attraction in fact, to thoughts of the singings *before* my time: those colorful early convention years and the tapestry of life surrounding a ritual so central to the community's interest. It sets my imagination a-runnin'. I could fantasize about having the lemonade or Co-Cola concession the day of, or the hat and bonnet business beginning a few weeks out from, the big event. But even more – for just one time! – to enter the forbidding past and mill about in that teeming host, hear the bursts of music from out the high windows, push my way inside the hallways and into the courtroom itself, with all those old men crowding the bass, standing against the walls – most of them surely thankful on a hot July day for the big ceiling fans that labored above them, further sweetening the harmonies they made. Ah yes, to be there just once. . . .

21

Amanda

Amanda Denson Brady (1941-2008)

I've certainly felt I understood, at least in broad contours, the figures portrayed in this book. But there are few I felt I had better insight into than Amanda – my generous, exasperating, indomitable friend, who left us all too soon.

Early connections before we ever met set the framework for that understanding. Amanda's Aunt Ruthy had taught my father and many years later had guided my entrée into the world of Sacred Harp. In her youth, Amanda had spent many weeks in my hometown visiting Miss Ruth. We both had attended Auburn University, though just missing one another (she was two and a half years older). So if our paths had not crossed in the early years, they had come close. "We've chewed the same bark," she would say. And then over the years, especially after she moved to Birmingham, we spent much time in one another's company and confidence, traveling many hundreds of miles together, "roaming on up to," as she would put it, this or that distant singing location.

Amanda had as distinctive a personality as anyone I've known. Included in the mix of traits was an instinctive intelligence for social interactions, for personal communications. It was as if she wielded special antennae for such, though in her overextending enthusiasm or passion for helping, she sometimes failed to sense a perhaps natural reluctance on the part of the person now bathed in her kindly sight. Anyone trying to follow her through the precipitous moves, the twists and turns, the sweeping entrances and moist exits, the propelling force of her inveterately optimistic life surely had to find it a dizzying ride – a little, I imagine, like trying to keep pace with Auntie Mame.

Amanda at the Chattahoochee Convention, Wilson's Chapel, August 2002. (Photo by Martha Beverly)

I first knew of Amanda from Miss Ruth's references to her favorite niece. Amanda was abroad, married at the time and with two or three and then four children, and not often in evidence at local singings in our area, only swooping back down occasionally for one of the signal Sacred Harp events. It was at Holly Springs Church in Georgia that I first saw her, but I had heard of her often from Miss Ruth. In time, I would find that all I had heard about Amanda and her attachment to Sacred Harp was true - and then some.

Sacred Harp, she would often say, was the great love of her life. Aunt Ruthy was the formative influence in that life. When she was eight, Amanda had lost her father, Howard Denson, to throat cancer. A few months before his death in 1950, Howard had written to Ruth, "I have always come to you for advice and guidance and you have more influence on my life than any other person in the world." Those same words could have been written by Amanda. In Ruth, both brother and brother's daughter found their life model and most solid support.

Amanda's mother, Howard's second wife, had no interest in nor sympathy for Sacred Harp, a fact that surely contributed to the distance between them. "I learned early in life that Sacred Harp is a privilege," Amanda would say to me, recalling a recurring pattern from her childhood and teenage years: trying to cajole her mother, to slip around to get ready and then leave unobtrusively when singer and friend of the family Toney Smith or others would come by to pick her up in her hometown of Tuscaloosa and take her to singings. She especially treasured the few weeks each summer when she got to stay with Aunt Ruthy and go to singings with her, Uncle Paine and sometimes Aunt Annie. On the way, she would sit in the back seat as Paine drove, and he and Ruth or Annie would tutor her, have her practice her songs to lead, always without a book.

Traveling to and being at singings was, to Amanda, sweet air to breathe - the essence and best of life itself. She never lost the sense of that. No matter how much we had sung, no matter how tired the voice, she was always ready for more. Sacred Harp Publishing Company board meetings, which the two of us attended together for a number of years, always opened and closed with a song and prayer. Amanda and I, like other board members, would often at the end of the session find ourselves weary from the early-morning travel (to Carrollton, Ga., from, in our case, the Birmingham area) and the sometimes frustrating gives and takes of the meeting. But one parting song was never enough for her. She always called for another . . . maybe another still.

As her son Howard said, the picture was much the same at home: "She'd be listening to her recordings. You'd walk in and she'd be 'leading' [bringing in the parts as she sat], snapping her fingers with the music. She would do that all night long."

Amanda and Aunt Ruthy at a convention in Georgia, in a clipping from probably the summer of 1944. (From the collection of the grandchildren of T.J. and Lola Akers Denson, used with permission)

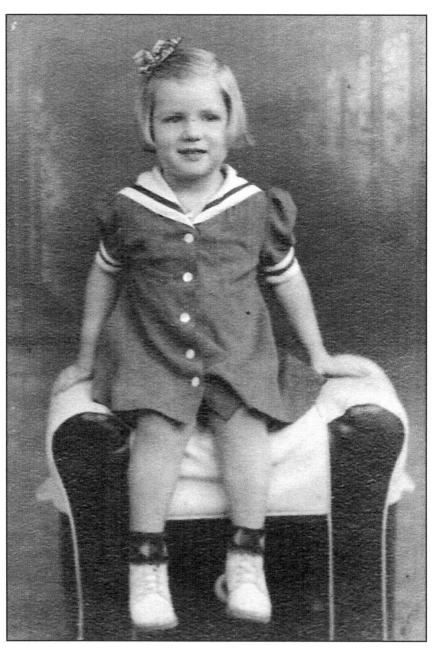

Always on the edge of her seat: Amanda, about 1945. (From the collection of the grand-children of T.J. and Lola Akers Denson, used with permission)

Amanda with parents Marjorie and Howard Denson and younger sister Willie Carolyn, about 1949. (From the collection of the grandchildren of T.J. and Lola Akers Denson, used with permission)

A Sacred Harp Heart

I don't know that I knew anyone who loved the *music* of Sacred Harp (and especially the minor tunes!) more deeply than Amanda. But that was only part of it. The extraordinary gifts the Denson family had given to Sacred Harp and the shepherding way her father's siblings had transferred their knowledge of the tradition to her meant that it was for her a deeply personal thing, a sacred trust. ("Our family has an anointing for this music," as she once put it in an e-mail note; and indeed her great-great-uncle, James Denson, was represented by the composition CHRISTMAS ANTHEM in the songbook's very first edition.) But it was still more than that. Sacred Harp was the frame of reference for her life; it represented a way, the best way, of facing the world – and God. And when she spoke from time to time of someone having "a Sacred Harp heart," she used a phrase that may have best captured how she herself thought and felt.

If all were children of God, Sacred Harp singers were to her somehow a purer strain, a more consistently principled people. A conversation with Amanda that Dave Richardson from the U.K. once related to me seemed perfectly in character. On learning that some woman in the Sacred Harp community had separated from her husband, about whom Amanda apparently knew little, Amanda had remarked, "Well, it must be *him* – she's a singer. . . ."

Amanda had not lived an easy life. She was married three times over a considerable span, with the first two marriages ending in divorce and the third, after a few years, in her husband's death. The latter brought to a close a partnership that seemed – in retrospect and once again – too hastily entered into, and that close friends and family would have been hard pressed to describe as truly happy. (Amanda would often later quote with amusement the gentle plea from Howard, her youngest, after she became a widow: "Mom, let's not get us another husband. . . .") A single mom for much of her children's youth, she had sent all four through college and started them on successful individual paths.

As the wife of a naval officer in her first marriage, Amanda had experienced, and relished, life abroad. As well as residing in several U.S. states, the family had lived in Barbados, Iceland (twice) and Wales. Even before the dissolution of that first marriage, Amanda and the children had formed an exceptionally tight bond. For the youngsters, moving so often meant a familiarly chilling pattern: exchanging friends for strangers. As they were settling in to one of their destinations, Amanda had said to them, "I don't care if you don't have a friend for six months, we have each other!" It was a lesson they learned well. As daughter Mandy said, "If you tied up with one of the Bradys, you bought into the pack of us!"

Particularly in her life abroad, Amanda honed what were surely natural skills as a hostess. She carried always a perspective of more sophisticated society: Junior League, bridge-playing, evenings on the veranda with servants circling with drinks and hors d'oeuvres. But she also retained a closeness with the common touches of rural Alabama and Georgia, with the humblest country churches and the variably proud and humble people who filtered through them, the ones who brought forth the incomparable music.

Her way of seeing, of making her way through the world, was characterized by this teetering balance between big-city and country living. At some point in her youth a disparaging remark about country life or folk had brought a heartfelt retort from her dearest relation: "Amanda, don't forget where your roots are!" It was, she knew, Aunt Ruthy "teaching school," and that lesson, altering her early perspective, remained with her.

At a few points in her life Amanda had lots of money and at great stretches almost none. "Money makes me tired," she would say – or frequently, "Easy come, easy go." In money was no security; security was found only in her great faith and in the binding power of family love.

For several summers when the children were young and the family was still living abroad, Amanda would gather up her brood to take them back to visit the home folks and go to singings.

"We would fly back in from foreign countries," middle son Tim remembered, "and there would always be a car on loan for us from various family members. We would have it for a month or two, and we would literally drive the South, but especially Georgia and Alabama. We were just up and down the road.

"When we'd stop to visit, you know how kids are always asking, 'How long are we gonna be here? When can we leave?' We knew we'd better not even ask. Because we were leaving when she *decided* to leave. She loved visiting with all those people - every one, every time. We left no one out. And for us boys, she tried to put us around those older men - Hugh McGraw, Toney Smith, D.T. White. She wanted her boys to be interacting with them, to see them as role models. She wanted us shaking their hands and looking them in the eye."

One summer in particular was marked in memory for eldest son Jim. "We came down for two and a half months, traveling the South," he said. "We'd stay with family, and between singings when there wasn't family nearby, we'd pull into a roadside motel for a week." A visit with Uncle Bob Denson stood out. Amanda had taken her flock inside for the start of the visit and then, past a point, had sent them outside to play. "We stayed out there for maybe three hours or so," Jim said. "It was hot. We just kept playing, trying to throw rocks at the signposts. . . ." As Tim had said, they knew they'd "better not even ask."

Aunt Ruthy was often along for the ride during their visits in Alabama. On one occasion she and Amanda were in the front seat of the station wagon, with the kids in back. Howard, only five at the time, was in the very back section, where people usually put their dog, if they were driving with one. Hearing that fact remarked on, he, "being a wise guy," began to bark - and kept it up. It didn't take long for the racket to ride on Miss Ruth's nerves. "Amanda," she said, showing that combination of firmness and finesse she was known for, "we're going to have to put that *dog out!*" As the adult Howard said, "And that was that." The little episode was one of Amanda's choice memories over the years, and, as example of the sometimes towering presence of great-aunt Ruthy, it stayed with Howard as well.

Mandy had another memory of Aunt Ruthy from those summer trips. The family would be staying in a motel between singing locations and usually would have Miss Ruth in tow. If Amanda had arranged for a hair appointment and was gone for the morning or afternoon, Miss Ruth would focus on Mandy's apprenticeship. "I would be at the foot of the bed, facing Aunt Ruthy, like facing the tenor," Mandy said, "and she was there with a fly swatter to keep time. Invariably she would have me go over my lesson for the next day, leading without a book. . . . I don't know how the boys got away without having to do that! She set a very high standard for the Denson women."

Preserving family heritage, for Amanda, carried over to the formulas for those things in life most piquant and perishable – the special dishes her aunts and older cousins were renowned for: Cousin Belle's egg custard, Aunt Annie's cobblers, and so forth. On one of the summer trips south, Amanda had determined to take the measure, literally, of these homemade recipes based on "a pinch" of this, "a little handful" of that . . . . Visiting each of the notable family cooks in turn, she had them make their signature dishes and precisely measured out their fistfuls and spoonfuls and dashes of this and that. She intended to have these recipes published eventually, to make a cookbook for her grandchildren. "A recipe not shared will soon be forgotten; but when it is shared it will be enjoyed by future generations," she wrote in a 2005 e-mail note. But that task, like others, was left unfinished. (The two recipes mentioned above, along with "Aunt Ruthy's sour cream pound cake," did find a sharing place in Kathryn Eastburn's book *A Sacred Feast: Reflections on Sacred Harp Singing and Dinner on the Ground*.)

After some years of living in the Washington, D.C., area when her children were out of the nest, Amanda decided to settle in old family territory – Winston County, Ala. – and selected the town of Haleyville. Ultimately that proved too small a place, and she moved to Birmingham, where she got her real estate license and sold houses, or put people in them. As much as providing financial support, this career gave her an opportunity, as she often said, to help people. And when there was a conflict between the two impulses, it was usually the livelihood part that came up second. Each client was, from the start, a new best friend, someone to shower with kindness, canny advice, curb-appeal analysis. . . .

Family Pride

Spending even a few minutes in Amanda's presence would have led almost anyone to see that she was distinctly and proudly Southern. And central to that was her pride in the Denson-Burdette pedigree (her grandmother was Amanda Burdette Denson, author of the song KELLEY). "They had class," Amanda would often say about the previous generation of her family – Howard, Paine, Ruth and sisters – and their good singing friends.

Amanda and I were riding together once after I had received two CDs of reissued 78 rpm Sacred Harp recordings from the 1920s on, one by the small Birmingham-area ensemble called the Allisons and another, I thought, by the Denson Quartet – though that second collection actually included several other groups as well. Being particularly busy at that stretch, I had not taken the trouble before our ride to inspect either the recordings or their liner notes. I had the CDs with me, though, and plunked one into the player as we rode.

We were both eager to hear the Denson Quartet, about which we had heard so much over the years, but by mistake I had started the Allisons instead. What we then heard was a quartet-like sound, distinctive but certainly not impeccable – and piano, and an un-artful one at that. Amanda, who played the instrument, was crestfallen: "I can't believe they're using a piano!" That her esteemed relatives had had the poor taste to use a piano with Sacred Harp classics, and clunky piano playing to boot, was just about more than she could take. (Now, it should be said that the great Whitt Denson, accompanying himself on the piano on a famous recording of his own overdubbed voice for all four parts, was always and in all quarters given a pass.)

We listened for more, and the unhappy perception settled in on her. "I just can't believe it!" she continued to say. As we reached our destination, but before I had caught the misidentification, she at last managed resolve. "Well, we just have to rise above it!" she said, and stepped out of the car, every bit a Denson and proud of it.

I may at times have associated one or more sayings with this friend or another, but nothing like with Amanda, where the number and variety would have overwhelmed anyone's tendency not to notice. Oft-repeated phrases served as sure steppingstones of thought. As Howard said, "Mom was a quote machine." Thus the season, if not the day, was textured with the little fragments that summed up feelings: "Tickled me"; "Touched my heart"; "Makes me cry." "God is good all the time!" one heard frequently. "Nothing happens to you that doesn't sift through God's fingers first." "You lie down with dogs, you're gonna get fleas." With the latest update on one or more of her grandchildren: "God forgive me, I am so proud!" But about some character perhaps not to be trusted: "I feed her with a long-handled spoon." "We're loyal dogs," she would encourage; "We're first-team players!" And from the children's youth, there was Mom snapping her fingers and threatening, "*Get happy!*" And in that same vein: "We're gonna have fun if it kills us!"

"That says" was one of the phrases one frequently heard from Amanda, as in "That says we weren't supposed to go," or, from an e-mail note she once sent, a mention of a look on someone's face "that says you better get it right (I know that look as I am sure you do too)!" Amanda expected, and generally found, a simple or at least straightforward explanation for things. The world, after all, spoke for itself – and so did people's actions. If I suggested that the situation might be a little more complicated than that, what I usually got in return was the pointed silence that says, "Well, I doubt it."

Picking Amanda up at her place for another singing jaunt would see her tripping out to the car, cradling or now retrieving loose paraphernalia, and greeting the driver with "Morning, Glory!" – to be followed, a few miles into the ride, by "Aren't you glad we're doing this?!" or my favorite, "*Don't you just love us?!*" when "us" meant the two of us or the three or four who formed the group of the moment. And yes, I did love us, couldn't help but.

The Toughest Challenge

In another e-mail note to me after she had moved to Birmingham, Amanda wrote, "God has been so good to all of us," and, in a nod to the old Irish saying, "The test of the heart is trouble and it always comes with the years; I'm just so thankful we haven't run up on something that's too hard to handle."

Cancer would prove the greatest challenge. Amanda had lost her father, her mother, her younger sister, Willie Carolyn, and her third husband – smokers all – to throat or lung cancer. A near-lifetime smoker herself, she in later years steadfastly disregarded stern or impassioned counsel on the subject from medical advisors, family and friends (and I did try my best. . .). When doctors lectured her on it, she used to tell me, she would "just turn and look out the window." It was an addiction she was unable or unwilling to shake – until it was too late. Eventually she had two surgeries for esophageal cancer and after that had most of one lung removed. When the throat cancer resulted in the removal of her voice box, she hardly missed a beat. "I have nobody to blame but myself," she said, and never complained. And didn't curtail her singing schedule at all, or forgo a seat in the alto section for that matter, the little cloth flap at her throat becoming just an ordinary part of the scenery at sessions throughout the territory. Going to singings and hearing the music, seeing the people remained a supreme pleasure.

Even when lung cancer overtook her, she remained stoic. The closest I heard to a hint for sympathy came once when we were on our way to a singing. Trying to withstand a surge of nausea, she scribbled a note: "I don't like to complain, but I'm so tired of this." Even in the midst of that long stretch of illness, she could write in an e-mail, "I'm feeling good, and I'm happy, and I'm doing what I want to do. Life can't get much better than that!" And in a note to Jim close to the end: "We've had fun, haven't we?"

Two days after her lung surgery, I visited her in the hospital and found her sitting up in the middle of the bed and as animated as at any time I think I had ever seen her. Pain medication can be stimulating, but this was beyond remarkable. The two of us were shortly joined by Rodney Ivey, who was passing through the area on his way back to north Alabama from attending a singing. Writing notes, Amanda insisted that we sing for her, and we did. At the end of each tune, she would quick-clap her hands in pleasure and request still another and another.

Well before her surgeries, when I once remarked to singer friend Jim Carnes about what a beautiful, fluid leader Amanda was, he put his finger on a perception that bettered mine. "It's not just that," he said, "It's that *that* is her element," the medium, in other words, in which she seemed to move most naturally.

Most of the time, Amanda led without a book, usually rendering one of the old fuging songs she had memorized from her youth. With a beaming smile and warm eye contact with the front-bench singers, she would flow across the square, both hands gracefully calling forth the part entrances. Following the singing of the notes, she would always, as she had been taught as a child, call for "Words . . ." – with an encouraging uplift on the second half-syllable. She rarely led any of the several dozen songs composed by one of the generations of her family; asking for one of these songs so important to her would have been, she thought, unseemly. If she suddenly had in mind to call up a tune she didn't know by heart or had never practiced leading, she was not the least self-conscious about abandoning her free-form leading style. Holding the book up high, close to her face, with reading glasses on, she would dig out the melody line and direct the class with her free hand.

That latter image is an inescapable symbol to me of one of Amanda's great strengths – and a corresponding weakness. The scrutiny she brought to bear on any issue that engaged her was so unblinking, the focus so intense, that everything else for the moment tended to scatter out to the peripheries. Drawing so near to the issue at hand – the newly emerged need or problem – meant an impressive magnification of whatever powers she had available, but often meant loss of perspective, of proportion, as well. To the act of problem-solving she brought creative thinking and a formidable will, as well as the ability to marshal support, or rescue, from an amazing network of friends and connections she had woven over the years. She never shrank from problems, but faced them straight up. As Howard said in his eulogy remarks, "Mom always had a plan."

Amanda always said that I was good driver – though her presence in the front seat, or sometimes leaning over from the back if others rode with us, certainly raised the level of difficulty for me. I drove the great majority of the time, and she would, after settling into the car and catching up on small-talk necessities, produce the newest set of photos of grandchildren or of latest family gathering and eagerly thumb through them for me – as I tried to take on a tight curve or stay off the shoulder in a rocky area. My protests about this – "Now Amanda, I've got to watch the road . . ." – were fairly ignored; it was like trying to hurl peanut shells against a strong wind. On she would go, drawing attention to this or that feature of the photo or asking for an opinion. Did I not think that these were the cutest? Did I not here see a resemblance? After she had lost her ability to speak, she would write vigorously on a notepad – a wicked left hook in action – and, after nudging my arm with her pen, would point to a sentence or two just completed. When I responded, she would then flip a page and continue the conversation. She rode, in other words, with blinders on, as seemingly oblivious to either hazard or lush landscape as she was to the prospects for failure with any of the projects (or partners) she undertook. Her focus remained singularly on the subject at hand, and her trust in me as driver, or in God as protector of our little vessel, seemed unquestioning. And on we drove, finally without accident, I must say.

'There Must Be a Way . . .'

In the free-ranging discussions we had while traveling, we sometimes disagreed, but those disagreements were usually respectful, and often humorous. And when we came to the same conclusion, as we frequently did, we could have agreed as well that our minds had probably taken different routes in getting us there. Our conversations in a number of those years often circled around a single issue: how to reverse the decades-long trend of declining numbers in our local and area singing communities. Why was this challenge so difficult? How could people in general remain immune to Sacred Harp's obvious charms? "There must be a way," she would say. "There must be something we can do. . . ."

After a few years of this, feeling we had long ago exhausted the subject (we inevitably came up dry on tactics), I finally settled on a bedrock conclusion: "If it were easy, then Aunt Ruth and Uncle Paine and Cousin Bob and the rest would have come up with the answer. If it were really simple, they would have figured it out." Such was her veneration for these forebears that the answer quieted her; and that interpretation became the standard for us. As we then from time to time neared the subject, she stopped pressing for a solution. If it had been beyond the ken of that revered generation, who could wonder that it would remain a challenge for us, too?

She never stopped trying, though. As we were leaving the Cullman courthouse singing one year, a man walking on the sidewalk beyond us shouted out across the parking lot: "Was there a singing held there today? What kind of singing was it?" He was a minister, he said, in the brief conversation we had across the good distance, and he seemed at least vaguely interested as we tossed back a few defining statements about fasola singing and the day's event.

I've certainly made my own attempts at proselytizing over the years – as weary friends and relatives could attest – but I didn't think this a very likely prospect. Amanda, though, went over to him across the way and made him a gift of her book, with encouragements for him to use it and often. We didn't see him or the book again. But Amanda wouldn't have been put off by that. It was all part of what she saw as her mission.

Hunter and Suzanne Hale could bear witness to the impact of

that missionary spirit. Sometime residents of the D.C. area but frequently working abroad at the time, they had observed a Sacred Harp demonstration at the Arlington County Fair. Of the two first-timers, Hunter was initially more intrigued. At the next D.C.-area monthly evening singing, he walked into the foyer of the host church to check out the experience from a participant's point of view. Amanda, with loaner book, was there to greet him – as she was with so many others at many other singings and conventions over many years. Taking the book, he mentioned that it would have to be a brief visit: his wife had a headache and had stayed in the car outside. That was all Amanda needed to hear – well, that and the location and model of the vehicle. A Coke and two aspirin in hand, and she was out the door and into the evening air. A tap on the car window led to a warm introduction and encouragement, and in no time she returned with Suzanne. "I hadn't really felt like going," Suzanne would later say, "and I wasn't in good spirits." But Amanda prevailed. Suzanne walked back outside maybe a couple of times, she said, and each time she came back in, "the music sounded better and better."

The inoculation worked, and Hunter and Suzanne in time became dedicated singers. The interaction on that evening turned out to be no trifling event. Suzanne was then in the Foreign Agricultural Service, and Hunter had a law practice in Japan. The two of them were soon introducing – in some cases, reintroducing – shape-note singing to thousands of residents of Japan, of the mountains of China and of the Micronesian islands: principally Pohnpei and Kosrae. Protestant missionaries, in some of those locations, had long before carried over, along with solfege, a few standard hymns included in the Sacred Harp canon. Having a *Sacred Harp* songbook meant an exciting addition – "New tunes!" – for some of the people the Hales came to know and sing with.

For the Hales, Amanda and her determined, generous way, the "gentle grace of [her] spirit" had been pivotal. "For that evening and every time we went," Hunter would say, "she was the person who graciously welcomed us, who had an interest in what was going on in our family. She was just the soul of the singing, welcoming everyone who came. She represented the soul of Alabama hospitality." By several reports, Amanda's years in the D.C. area attained near-legendary status, with a good many other singers along the middle-to-upper eastern seaboard finding in her a mentor and guiding spirit.

At home at last in Alabama, she was ever energized to help. One year an out-of-state friend had been staying with me during the National Convention, which ended on a Saturday. The following day, with Amanda joining us, we attended the much smaller singing at Little Vine, out from Birmingham. We drove up to the country church with Amanda in the front seat and our friend in the back. The two were engaged in light conversation when the friend touched on what she surely intended as only a brief reference to a concerning family matter. As I was getting out to retrieve our songbooks from the trunk, Amanda responded with a Bible verse she thought might apply. At that point the conversation plunged deeper, and I left the two of them in the car and went inside. They remained in the car the rest of the hot morning, talking across the seatback. Tears were shed – cathartically, I'm sure, in the case of the friend. At noon, as lunch was being spread on the tables, the two emerged and joined the company of singers. We had gone to the place to sing, but once Amanda heard what sounded like a cry for help, or inadvertent hint of need, all else was put aside. Only when they had thoroughly sounded out the issue did she free herself again to resume the day's agenda.

Giving help was the essential thing; receiving credit for it was unimportant to her. In one case I remember, the two of us had a mutual friend in another state, someone I was closer to than she, someone who was known to be struggling financially. Upon a mention of that situation, Amanda handed me $50 – "I'd give you more if I had it," she said – and asked me to send it on. "But don't tell her who gave it to you." I did as I was instructed and only told the friend years later, well past Amanda's departure from us.

When she was in the midst of her lung-cancer treatment, I had to be amused at this e-mail from Amanda about a visit to one of her doctors: "I thought when I went to her that she was supposed to help me. I know now I'm supposed to help her. She has a [family issue, tossed off in a phrase], and I spent most of my visit giving advice on that topic. I picked her up a chicken salad sandwich and limeade at that good shop in Mountain Brook [Birmingham's classiest retail area] since she was good to work me in on her lunch hours. Soooo we get along, and I'm doing my part." Indeed. Who else but Amanda would take a sandwich and drink (along with advice) in to her doctor's appointment – for the doctor?

Mandy tells a story from her childhood that speaks to the softness of her mom's heart:

> One time when we were driving through the country on our way to a singing, we were going down this little road and a bird flew out in front of us. It had mistimed its flight. We hit it, and it died. She stopped the car, and we all got out. She was crying. We dug through our baggage and found a shoe box with tissue in it. We wrapped the bird in the tissue and buried it in that box before we continued on to the singing. It just broke her heart. That she as a grown-up, after driving for all those years, that she would cry about that little bird . . . . We were maybe all crying, but that she was crying! . . . She just was incredibly tender-hearted. She had a real soft spot for the underdog and the wounded.

An Iron Will

Surely Amanda's children knew her best of all, and the summing-up descriptions they give are all of a piece.

Jim, first: "She had two big loves – Sacred Harp and her children. It was hit-and-miss with her partner choices, but she loved those two things the most. I think Sacred Harp took her back to a time when life was simpler – and then she loved the heritage part of it, the family history. Mother really loved people, but Sacred Harp was the thing in her life that she had the most uncomplicated love for. There were unquestionably complexities in her life – some of which she contributed to – but I think the love she had for Sacred Harp was possibly the most pure thing she had."

"Mother was a complicated cookie!" That was Mandy's half-joking summation. But then, more seriously: "the fullness of humanity in one person." She was, Mandy said, "gracious and tenacious in equal measure. She never met a stranger; everyone was just a friend she hadn't yet gotten to know. And if she was focused on her family or on Sacred Harp, there was no changing tack with the wind."

"Her iron will" was what Howard saw as the essential trait: "If it was *dead wrong*, she was still going to see it through. Even as a child, I knew. . . . Her level of pride in you, in the Denson name . . . . She was so proud. She lived her life around the family and the kids. God was number one – there was no doubt about that – then it was 2-A and 2-B" [Sacred Harp, of course, being one of those].

Tim could join the others on the same pitch: "She would fight tooth and nail for what she believed in. She was loving but at the same time tenacious. And it came out in a lot of different ways. She was full-throttle, no matter what she did. That was just her way. She was tenacious in her love for people, for Sacred Harp, for what she wanted done or what she didn't want done. She was tough – and wouldn't quit until it was done the way she wanted it done. There was no turning back."

The point could be extended further still: "It affected all her children," Tim said. "My friends will say to me, 'How do you always cut to the chase? How are you so tough-minded?' And I know exactly where it comes from; it comes from her. It's just a trait we all got from her. That's really who she was."

A story that Amanda often referred to, and that Howard later recounted to me in detail, well depicts the core traits her children speak of. It was 1988, and Amanda had relocated the family to Georgia. Howard, still at home at that point, then flunked the ninth grade – twice. In that oft-used phrase, it was a matter of not applying himself. . . . "I didn't have any interest in it," he would tell me later. "I was chasing girls and stuff. . . ."

Desperate finally, Amanda laid everything else aside and took on the challenge full-time. "She was going to straighten me out," Howard said. "She didn't give me an option. She said, 'We're moving.'" Amanda knew of a private boys' school in the D.C. area, an institution where the required formal dress – blazer, tie and dress shoes every day – bespoke the school's seriousness about academic rigor and discipline.

"There was no real reason for them to accept me," Howard would say, "but she was determined to make it work. We drove the 12 hours there from Georgia. We went in, and she had my grades written on a paper sack. She wasn't going to take no for an answer. That was just the jewels in her crown. She told the headmaster, 'You're my only shot.' We cut a deal with him. They allowed me to go to summer school, and if I made it then, I would be accepted.

"So we did a test run. It was a one-hour drive either way [from Virginia, through the District, into Maryland]. She would take me there and wait in the car for the three or four hours I was in class and then drive me back. That's how bad she wanted it. She would do *a lot* for the family."

Howard could look back with gratification, as Amanda always did, on a remarkable turn-around. After his sophomore year, he received, from President George H.W. Bush, the award for Most Improved Student in Prince George's County. After his junior year, he was inducted into the National Honor Society. Amanda received no award but gained a touchstone she would keep always: "If we could turn that situation around, we can do just about anything. . . ."

Amanda and the Masters

Many Amanda stories drew my attention and wonder over the years, but one, for drama and panorama, tops the rest. Tim (Timothy McGuire, "Guire" to his family) told the story in the eulogy the

brothers gave for their mother, and, because it seemed so quintes-
sentially Amanda, I asked him to relay it again in more detail so I
could share it with others. The incident was from a weekend in April
1999, when Amanda was staying with Tim and his wife and their
two children at their home near Clemson, S.C. That Friday about
midnight, Tim received a call. It was the weekend of the Masters Golf
Tournament in Augusta, Ga., an event he had always dreamed of
attending. The unexpected call was from a benefactor who had arranged for him to have two of the highly prized tickets. They would
be waiting for him at his host's home in Augusta the next morning.

Amanda, concerned about the late call, had come to stand beside Tim as he finished the conversation. "Guire, who was that?"
Though the names of several good buddies must have raced through
his mind when he was thinking of whom to share this windfall with,
he knew, as he turned to face his mom, what he should do. He briefly
explained, and then: "Would you like to go with me? "Oh, I'd love
to," she replied.

Though Amanda may have played some golf in her youth, and
did at least play when the family lived in Barbados, she didn't keep
up with the who or the what of the professional game and likely gave
little more thought to its rules and rituals than the average golfer
might give to those of Sacred Harp. But the Masters was also a social
occasion – one of the grandest in sports – and knowing the privilege
it embodied, she was pleased to accept this kindest of invitations.

They left early the next morning for the more-than-two-hour drive
and arrived at the home of their hosts, a local doctor and his wife,
who often shared tickets with good friends. Before they headed to
the club, the doctor reached over on the counter to pick up something – and handed Tim two clubhouse passes. This, it might be said,
was the great prize: entrée to the sanctum itself, the clubhouse, even
the locker room – and the chance to mix with sport celebrities from
around the world. At that point, the doctor's conversation turned
momentarily stern: "Whatever you do, do not get these two passes
taken up. *Whatever you do . . . .*" It was understood that the surrender

of the passes, for any violation of club policy, would likely mean the permanent loss of clubhouse privilege.

The first part of the day, warming up, went well. They took in the scenery of what is often said to be one of the world's most beautiful places. Their host showed them the best views, the best sites from which to see great golf. They settled on the grandstand between the par-4 No. 3 green and the par-3 No. 4 tee box. After being seated for a short while, Amanda disappeared and was gone for maybe up to 15 minutes. (No one who knew her would doubt that this included a smoking break.) By that time, Davis Love, a PGA fixture, was coming off the No. 3 green and striding over to the No. 4 tee box.

The gist of the story now in Tim's words: "Right as Davis Love is approaching the ball, I see her coming to the stairs of the grandstand. She's on the bottom row, and we're 30, 35 rows up. . . . I see this frantic look on her face, a panicked look . . . and she's scanning the grandstand – and it's packed. Her eyes locked with mine. And I'm like, "Oh, this is not going to be good! Oh my God, what has happened? . . ."

As Love was in the middle of his backswing, a plaintive cry sliced through the moment. "Gui-i-r-e!"

Amanda was crashing through one of golf's ancient taboos, shattering the reverential silence of the crowd now transfixed on the golfer at his crucial transaction with the ball.

"I'm thinking, 'I can't believe this!'" Tim said. "Our host was mortified! I stand up, trying to wave her down, to get her to stop – and she's now yelled out my name twice! Love, who didn't exactly get off a great ball, looks back now. . . . He's staring up at the grandstand. . . . By now a marshal has kind of moved her off, and we're scrambling down the stairs. And I'm saying, 'Mom! *You can't do this!* You can't do this *at the Masters!*' Our host was just mortified, he was shaking his head. . . ."

And Amanda's story? A boy, whose mouth was "wired shut" and whose parents were somewhere on the back nine, had, right in front of her, fallen out of a tree he was climbing up in. "There's nobody here for him!" she said. Amanda was as quick as anyone I ever saw in putting one and one together to make a simple conclusion – and she had quickly made the determination that the boy needed a medical check. Their host was an orthopedic surgeon, so . . . . As Tim said, "her motherly instinct just took over." A child in distress, or potentially so, and Amanda to the rescue, no matter the setting or circumstance: It could hardly have been written up better.

Late that afternoon, after things had quieted down, and while Amanda was sitting on the veranda sipping a drink and enjoying one of the clubhouse's ordinarily spectacular sunsets, Tim was still out, making the most of his unforgettable day, and lately securing player autographs on a poster of the course's famed Amen Corner. As he neared the clubhouse, he saw, walking parallel to him, Davis Love, who had just finished. He walked over closer, asked Love for his signature and got it. As Love was putting pen to poster, Tim took the opportunity to mention "that tee shot on 4" – and saw an exasperated look: "Yeah, what was *that?!*"

"That was my mother that yelled in your backswing," Tim said, and gave the brief explanation. He got from Davis Love "sort of a wry smile." He had also gotten that day an Amanda story that will live on in family lore. Amanda never mentioned the incident to me, but if she had, I can imagine her saying – as she did on other occasions about other incidents – "Can you believe I did that?" surely followed by, "But the little boy had his mouth wired shut, and his parents weren't there, and . . . ."

The Last Song

The downward spiral of Amanda's last years was slow and painful, alternately gruesome and inspiring. For the last year or so, she was in a nursing home near Newnan, Ga., where Mandy, an Episcopal priest, then lived. Over the last six to eight months of her life, Amanda, Mandy said, had continued to insist that she would make it, that she would triumph over the disease. During that time, though, she increasingly had trouble breathing, momentarily making her panic, which made the situation even worse. When they were together in those instances, Mandy would sometimes sing, and that, she said, would seem to calm her mother and Amanda would get the oxygen she needed. In one of those episodes over the Thanksgiving holiday, Mandy had done this, singing what was known to be Amanda's favorite song (the title of which she had chosen for her e-mail address), THE CHILD OF GRACE.

Rarely leading together, though often in one another's company: February 2007, after the throat and lung surgeries. Burnham and Brown Memorial, Wesley Foundation, Jacksonville, Ala. (Photo by Nate and Norma Green)

This time, when Mandy finished, Amanda had managed to whisper, "When I die, I want you to sing that for me." "I think that was the only time she acknowledged that she knew she was going to die," Mandy later told me. "But then she said, 'But that's not going to be for a very long time.' And we both agreed that it would not. She lived on sheer force of will for a very long time. It was hard for her to admit that she was vulnerable."

At Christmastime, about six weeks before she died, the family managed to check Amanda out of the nursing home for a few days and take her to Tim's house in South Carolina. Tim and his wife had already bought presents for their two children – "from Gran." At their house, Amanda was "pretty much out of it," Tim would say. On Christmas Eve, about 9:00 in the evening, though, she roused herself from the sofa and told Tim, "We need to take a ride." Take a ride – *what for?* he asked. "I'm gonna buy the children's gifts," she said. He of course resisted, pointing out that he had already gotten gifts for the kids in her name – and in any case, "none of the stores are still open!" But she insisted. Calling around, they found that a nearby drugstore would be open all night, and at about 10:00 they set out to shop. "She started going up and down the aisles," Tim said. "At about the third aisle, she was winded. So she just sat down in the aisle, and we would bring things for her to look at, and she would nod yes or say no. That's how she shopped that last time. She was determined to do it her way."

Amanda died in early February. Mandy, seeing that the end was near, had called her brothers, and within a day all of them were there: the five of them, the original and essential family unit, together again. Jim had just had a baby born a couple of days before. He had over-nighted the photos of young John Joseph to Mandy, who showed them to her mother – just before, as Jim put it, she went over to "that unreachable place." "Flipping those pictures with Mandy," seeing this confirmation that there had been a safe delivery, was, he said, "her last conscious moment, her last conscious act." For Tim, it was more of that "sheer determination" he had witnessed so many times before – and would witness maybe one more time.

For two nights, the children stayed in the room with Amanda, taking turns trying to rest, with at least one of them staying up with her, talking to her and doing what Mandy called the "end of life work." On the second morning, they decided to go, by pairs, to get breakfast. "When the first set came back, I had had the privilege of standing vigil," Mandy said. "There had been sort of an intangible shift. I can't tell you how I knew, but I did. I said, 'I think we should sing CHILD OF

GRACE. Nothing would please her more than to have her four children sing that song for her.' So we gathered around. We sang the notes and then sang both verses. When we stopped, as the last note faded, she took one last, deep breath and was gone. . . ."

"It's like she was holding on for that," Tim said. "She had done her part, and now we had done what she had requested." It was complete.

To close this chapter, let me draw up one more bright memory of Amanda. It was from a visit that Jim Carnes and I made to the D.C. area in 1992 for the Potomac River Convention. Amanda was then between housing situations and was staying with good singing friend Steven Sabol, who had invited Jim and me as well to stay with him on the Sunday evening following the close of the convention. Amanda and Steven, a scientist, were devoted, if unlikely, friends. Sacred Harp was the connection between them; supporting and growing the local singing, their common goal. As the two of them would say, their minds "didn't work the same way, but we made a great team!"

As the de facto hostess for the evening, Amanda played her role beautifully. She and Steven planned a dinner for us and a few other singing friends, maybe ten in all. To use one of the phrases one frequently heard from Amanda, she "knew how" – knew how to do, knew how to maneuver in someone else's kitchen, to work with scant or ill-suited supplies and whip up a meal out of next to nothing. As she said to Jim and me, "Honey, I can turn a shoestring into a gold rope!" Steven's pantry was evidently well-supplied, though, and following the two days of singing and cooking for the convention, she had prepared a marvelous meal for us: a roast, a beautiful salad, potatoes, asparagus and a fine dessert.

The details of conversation from that evening have left me except for one key exchange, just as we came to the table. Steven and the other guests were already gathering round, and as Amanda and I started to take our seats, she commented to me that she so hoped she was "like Aunt Ruthy." I came back with some point of assurance that she was indeed. The others' conversation had come to a stop, and I was aware as I answered that Amanda and I now suddenly had the floor. I expected the topic to be put on hold for the moment. But no. "Oh, tell me how I'm like Aunt Ruthy!" she implored, as we moved our chairs closer to the table. Her focus was at that point locked in, the context of the moment suddenly as distant to her inner eye as any foreign shoreline. No one, I think, had yet so much as lifted a napkin; all were at attention until being released to begin the meal or until she and I resolved the request hovering there, the question now so imperative.

I was struck with an answer, and certainly felt it true: "Well, for one thing," I said, ". . . *charm*." This was, I think, about the last thing she expected to hear, and for an instant it stopped her in her tracks. Recovering quickly then from surprise, she pressed her hand on my arm. "Oh, you're just saying that because you love me!" "See what I mean?" I said. The other guests, who saw, heard and knew, burst into laughter, and we went on to have a great meal and an animated conversation – what another guest, speaking probably for each of us, would later say formed one of the most memorable evenings of her life. Amanda, with friends, sparkling conversation and the culinary creations of a superb hostess. It was gold rope all the way.

22

Singing Days at Antioch

I don't suppose I ever heard better singing than in my hours at Antioch, the home church of the Woottens, in Ider, in early April of many years, when spring would just be bursting upon us. Beauties of sound and spirit made up the day each time. Family singing with family made for a fine blend of voices – and oh, that alto! More than in other places I visited, the strong male trebles there, alternating on the high notes with the powerful tenor class, brought a thrilling effect. The thrill once carried me over into a sensation I had never experienced before, and haven't since. It may have happened in another song as well, but I do remember that it happened in LIVERPOOL, the number I would hold out for if told I could have only one song in the entire book. . . . At a point, in the peaking rush of all that harmony, with so many bold, wonderful voices around me, it seemed that not just we but the song itself began to sing! It seemed to just catch fire and burn across us.

I first knew the singing there by reputation. Someone around my hometown area had once mentioned that hearing "those boys up on the mountain" sing 163 top, MORNING, would "make the hair stand up on the back of your neck." Some years later I followed Hugh McGraw to meet the purveyors of such magic. On another occasion, when I had picked up old singing buddy Carl Hughes in Rome, Ga., and headed for Antioch, he mentioned admiringly a note about the disciplined singing one would find there in "singin' with those boys" (as he had done many times over the years): "Sing out on a rest up there, and you'll *embarrass* yourself. . . ." (That then led him to reflect on an occupational hazard, and inevitable embarrassment, for those, like himself, who made a habit of chewing tobacco before and during the breaks at singings: brown dribble down the front of one's shirt.)

A few brief scenes I noted from some of those years of singing at Antioch:

On one particular day: Before a dining hall was added to the main building, the dinner tables were down a slope from the back of the church. And before the meal, someone was asked to pray. Someone else clapped and called for attention to the prayer, but the sound was swallowed up. As the prayer began, quiet rippled up the slope, surrounding and surprising groups of threes and fours. Chastened, they stopped mid-sentence and bowed their heads: ". . . and dear Heavenly Father . . . ." Abruptly the wind shifted, took the prayer from our ears and flung it toward the field beyond.

Back in the session, Antioch's minister was called to lead, and did so with a friend. "I just told Brother Watkins," he said, as they stood before us, 'you won't hear nothing n'better'n this till you get Home.'"

Mack Wootten sat slumped somewhat on the bass bench, his mouth open as if to taste the air. He half-mouthed the words of each song, smiling broadly as he watched the leaders' faces.

And when he stood up to lead: "I may not make it another year. . . . If I leave out, just say I took a shortcut Home."

The 1990 session was one of some impact. Kathleen Thro of St. Louis had recorded the singing. She then made that recording available for a tape cassette that she, Jim Carnes, David Ivey and I produced called "Bound for Canaan" (it would end up being selected by the Library of Congress as one of the best folk recordings of 1990). The recording would prove to be popular in our singing community, but one of the songs from it, PASSING AWAY, drew particular interest because of a woman's spontaneous cries during the singing.

I had a few times before, in singing sessions, been witness to someone "shouting" or "gettin' happy" – those phrases used to describe an expressive form of ecstatic experience. (Two specific memories from years back still linger with me: At the height of some vigorously rendered song early in my singing days, Vera Alexander Lowe, sister of singer Jewel Alexander Wootten, suddenly began to cry out. Held onto then by a couple of others, she just began to dance in place, her feet almost running out from under her. Another time, at the Cullman courthouse convention, with the singing effect in the afternoon session growing warmer and warmer, a Mr. Grimmett, when the treble run in the song FILLMORE seemed to fly up to the ceiling, found his cup overflowing and began to holler out.)

Wootten nephews and cousins in full cry: (from left) Jeffrey Wootten, Terry Wootten with granddaughters KayLee and Karalina Mann, Shane Wootten, Marty Wootten and, around the corner on bass, Phillip Wootten. (Photo by Laura Densmore, 2008)

Such experiences are surely in part the result of a cumulative building throughout the day – song after song, memory after memory – until at a point something just explodes. The rising steam, from a kettle now heated so, must somehow escape. . . . That day at Antioch, the woman – not a regular singer but a member of the local community who usually attended the annual sessions and whose husband had died a few months before – stood, just moments before our singing of this, the closing song, and began to speak fast and forcefully. She was almost flinging the words out, as if her slender body were being beaten by the thoughts that came too fast and hard for her to handle otherwise. "This is my eat, and this is my drink!" she nearly chanted. When she paused as if to catch her breath after several minutes of this non-stop speaking, Terry Wootten sounded a pitch for PASSING AWAY, and we started singing. At that point, it seemed as if her voice went up in flames and she just soared. It was an electrifying experience.

Children's lesson at Antioch, 2001. (Photo by Laura Densmore)

In the following months, as our little production team was preparing the recording, we debated about whether to include the song, knowing that it might bring embarrassment to some and distaste or confusion to others. (One example of initial confusion was relayed to me by a couple who, at first mistaking the woman's cries, had looked around to see "who let the cat in.") We felt compelled at last to include it, as it had represented the emotional climax to the day. Indeed after the first and last verses were sung, someone – there was no leader – had launched into the passed-over second verse, and the class followed and then went on to repeat the chorus: no one in that moment wanted to let it go.

In the old days, such experiences were surely not unusual. The minutes of the 1943 session of the Warrior River Convention, meeting at Mt. Moriah Church at Oneonta, recorded the following comments about the convention's parting hand: "Many shouts went up, praising the Lord for the blessings He poured down upon us during these services."

One of the things I appreciated so about the singings at Antioch was that the Wootten family and others of the community of singers there were not embarrassed by any show of emotion, but warmly encouraged participants to express and share their feelings.

The song NEW HARMONY has a tie-in here:

I want to live a Christian here,
I want to die a-shouting.
I want to feel my Savior near,
While soul and body's parting.

It was one of the favorite songs of Beulah Haynes Wootten (1884-1967), mother of the seven senior Wootten siblings I sang with in those years. "Sweet Is the Day," an affecting film about the Wootten and Haynes family produced by wife-and-husband-team Erin Kellen and Jim Carnes in 2001, intermingles multiple family voices to tell of Beulah Wootten's death while in a church service and of the application of that song's words to the moment of her passing. By all accounts, her life had been rich with the things that were important to her. Early on, she had taught her husband to sing Sacred Harp and had always prayed that her children – and especially the boys! – would in their turn be good and faithful singers. The decades of her later life saw that hope fully come to fruition.

Mama Wootten was, as youngest son Freeman put it, "a shoutin' woman." And as the children and grandchildren relate in the film, she had always prayed to be able to, in the words of the song, "die a-shouting." Following a sermon by her son Postell, the handshake before the break for lunch had launched a song – and shouting. "It was a good day," grandson Marlon Wootten remembered, "and she just enjoyed it, and she just went right on rejoicing." From her daughter Olivia: "She got to Postell to hug his neck and got happy and had her heart attack right there." Though she was rushed to the hospital, the family knew that she had died in their presence – and in receipt of her fervent wish. As Freeman said, "She was granted that privilege. . . . She got what she'd always wanted." Her tombstone carries the words: "I want to live a Christian here and die a shouting." Surely the family's honoring of that unforgettable memory underlies their embrace of the emotional surges, the rejoicing, the happy expressions of faith and longing that are the source and product of their singing.

Finally, from a less emotionally charged but still memorable incident from my visits to Antioch, this note from the 1997 session: During the announcements at the end, a fellow, from the back of the church, who was making video and audio tapes of the singing, asked to be recognized, and then said that he wanted to say something about the chicken served there that day. (I had seen the great portions of smoked or barbecued chicken as I went through the line, but didn't think I could handle that much at one time.) Maybe not his exact words but close: "Whoever cooked that chicken . . . I don't know if that's a secret recipe or not. But if it is, I sure hope you'll tell at least one person how to do that before you die. . . ."

23

Tat Bailey

Tyrus Cobb Bailey (1913-2013)

They're called minced oaths, those safely off-center phrases we've used or heard all our lives: By golly! Darn! Shoot! Gosh dang it! – and so forth. Useful implements in the lexicon, they allow a person to blow off steam without having to resort to the heavy-duty stuff.

Ben Berry of Red Hill, a little community near Arab, in the northeast quadrant of Alabama, in the early decades of the 20th century may not have known about lexicons or minced oaths, but he was determined not to curse or blaspheme. So "By gad!" was what he tended to come out with whenever he was provoked.

Berry's grandson, T.C. "Tat" Bailey, remembered that expression well – and remembered in particular his grandpa's response when a new-book singer needled the oldster about the *Sacred Harp*: "Why do y'all sing the same old songs year after year?" the fellow had baited him with. "Seems like you'd get tired of 'em."

"By gad, when they come up with better songs, we'll sing 'em!" Berry had replied.

That competitive tension, sometimes oath-provoking, between the old-book *Sacred Harp* and every year's new gospel-song collections was a theme circling through the 1910s, '20s and '30s in the countryside where the Berry and Bailey families lived – the years of Ben Berry's later life and of Tat Bailey's youth. Berry was a dyed-in-the-wool Sacred Harper. His son-in-law, Frank Bailey, Tat's father, was a new-book singer who taught at least one singing school in the then more fashionable seven-shape system. Tat, caught in the middle, preferred the old-book sounds, as the rest of his long life would show.

Grandpa Berry, who was born in the last year of the Civil War and who died in 1939, was a blacksmith as well as a farmer. "He shod horses for ten cents a shoe," Tat remembered. His grandpa also liked to play with the hardware itself: "He'd go down to the store and pitch horseshoes every day if he could." But Berry was a tribble with "a keen voice," and singing the songs of the *Sacred Harp* was his great love.

Ben and Martha Berry had raised their ten children on 30 acres of hillside. Their daughter Mamie, Tat's mother, died when Tat was nine. Both before and after that pivotal event, Tat and his siblings, three brothers and two sisters, found their father a difficult master. Soon a stepmother and four stepbrothers and -sisters complicated their emotional attachments. So the tug from their Berry grandparents was strong.

Getting to see grandpa, though, required effort. "After Momma died, we'd walk about five miles through the fields over to Harmony Church to see him, to hear him sing," Tat said. "We'd be barefooted, and it'd be dust and sawbriars all the way. . . ." His grandpa had to walk about ten miles to get to Harmony, he said. "He never did have no transportation. He'd walk out there, and he'd be in the church singin'."

"When he got old, he would sit at his window and sing by himself, in his little old house," Tat said. "Three months before I went to the navy, I stayed with him, and he would sit at his window and sing. . . . Them notes just *rolled* out the window."

Those early sounds of his grandpa singing were imprinted on Tat, as was the fasola singing he heard at the Cullman courthouse. "We'd ride in an open-bed [Model T] truck with Wyatt Nolen to the

Cullman singing . . . hang our legs off the back, barefooted. Our eyebrows would be covered with dust. People today don't understand how dusty it used to be. We don't have dust like we used to have – it's all blowed away!"

Once they got to Cullman, though, they found things, well, very *uptown*: "Oh man, the Cullman courthouse with the balcony around it on the inside, those big fans a-turnin'! . . . It was one of the few places that had electricity back then. We didn't know what electricity was till we went to Cullman. They had their own power plant, had that for a long time. They had a water fountain there. And the whole place was full of people. I'd listen to 'em sing. And there'd be so many people out in the street you couldn't even walk. You'd have to push your way through the crowd to go get a Co-Cola. There'd be people there from up in Tennessee. And a fellow by the name of Al Richter had a fruit stand on the corner there, selling bananas."

And then there was the singing convention at Guntersville, the Marshall County seat and eventual site of Lake Guntersville, what was to become the largest lake in the state. Tat remarked about one unforgettable trip to the courthouse there: "Pappa took us in his old Model T. You had to cross [the Tennessee River] by ferry boat. We started down that steep hill and a wheel broke. A guy wire caught us, kept us from tumblin' on down the hill. We'd liable to got killed if that guy wire hadn't caught us." So they had plenty to sing about that day, or at least to think about, gratefully, while others sang.

Though he grew up around it, Tat himself never learned to sing – what he later called, as he neared and then passed a 98th birthday, "my only real regret."

He never attended a singing school. "In the summertime, we had baseball on our mind and swimmin' hole on our mind – didn't want to go to no singing school." Baseball was a natural interest. His father loved the sport and had named Tat, at his birth in 1913, after Ty Cobb, then in the prime of his record-setting career. A neighbor, though, was responsible for the nickname. "He put the 'Tat' on me," the honoree said, though "Pappa never did call me Tat; he didn't like it. He always called me Tyrus – 'Tarse,' the way he said it."

There was the time, though, and memorably so, that a singing school of sorts was briefly brought *to* the Bailey youngsters. Their daddy experimented with teaching the four boys the *do-re-mi* seven-shape system, calling them in one by one, in order of birth, to try the scale from a blackboard he had set up in their living room:

He called Keith in, the oldest first. He'd write the scale and try to get Keith to sing it. *He* didn't do no good. Well, he whupped him ["Spanked his ass," in the version he first told me]. Then he called in Girtes [rhymes with Curtis]. Me and Girtes had been pissin' all over ourselves, waitin', scared to death. Girtes would miss it, and he'd spank him – for not knowin' how to read that scale! Same thing with me. And then Vogel – Vogel never did get no whippin' though. . . . He was high-tempered, my daddy was. He thought you ought to learn everything easy.

It was a method of shape-note pedagogy that, understandably, may have quickly gone extinct – one hopes so, at any rate. The Bailey boys, as it happened, failed to acquire the targeted skill, and the experience hardened in them an early disaffection for the new-book system and their father's music. "We rebelled on him," as Tat put it. But for his grandpa – and for his grandpa's singing – he kept a kind of awed love. One of his stories brought that point home for me keenly.

As a teenager, Keith, Tat said, had a bicycle that he used for delivering the afternoon newspaper in Cullman, some 20-plus miles to the west from where they lived. One Saturday morning Tat, then about 13, slipped off with Keith's bike. He had in mind to ride the couple of miles to the little community of Joppa. By the time he got to the outpost there, he had conceived a bigger idea: He would ride on in to the town of Arab, some four miles to the east, and then, another dozen miles or so, on down the mountain to Guntersville. It was the date of the big Marshall County singing convention. He knew his grandpa would be at the courthouse there, and he wanted to go in and see him sing.

It was a long ride – and not without complication there at the end. By the time he got close to the courthouse, several boys from the outskirts of town had started chasing after him, wanting to ride the bike. It occurred to him then that if he went into the courthouse, he might not see the bike again. He was trapped. He could hear the singing through the open windows, but was not able to go inside to see his grandpa. Disappointment must have been as palpable as his growing sense of hunger. "I didn't have no dinner," he said. The trip, after all, had been sketchily conceived. And he still had to go home to face a charge that, over the hours, was surely being upgraded from petty to grander theft.

Heading back home at last, he found he was running out of fuel – and had the tough mountain climb ahead. Hungry and thirsty, he had to push the bike up about two miles of mountain. Along the way, he came to a spring with water running across the road. "I got down on my belly and just drank and drank and drank." At last he passed the home of a family he knew. "They gave me some dinner," he said – "some cornbread and cabbage." "It was about dark before I got home, and Keith still had to go on to Cullman. I didn't get no whippin' – I was surprised I didn't – but I mean I paid for that!"

Up in the Crow's Nest

In order to attend Cullman high school, Tat, along with Girtes, boarded at a home within the city limits. "We batched it," as he put it. In his senior year, he and good friend Julie Woerner were elected cheerleaders. "I guess they thought I was a pretty cute kid," Tat told me – and said it as flatly as if he were rendering an ordinary verdict on the day's weather. On his head and Julie's, then, was the responsibility for "making noise" and cheering their football team to victory: "We had 15 'rah's' we did. We had to make 'em up. We didn't have no band to make music."

From the navy years, about 1936. (Courtesy of T.C. Bailey)

Tat left school before graduating and in 1933, after a stint selling magazines over a sizable territory in the state, enlisted, along with brother Keith, in the navy. Girtes had entered the year before, and three or four years later Vogel would join as well. For about a year and a half, the four of them served together aboard the destroyer tender the USS Whitney. "I couldn't go to the toilet without runnin' into one of my brothers," Tat said.

The siren song that haunted him out on the waters was not a new song; it was the strains of Sacred Harp singing, that distinctively churning, rising and falling a cappella sound playing over and over in his mind. "I dreamed about 'em while I was out in the ocean, out in the Pacific," Tat said. "I thought, I'd just give *anything* if I could hear fasola singin' again. I'd be up in the crow's nest, up in the tower, on watch - boy, I'll tell you, I got lonesome! - and I'd think how *good* it would be to hear a Sacred Harp song."

After six years in the navy, and after Ben and Martha Berry were gone, Tat, who had married a local girl in 1937, came back to civilian life and began a career in civil service. For seven years, including the World War II period, he worked in ship repair at the naval shipyard in Portsmouth, Va. After that he worked for three years with the Arab water works system, then for seven months at the naval air squadron in Jacksonville, Fla., and finally for 17 years at Huntsville's Redstone Arsenal.

In Alabama again, he came back to Sacred Harp singing. Tat and his brothers and sisters were tight-knit, the brothers particularly close in their interests, but none of the rest had taken to Sacred Harp as he had. None of the rest had been touched with such a tender nostalgia for it. Never a singer, Tat was now drawn to Sacred Harp singings in the area. His 1921-vintage Model T became a familiar sight at singings around Arab, in nearby Blount County, at Guntersville and at Cullman.

At one courthouse singing in Cullman, he remembered Paine Denson, up from Birmingham, saying to the big assembled class, "There's a song in this book for *every human idea*. If you can't find it,

I'll find it *for* you." "That's a phrase I'll never forget," Tat said. "He was a dandy." Paine's sister Ruth, too, had left an impression: "She could open her mouth *this wide*," he said, laying one palm atop the other and springing the two of them open like a trap. "I'm tellin' you, she could *sing*." From those early years, one singer drew his wonder more than the rest, though – Dock Owens, from the Marshall County side of Sand Mountain: "He had the biggest mouth I ever saw – looked like he could swaller a watermelon. But you didn't need but one bass singer if you had him. . . . Didn't need nobody else."

The man and his Model T. (Courtesy of T.C. Bailey)

Although Tat's mother died too early, the rest of the family lived long enough for some mellowing and some fence-mending. "My daddy, he didn't like his daddy-in-law," Tat said. "But then he came to love the old man before he died." And despite his tough exterior as a young father, Frank Bailey showed himself in time "a loving sort."

That late-demonstrated affection reached out to include the old music as well: "Pappa didn't really like fasola singing till he got old. Before he died, he'd got to where he'd go to them fasola singings . . . enjoyed those old singings in his old age."

Early on in high school, when he was delivering the Birmingham newspaper in Cullman, on a bicycle as his elder brother had done, Tat had found himself awed by a big rock house owned by the Vogel family [from whom Frank Bailey had gotten the name for his youngest son], descendants of German immigrants. "I wanted a big rock house ever since I saw that Vogel house in Cullman," he said. "It was like a *castle* built out of native rock." In later years he had a local artist do a water-color painting of the house, as he also did with another Cullman favorite, an antebellum-style home with big columns across the front.

In the mid-'60s, freed from a long, unhappy marriage, Tat devoted himself to building his dream of a big, two-story rock house with columns, a combination of sorts of the two Cullman prototypes. He didn't do all the work himself, but did the extraordinary prep work for it: "I was the main 'head doctor' on it. I brought in rock from five counties, bought up old fireplaces from all over, hauled 'em up here with a winch."

His two-acre estate now appears an eccentric's fantasy. A big, wide rock archway leads a visitor in. A decorative fence, thigh-high rock pillars connected by horizontal bamboo poles, flanks the curving roadway on the left. To the right, a little pond, carrying the reflection of the house above it, is bordered by a short, old-fashioned-type covered bridge that he built himself. A log cabin, a rudimentary wishing well, an old-style outhouse (a three-seater, including one sized for a child), and rock statuary everywhere show that this is not your average sideyard-backyard lot. At the back entrance, a wooden plaque hanging above the rock walkway carries this inscription:

Tyrus (T.C.) Bailey
"The Singing Hills"
Fry Gap Mountain
This Home of Love I Built

Whence the obsession with rock? "I've hauled rock and messed with rocks ever since I was a little boy," he told me one time. "In the summertime we'd plow 'em up and then the next spring we'd pile 'em up and haul 'em out down next to the creek. As a six-year-old boy, I'd have to pry 'em out of the ground. That whole hillside was filled with rock." The permanence, the strength of rock must have been a major part of the attraction for him. I once heard him earnestly tell someone at a singing, "Rock is the most important thing on earth – it keeps everything from sinkin' into the ocean!" and then later, "Rock is the foundation of the earth. It keeps us all from livin' in a mudhole."

A Day in the Life

I had known Tat Bailey for years, and my mother's family, living in or near Arab much of that time, had known him for longer. An electrician by trade, a handyman by reputation, he had won the family's gratitude by an act of neighborly service: on a Christmas morning, with my elderly grandmother expecting a houseful of children and grandchildren, Tat had answered the call to resolve a day-threatening plumbing crisis.

For years I saw him around the fringes of singings, often with tape recorder, trying to capture the day's glories. We had talked before about his abiding love of Sacred Harp, he had told me about Grandpa Berry, and he had invited me to his rock estate – even told me about the rock tomb he had built for himself. I had seen him at a singing or two even when he was in his 90s and no longer able to drive. But I had lost touch with him until I saw an online photo from a July singing at Henagar in 2010. There he was, in overalls and amazingly now 97, pictured on the floor with Rodney Ivey and Geraldine Sharpton as they led a lesson.

As the weeks went by, he stayed on my mind. The United Sacred Harp Convention, meeting annually on the second weekend in September, was that year to be at Zion Hill Primitive Baptist Church near Snead Crossroads, maybe less than an hour's drive from Tat's mountain home. So I decided to try to find him and offer to take him to the singing. It took some doing to obtain his telephone number, but when I finally had it, I called, about a week before the convention, and spoke to Angie, the younger cousin now staying with him. "He'll be thrilled to death," she said. "He won't sleep a wink tonight." She put him on the phone, and he enthusiastically assured me he'd be up for the trip.

Early that next Saturday morning, I found a feebler Tat Bailey, no longer steady on his feet but eager to take in the day. Angie had packed a bundle of supplies for him and handed me pain pills to give him as needed.

I had assumed a straightforward drive to the singing site, and had looked up the directions online before I started. Tat had other ideas. "Turn left here," he said, as we were about to pull out from his driveway – the opposite direction from where I had planned to go. "I know all these roads," he said, and I knew that he must – these roads that he had hauled many tons of rock over. From that point on, he directed and sent us, with running commentary, on a circuitous route over the mountain.

We hadn't driven far when he said, "Turn down here. I want you to see something. It won't delay us long." It was Red Hill, an edge of the little community his mother and his grandfather had grown up in. Later he worried – "I'll make you late" – but still pressed me on to see just a few more sights along the way, if we could take a moment. I was up for all and told him so.

He reflected constantly now, he told me later, on cemeteries, grave plots, monuments. He frequently thought of his beloved kin, of all his contemporaries now gone, and was proud that some had a proper resting place, bothered that not everyone did. His cousins down in Florida, he was told, were buried in a cemetery that was well-kept, but he had not been able to see it for himself.

The cemetery at Red Hill, where so many of his Berry kin were buried, satisfied him most. (The grave of Ben Berry has this epitaph:

Here lies the dust of NBB / His spirit sings at home.) Two relatives had purchased an extra two acres, room for the cemetery to expand if needed. "There'll be plenty of room here," he said. "This is the best place in the world to be buried! You dig down and it's just red dirt, you won't even hit a rock. And it's so high above the water table, there's never gonna be a problem with moisture."

His mausoleum is the first thing you see on the right going in, set off by itself, on the outer side of the circular drive that circumscribes the burial area. The tomb is made of rock. "The walls are 17 inches thick," he said. A marble portal, inscribed with his name and birth date, lies in front and is to replace the temporary entrance portal. Around the tomb are the words "fa sol la mi," the notehead symbols themselves and key phrases from the songbook: "'Tis finished," "Complete for sinful man."

Some minutes later, back on the narrow upland roads, we stopped at another cemetery, Pleasant Grove. He was much impressed with it, with the size of the monuments ("bigger than you'll see most anywhere") and with how well-kept the grounds were. Though we didn't stop and get out, he wanted me to see his grandmother Bailey's stone ("that narrow tombstone there," as he pointed, "there just beyond that cedar tree"), and we looked at the sloping ground in a crowded and shady area, with a number of smaller, darkened stones slanted by time.

On Vaughn Road, the long-ago-paved route we took early on, Tat said, "This used to be the muddiest road I ever saw – so muddy a mule couldn't hardly pull a wagon through it." And then up over the mountain: "This was the toughest road I ever remember goin' over. All those big rocks in it! Oh, my gosh!" (showing that he, too, could mince an oath).

Tat had contracted shingles two years before, he told me as we drove on, and the condition had settled in his right eye. The shingles had moved on but had left him with excruciating pain in his eye and the entire right side of his face. "I can touch the left side of my face and it's fine, but sometimes just touching my nose on this right side hurts me so bad I can't stand it." He had been to Huntsville to have the nerve-ends "zapped," but the costly procedure was unsuccessful, had not eased his pain and now had left that area partially paralyzed, he said, though I couldn't tell that it affected his countenance as he talked.

We turned at last onto Highway 75, the main route we would need, and then onto the little destination road. Neither of us had been to the church before, but Tat admired the one-mile stretch of road, at one point overarched with trees.

Before we got to the singing, he made a request: that MORNING SUN would be the last song sung for the day! "I don't want to dictate," he said, "but if you can arrange that, I sure will be grateful." Even though life for him was now deep into the twilight, he had fastened on the words "Your morning sun may set at noon, / And leave you ever in the dark." I told him I would try.

At the singing, he said repeatedly, "Go on up there on the front, I want you to be happy." No, I assured him, I was content where I was, a few seats back from the front – and wanted this to be *his* day. He still had an eye for the ladies. When I returned from the first morning break, he motioned me over: "I want you to meet one of the prettiest girls you're ever gonna see – look here, she's from Georgia!" We met and spoke briefly; he had struck up an acquaintance with her as she had started to walk past him. She was complimented, and he seemed pleased with it all. His pain had now surely subsided.

Close to the lunch break, and then once or twice more in the afternoon, I offered a pain pill. He waved it off each time, and took nothing for pain until at least after I parted company with him.

"Run off with some of these women! . . ." I heard him joke to the two singers in front as I turned back to him when we took our seats after the noon break. "No, my roaming days are over. . . ," he said, his voice trailing off, a soft and wistful landing.

During the session, following each of a number of songs I knew he must have heard a good many times before, I was surprised to hear him say, "That's a pretty song! That's the first time I've ever heard that. . ." or "I've never heard that one before, but it sure is pretty!" But many more times, when we finished a selection – 208, 216, 318, 142 and a couple of dozen more – he would clap his cupped hands together soundlessly and say, "What a song! What a song!"

On two or three numbers, with me singing close and leaning in to him, he joined in, especially at the end of SOUTHWELL, with the words that are already on his tomb: "Complete, complete, complete for sinful man."

With Tat, in the middle of that first MORNING SUN, United Convention, September 2010. (Photo by James Robert Chambless)

At the end, for the last song before the closing, I was called up to the square and brought Tat with me to lead MORNING SUN, the song I had previously requested, in an announcement to the group, to be kept in reserve. I steadied his arm as the large group sang, and he seemed almost to bounce with the pulsing music, his two hands striking up and down with the beat as he if were tamping down a cushion. When we finished, his voice breaking, he thanked the class and pointed out the import of that key phrase: "Your morning sun may set at noon . . . ."

"I'll remember this day for the rest of my life!" he said repeatedly, at the site and again finally at home.

Over the next couple of years, Tat accompanied me to several more singings, primarily in the northeast corner of the state – and joined me in the square each time, always getting to hear an inspired rendition of MORNING SUN. One of those occasions merits a citation: the Sunday of the Henagar-Union Convention at Liberty Church in Henagar in July of 2012. Though always a great singing, this one seemed especially strong. When Jeffrey Wootten stepped into the square to lead, he called for 460, SARDIS, pitched it just shy of the stratosphere and began beating time in the deliberate leading style of four beats per measure. The sound that ensued was powerful, bright and sweet. Midway through the song, Tat suddenly began to cry. He put his hands up halfway to his face, closed his eyes and just sobbed. As the song ended he said, "That's the best singing I've ever heard – it's *so* beautiful!" And then putting his hands forward, as if resting them on an invisible shelf, he said, "Oh-h-h, I just wish that sound would *hang* in the air! . . ."

The woman on the other side of him, an infrequent visitor from a far-off state, had seen him start to cry and, in full sympathy, immediately teared up and then busied herself wiping her eyes. A few songs later, at another high point, Tat again began to cry. "I've just never heard anything like it!" he said. Ecstasy – in this world – is fleeting. But Tat had tasted it, and he longed for more. On the way home, he remarked on his outburst, near-apologizing for it. This had never happened to him before, he said. "Those were just the most beautiful tones! Oh, I wish those tones could just stay in the air!"

Continuing Conversations

Tat was always eager for the trips we took, and Sacred Harp remained a favored topic for our get-togethers. "I've gotten a lot of pleasure out of it," he would tell me. At home he showed me the CD player that let him listen to Sacred Harp songs played loudly (Angie said) every night as he went to sleep. "I just feel sorry for people that've never experienced fasola singing," he would say. "I'm serious, doggone it – I just feel *sorry* for 'em!"

Whenever we rode together, he would sit slightly hunched and squint-eyed, never losing focus on the road unfurling before us. His hearing was poor, so our conversations tended to be one-sided. He liked to talk, to reminisce, and I would prompt him with volume-enhanced questions or brief rejoinders ("Say they did, huh?"). He frequently mentioned his brothers, all of whom had moved to California earlier in their lives – and had died, and been cremated, there. "I'm against cremation," he told me at one of those references. "I just can't stand the thought of it. I don't think God intended for us to be burnt after we die."

He had made arrangements of a different sort for himself. On a trip to Long Island many years before, he had seen and much admired a special rope plait in a hardware store there. He bought it and then, over time, as he conceived the idea of making his own casket, decided to use the rope for the casket handles. The wood he would use had some history of its own. There was an old house in the area where, he said, "a Yankee was hidin' after the Civil War, and they shot him through the wall." The woman who ultimately owned the house had dismantled it and had let Tat have some of the lumber (including a piece he would show me with a bullet hole through it). Borrowing a buddy's woodworking shop, he used pieces of the old lumber, along with cedar, to make the big, heavy box. He had positioned six hammers in a wooden tray inside it, one for each pallbearer to use in nailing the top shut.

Meandering from one cluster of memories to the next, as we rode, Tat would often pause in between for some introspection. At least twice he told me a story of "kidnapping" his wife early in their married life. He had loved his old Model T and enjoyed giving the town kids rides in it, taking them for ice cream – a treat that he said those individuals, now well into senior years themselves, still remarked on whenever he saw them. His wife, however, on supposed safety grounds, refused to ride in the vehicle – from his point of view, peevishly so. Determined to have his way – "You'll take at least one ride in it!" he promised himself – he drove the Model T around to pick her up one day at the back entrance of the store where she worked. "I knew the hour she got off," he said. "I backed the car up to the curb, throwed her butt over into the back seat!" – from which, with the door now shut, it was nigh-impossible for her to free herself. He seemed in the telling, even at this far distance from the event, a bit more surprised than I that, by the time they got home, "That was the maddest woman I ever saw in my life!"

Pulling back from that scene, he eased into a confession of sorts: "I can be stubborn as a bull when I want something! I'll do almost *anything* to please my mind. And that's not a good thing, either. . . . But I was raised up to be stubborn. My brothers used to whip my ass, but they didn't do it often!"

I'll do almost anything to please my mind. Rarely in conversation do we chance to hear a single statement of self-disclosure that seems to strike like a lightning bolt across the blurry background of someone's life. But I don't think Tat ever said anything to me that brought hotter light to bear on his formidable, almost otherworldly blend of supercharged will and inviolable eccentricity. It could extend all the way back to encompass the 13-year-old's "borrowing" of his brother's bike (company car) to ride all the way to Guntersville just so he could hear his grandpa sing; his shaking loose heavy rock from hillsides in five counties and finagling stones from old hearths and chimneys so he could erect a rock house befitting his outsize, Gatsbyesque teenage dreams; his stocking his estate grounds with nature-sculpted rock statuary – here a huge turtle-like form, there the big slab in the shape, nearly, of the state of Alabama; the "flying jenny" contraption of flat, oblong stone, maybe four-and-a-half feet across, mounted on an old wheel assembly, for really giving a guest a whirl; his custom-built and hand-inscribed mausoleum; the wooden casket trimmed out and waiting in the lower room of his house, the chosen vessel for his next-to-final passage. . . .

Tat conceded in a few conversations that his life at times had been messy. "I spend a lot of time looking back over my life, looking back over the mistakes I've made," he once told me. "I'm bad on mistakes. . . ." He had also, especially in his youth, had a number of close calls with the death angel – like the time he was sucked into a whirlpool in the creek below the bluff where the Bailey boys swam, emerging gurgling and dazed, after what seemed to his brothers like several minutes, a couple of hundred feet beyond where they had seen him disappear. As an adult, cutting grass, he had slipped on the edge of a ditch and tumbled in, with the big lawn mower falling on top of him and almost cutting his leg to pieces. Or the time he was taking down a tree with a chainsaw and had it snap back and fall on him, breaking his neck and requiring a steel "halo" to be affixed to his head for months (probably the only time past infancy that that word would have been associated with his person). And what a number of other stories Tat could relate! Through it all, like his old Model T, he just kept on cranking and rumbling.

In early March of 2013, on the eve of his 100th birthday, amid a houseful of family, friends and admirers, a dozen of us met up to dress the occasion with some of his favorite tunes. "Anybody that don't like Sacred Harp singing, show 'em the door!" Tat trumpeted, in between songs. "Just show 'em the door!"

Over the following months, he began increasingly to stay in bed and just gradually seemed to slip away from us. He died peacefully at his home in late September. He was buried in a bold outfit he had exulted in assembling long before the date of departure: pants, coat, shirt and tie in stripes and shards and spangling stars of brightest red, white and blue.

T.C. "Tat" Bailey. This was to me, finally, a most endearing man, possessed of so much love – surely enough to wash over a sheaf of mistakes he may have made along the way in a long and active life, his wayward, song-haunted sojourn here.

24

'. . . and All and Everything . . .'

Her name was Mae Abercrombie. She was a right pretty woman of middle age when I knew her in my youth, a mid-distance neighbor and a seamstress. She could sew all day – and talk. Though we sometimes joined her in little conversations when we passed her yard, it was when Mae came to our house once to make draperies that I experienced fully the texture of her speech, the gossip and ruminations with which, like the steady whirring of a machine, she filled the open minutes and hours. My mother was the primary listener, the intended audience, but I was close by for much of the time on what I guess was a rainy day and so got an extended dose. I don't remember now a single thing Mae said on that or the other occasions – except for the tag line she put on many of her sentences and maybe most of her paragraphs, the little knot she would tie at the end of the thread: ". . . *and all and everything.*" It was her version of the little codas that people sometimes use, or overuse – "and so on," "and so forth," or the King of Siam's *et ceteras*. A typical sentence from Mae, then, might come out something like: "And then of course he got mad and went home, an'-all-an'-everything. . . ."

It was the most capacious of closing devices, a snatching-up of most everything in sight (or imagination) and then some. . . . Sometimes she would gear down and use only the short form – "and all" – but most of the time she used the longer one with its built-in redundancy. We all may have our own verbal tics, but what I, even as a youngster, found puzzling about Mae was that she seemed not to notice at all in her speech what surely anyone else would notice most of all. She didn't make the phrase a point of emphasis; she said it perfunctorily, almost running the words together. But she was *bound* to use it.

As I've tried to bring together this memoir, readying many of the little incidents or fragments of dialogue too short or disconnected to merit stand-alone treatment, Mae's signature phrase struck me as a whimsical but useful vehicle for setting them all up together.

What follows then, in near-random order, is a train of little reminiscences, a whole bunch of my *all and everything* from a 45-plus-year Sacred Harp experience. I don't intend a perfunctory treatment of these memories, though, or mean to give them short shrift. I cherish them each and all. And as Mae Abercrombie's non-stop talk used to do, I hope that together they will help fill, somewhere for someone, an otherwise empty hour.

A Day at Mt. Lebanon

SUNDAY, JUNE 28, 1987

At this his home church near Fayette, Ala., Hamilton Ballinger, 84, led a song with his ten surviving children: one daughter and nine sons. As they sat down, Tressie Adkins said, "Not many men can say what he can – ten children and all of 'em can sing." It was a truth no one disputed. Later Ozella Chafin asked if I had ever been to Hamilton's house when all his children were there. "You should see it. There'll be about 90 of 'em there. There's so much love, you can't tell which one's children belong to which."

A Mr. Keeton, bald and trim, got up to lead during the morning session. "He spent all day looking for this singing one time and never found it!" D.T. White announced. "I didn't find it today, either," Mr. Keeton answered back, almost proudly. "Somebody found it *fer* me."

At noon, we took our recess. The men's and women's restrooms, back to back, were in a small building about 15 feet behind the church. I found the door to the men's restroom closed. Young voices on the inside sounded out: "You want to talk to them little girls or go play?" "Talk to them girls" was the reply. The door swung open, and three youngsters grinned and looked up, the sun splashing in their faces. They disappeared among the crowd, now gathering round the tables.

Mr. A.A. ('Lonzo) Malone thrust a large thumb, blue-black just under the nail, at one of his buddies, Mr. Arnold Moon (the two of them surely in their 80s). "Them blue-hull peas you said'd never make . . . I *shelled* a bunch this morning." The other reached for the thumb and shook it, chiding his cohort with a grin. "Six days shalt thou labor, and on the *seventh* shalt thou rest."

There was an explosion around the big oak where the table for drinks was stationed. Someone had opened a grape drink and in doing so sent lilac fizz in a radius of six or seven feet, showering a dozen or so of all ages. A squeal and the circle suddenly widened. The culprit was singled out. "It wasn't me," he said, tightening the cap and then loosening it again.

Larry Ballinger, as we ate, pointed out a large tree a hundred feet back in the grove. "Had five squirrels runnin' around in that oak one time. . . ."

After lunch, a member of one of the area singing families came in late and took a seat halfway back in the tenor. I noticed that when he didn't seem to know a song, he would just sit and listen. When he knew the song, though, he sang along – and did so with his eyes shut tight. Like a mockingbird on its roost at dusk that sings itself to sleep – or like a rooster crowing. ("You know why the rooster shuts his eyes when he crows?" my grandfather asked me when I was a boy. "'Cause he's got it up by heart.") On the last chord of the song he would open his eyes again.

Clarence McCool, one of my favorites, was as ever a model of skinniness. If he had been mean, it could have been said that there was nothing left of him but meanness. But he was a most congenial sort. He amused me by a reference to gospel singing as "little book, this *modern* music."

Mr. Malone, talking later with Clarence, remarked about the land where the local junior college (a sometime site for singings) is located: It used to be a big cotton field, he said. "This land could grow some cotton!" He was glad that the kids today "don't have to pick cotton the way I used to. It used to really hurt me." But on second thought, he and Clarence decided, a little of that would do the current generation some good.

"My grandson's been with us for the past three weeks," Lonzo said. "I just carried him home. He couldn't be still a minute the whole time. I don't think he rested at night. I told him, 'I wish you could drop sody [sodium nitrate] for just one day – carry it in your arm and drop from it all day like I used to do. Then you wouldn't have no trouble bein' still at night.'"

Azilee Adams

Azilee Mize Adams, born in 1926, was one of the unsung supporters of the National Convention. She was an alto, but not a prominent singer. Her cooking, her helpfulness to others and her steadfast attendance were her main contributions. For about 30 years, she joined three others of us ~ Sarah Beasley, Warren Steel and me – in attending every year's session.

She and her husband, Ralph, who died about 1988, had grown up in Winston County – he as a member of a large singing family, with siblings including notable singers Pernie Pelfrey, Ora Lee Fannin, Emily Jones and Kermit Adams (who at this writing is 93 and still a frequent leader at singings). It was Ralph's father, Azilee told me (Kermit later correcting somewhat that recollection), who built the schoolhouse in Double Springs, from rock quarried nearby, during the Great Depression – and who did so "on the credit."

Mr. Adams, according to Azilee and Kermit, had known that payment would be deferred, and waited patiently for it for a full year afterwards when the county was at last able to compensate him. That was surely one of many accommodations citizens made in those times.

In the early years of the National, Azilee and Ralph had put up many out-of-town guests for the convention. In the last few years, after a stroke had slowed her and she was no longer able to drive, I would pick her up early each morning during the convention and take her with me. Carrying the bountiful basket or two of food from her house to the car and then inside the convention site, I could attest to her prodigious cooking. In the years when the convention met in Homewood, Azilee's place was not far off my route. When it moved just over into Shelby County – the opposite direction from her home – I had to go out of my way a considerable distance to pick her up. But having her in conversation more than made up for the inconvenience. Aside from the stories she told, her lingo was always so appealing.

Azilee's house was hidden away in a fairly crowded, circularly plotted suburb that I found difficult to navigate. Each year when I would call to confirm the directions, she would refer me past a couple of "little *grassy* spots. . . ." The grassy spots turned out to be small neighborhood parks. Then, when we were in the car, she would direct me through a series of back-roads – "pig trails," she called them – that took us out of the main traffic flow and saved us time.

Once when the two of us had touched on a conspicuous absence at a singing convention, following an awkward change in leadership, Azilee had summed up her view of the matter in typically pithy style: "Some folks, if they can't be the big dog, won't be no dog at all."

And speaking of dogs: a sight I frequently noticed in the neighborhood when I picked her up each morning for the 2008 convention was young women walking or running on the sidewalks, often in athletic attire, and just as often with a dog on a leash. It was noticeable enough to remark on it, and I almost did. But Azilee beat me to it when we passed yet another young woman with her dog.

"Look there," she said and pointed. "I told my daughter, 'If I get to where all I've got to do is walk a dog, just get out the old shotgun and shoot me. . . . I mean it, just go ahead and shoot me.'"

Murillo's Lesson

By everyone's account, it's a great tune – and with its jaunty, patriotic fife-and-drum spirit, signally different from every other piece in the book. It's typically a song newcomers are attracted to early on, and, with ROCKY ROAD a close second, the one most often requested by non-singers at traditional sessions. (It was also, I should confess, the first song I ever led.) A scene from a good many years back frames it well: Dan Hopper, often the chair of the annual singing at Gum Pond near Eva, Ala., had just finished leading page 43, PRIMROSE HILL, at a small gathering, when an elderly woman in the back called out a question. "Was that Mariller's Lesson?" (At least, I could think, she hadn't confused it when we sang AMAZING GRACE.) "No," he said, and with a slight pause, "but we could sing that if you wanted. . . ." "Yes!" she said. "Sing that one!"

At the sounding of that always enthusiastic request, a virtual groan, with a few weary smiles, may pass through the class. For many veteran singers, the song – and ROCKY ROAD, too – has long since had most of the sweetness pulsed out of it. At Ider's Antioch Church, when number 358 has been called, I've in the past noticed Terry Wootten, front bench master and keyer of the music, looking back over his shoulder and shouting out for the back of the room: "Everybody listen up – we're about to sing MURILLO'S LESSON!" You wouldn't, in other words, want to have to sing it more than once because those in the back had not been paying attention as the tune first went by.

With all of that as perspective, I was a little surprised when an elderly Irvin Creel sounded the call for "Mariller's Lesson" when he was tapped to lead at Little Vine one year. I didn't know him and didn't recall having seen him before. He was announced as being 90 or close to it, as I remember, and it was evident he was related to the many other Creels in the room. I later found out he was the youngest brother of Charlie Creel: father, grandfather and great-grandfather of most of the Creels present.

As he stood before the class, Mr. Creel told a brief story accounting for his sentiments for the old warhorse. When he was a young man, he said, he was courting a girl in the community, the daughter of "Aunt Minnie Motte" ("Mote," as he pronounced it). On those occasions when he visited the Motte homeplace, he was called into the parlor, where Aunt Minnie lay. "Every time I ever went there, she was on her deathbed," he said. By Aunt Minnie's request, then, he would sing MURILLO'S LESSON for her, and she would join in.

Later, maybe after he and the young Miss Motte had parted ways, he got word that Aunt Minnie had died. He just had time that day to get to the funeral. Arriving, he was told that Aunt Minnie had requested, for the service, that he, alone, sing MURILLO'S LESSON. And so he did, and so he asked us now to sing it with and for him.

Like a soaking rain on parched ground: the story of Aunt Minnie Motte, a dying request and the figure of Irvin Creel restored sweetness to that song for me.

A Country Craftsman and the Song That Started It All

The thumping, robust songs of John Hocutt (1916-2005) have long been perennial favorites, each year placing themselves among the numbers that have "been used" most often at singing sessions across the now-wide Sacred Harp community.

I first saw John, a key front-bench figure, in action at the Cullman courthouse singings and at other sessions close around. We weren't immediately familiar. At that point at least, he simply wasn't the type to walk over and introduce himself to a visitor or extend a welcome. And feeling myself something of an outsider in those early years, I didn't press myself on anyone. I can't say I found John dour exactly; I did see an occasional smile, but it seemed a sheltered expression. Over the years, he seemed to me to have mellowed, but it was probably just that our early, stilted acquaintance had by then loosened up. In time he became one of my favorites, a figure with quiet humor and warming smile. Of our many conversations, one left an indelible impression: his story about the song that made him a Sacred Harp singer.

In typical stance: John Hocutt, 1998 National. (Photo by Joel Cohen)

He didn't grow up singing Sacred Harp, he told me. Surprisingly, it was new-book singing that formed his early shape-note experience. When he was about eight, though, he accompanied his parents to a Sacred Harp gathering. And it all turned for him when he heard the class break out number 53, JERUSALEM – in particular, that bold bass entrance in the chorus followed by a soaring tenor line.

To the unseasoned ear, especially to that of a child, Sacred Harp can seem a mishmash, a jangle - I think it must have seemed so to me the first time I heard it - with the melody submerged, hidden. I suppose it's not surprising then that it would be JERUSALEM with its surging melody, its strong, deliberate beat that would separate itself from the other songs in the young Hocutt's hearing and beckon to him in a way that it may not have to other family members. And that this childhood scene would remain all his life a stirring memory. (His brothers Harley and Owen (Woody) did later join him at a good many singings over the years.) That clarion call lifted him that day in that setting and ultimately placed him down in the center of a tradition where, surely, he would do his life's best work: singing, leading and composing Sacred Harp songs. He left us with sturdy, cleverly crafted pieces - among them, REDEMPTION, THE RESURRECTION DAY, ZION and A THANKFUL HEART - that unquestionably have done some beckoning of their own.

Ozetta

Ozetta Gilliland's name was found on convention memorial lists for the year 1998. Singers who had only come to Sacred Harp in the previous couple of decades might not have associated a portrait with that name, though many of the longtime crowd certainly would.

A sprightly type, no bigger than a minute, Ozetta slipped under the ordinary boundaries of life and lived to the age of 100. When I first took up Sacred Harp, I had the pleasure of singing with her husband, Celie (C.H.), on the tenor row, and later, when I started singing treble, got to sit with her on the other bench. The Gillilands were from lower Sand Mountain, around Albertville and Boaz, where Cecil, their son and also a singer, then lived.

I had not seen Ozetta for more than 20 years when she died - she spent the last years of her life in a nursing home - but she is framed in my memory in a single vibrant image. I see her, in my mind's eye, out on the floor at a big singing. Page 456 was her frequent choice, Marcus Cagle's SACRED MOUNT, and she always led a spirited rendition.

With her open book held down at her side, she would stride back and forth at a furious pace, exhorting the tenor class, her leading hand a blur of up and down, until – at the last second and quick as a rabbit (". . . till to the sacred mount you RISE . . .") – she would wheel to the tribble to ask for the high *La*.

She had that song down pat (as she did MILFORD, another favorite), and no one I ever saw lead – maybe not even, in his heartier days, the long-striding Edd Snell of the Wiregrass singers – put more motion into a lesson. Most anyone else, with more weight for gravity to tug at, would have been heaving midway through the course of notes plus words. But she flew, and led us swiftly with her. In my mind, I add her to that class of unimaginable number, the ones who have gone before.

Shades of Singing School

The singing schools of Colonial times were often described as providing a fresh diversion for the youth. Explaining in part the schools' "enormous popularity," musicologist Irving Lowens wrote: "No doubt the youngsters welcomed the break in routine provided by the chance to learn to read music, but they also used the singing-school as a place where they could make new friends, exchange notes, flirt, walk home together after lessons, and, in general, enjoy themselves."[28]

Old-timers in the South, remembering what must at times have seemed a long and punishing exercise in full-summer heat, didn't always describe their experience in idealized terms. Velton Chafin, right at 90 at the time, once followed someone into the square who had just led 209, EVENING SHADE:

The day is past and gone,
The ev'ning shades appear;
O may we all remember well
The night of death is near.

In one of the singing schools he had attended as a boy, Velton said, singing-master Joe Myers had had his charges sing 209 as their closing song "at 3:00 every day for four weeks straight." "It was about a hundred degrees in that church," Velton said, "no air-conditioning, of course. No fan." He mentioned a Calvert fellow as being one of the ones there with him during that late June-July stretch, and then added: "I don't think I ever saw one of those boys lead that song again. . . ."

And Not Just Singing Schools . . .

Just as I attempt to put a nostalgic gloss to the years before my time, something like Velton's anecdote pops up, bringing with it not only a bit of humor but a stiffening whiff of reality. And of course it wasn't only the last century's early singing schools that came up shy of the idyllic. Singing conventions like the century-and-a-quarter-old Cotaco Convention in the upper northeastern section of Alabama the fourth weekend of July emerged most years in sweaty mornings and played out through sweltering afternoons. The democratic spirit of those rustic events was ever-apparent. But Wilda Holmes, a participant at the Cotaco from her youth on, once mentioned to me another kind of democracy in those pre-deodorant days: "One thing about it," she said, "everybody smelled the same."

Singing for Tom Harper

POSTED NOVEMBER 24, 1996

Some 50 singers gathered at the funeral home in Jasper, Ala., Saturday morning (many of them missing the opening session of the Alabama State Convention roughly an hour's drive away) to sing for one of our best-beloved. Elder Ricky Harcrow made the stirring and sweet remarks that followed the singing. It was a fine class and a beautiful sound, particularly rich with bass. Leading songs were Elmer Conwill, Velton Chafin, Hugh McGraw, John Hocutt, Glenn Keeton, Joe Gilmore and possibly a few more I'm forgetting.

Tom Harper: Seated here, but most often remembered in stepping-off, half-bent-over lead-ing style. (Photo by Ginnie Ely, 1998 National)

The singers outnumbered the non-singers at the service – not surprisingly, I think, since Uncle Tom, at 93, had outlived the regular friends, neighbors and family of his generation. His Sacred Harp family, of course, was of all ages. He was someone who knew the great Sacred Harp world of the '20s and '30s. Sang with the teaching Densons. Frequented the courthouse singings of that era. As someone has commented, surely no one among us loved to sing or lead more than he. Even late in his life, if someone called out from the floor, "Uncle Tom, you have a request for a song?" – his reply, some three-digit number, would be sudden, and the group would laugh at the keen edge of his readiness. Such gusto in his singing and in his distinctive leading style, as he would stand (in those years when he could do so, and that was still very late in life) half bent over, slapping the air, palms down, to punctuate the beat. Singing Sacred Harp – and anyone who knew him would say so – seemed the very breath of his life. Ricky Harcrow said during the service that he had seen crowds at singings "almost come to shouts" watching Uncle Tom lead – and "seen him almost come to shouts himself!"

When Hugh McGraw stood to lead his songs, he mentioned that he first knew Uncle Tom in the 1950s. "I don't think I ever knew him to lead anything but 'class songs.' He loved class songs." Tom's daughter, Ila Ingle, smiled and nodded. And so, for the most part, we sang class songs for the allotted hour: ETERNAL HOME, MORNING PRAYER, SCHENECTADY, FILLMORE, ETERNAL DAY, MORNING SUN, A CROSS FOR ME, A GLAD NEW SONG and others.

With memories of many hours of singing with this sweet-tempered, grand old man still fresh, I leave this scene with the words to Tom Denson's COSTON, another of the class songs we sang Saturday morning:

> Dear friends, farewell! I do you tell,
> Since you and I must part;
> I go away and here you stay,
> But still we're joined in heart.

Broker Becker

Earl Becker was a real estate broker I came to know when I worked in the Florida Panhandle in the mid-2000s. Broker Becker we called him. He stood tall for his age: maybe late 70s, early 80s. He was a friendly sort and generally knowledgeable – including, as it turned out, knowledgeable about Sacred Harp singing in his youth in Clay County, Ala., on the east-central side of the state.

Earl grew up four miles from Cheaha State Park, which includes Cheaha Mountain, at 2,413 feet the highest point in the state (and more than 2,000 feet higher than the highest elevation in Florida). He went to Highland School in the community of Pyriton, the same school as in a photo in my 1978 book. He was raised by his grandparents and went with his grandfather to singings at Campbell's Cross Roads, just north of Ashland, in the mid-'30s – after the crops were "laid by," in late July or early August.

They ate well at those singings, Earl recalled. Mac Patterson, he said, would kill a calf and barbecue it. Earl's granddaddy would barbecue a goat. He remembered those old men, in their bib overalls and white shirts, sweating in the heat.

In the first school that Earl attended, he recalled that the teacher rode a horse or mule the four miles over the mountain each day to get to the little community of five families. That memory, in turn, led to his recounting his grandfather's thoughts on a practice that developed in his day: the busing of schoolchildren – "so they can get 'em to school, where they can take Physical Education – when, if they walked to school, they wouldn't need it!" The consumer market for two staples in today's world Earl was sure his grandfather would find just as stupefying: "people paying money for bottled water and pine straw!"

Not Buford's Bees, but . . .

Mr. Hugh, now a widower in his mid-80s, was about as far from a Sacred Harp singer as you could imagine. He was not, that I know of, at all musical – or interested in being so. His voice went way past being gravelly (though in that respect, he could remind one of an elderly Tom Harper) and on over toward sounding like heavy farm equipment scraping over pavement. That didn't stop him from using it, though.

He was tall and lean and a country dweller, like Buford McGraw, but only the connection with bees would have linked the two in my mind. Where Buford was terse, Mr. Hugh – he and I always exchanged greetings as Mr. Hugh and Mr. Buell – was talkative, and then some (and I thought "Uncle Joe" – or I – was hard to get away from). He had been a truck driver in earlier decades, and he could recall – and would love to tell you about – all his stops along the way, the distances between each, the fee he was paid for every lonely trip. . . . He spared no anecdote – like the one about how, when he was routinely driving overloaded at night, he would, just before the state line coming out of Louisiana (with highway officer parked nearby), turn off his head-lights for a mile or two, so he and his cargo could skip past oversight. He relished each tale anew. And funny how one reminded him of another. . . .

But where Buford summed up the bee as "curiousest and most peculiarest," Mr. Hugh filled in the considerable blanks around that summation. At a visit to our family farm in Shelby County, just south of the Birmingham area, he once became expansive about the crea-ture he, like Buford, found most fascinating. And Buford himself could not have been more impressed by those swarming back-field residents than was Mr. Hugh: "Them bees keep the temperature of the hive *steady* at 92-93 degrees, winter *or* summer. Why, they the smartest creatures God ever created! Them professors at Auburn and Alabama, with all their education . . . them bees know more'n any of 'em. Why, one of them professors would just walk into yo' house, but bees ain't goin' into a house that ain't theirs [hives, he meant]! Look at the Bible, where a man lived on honey and locusts. . . . Bees were there back in Bible days!" And so on.

Mr. Hugh was evidently not up on bee home-invasions, but he was ever alert to the possibility of encroachment by others. He was a lib-ertarian in spirit if there ever was one, fiercely protective of property and family honor (he had been arrested one time for knocking out a longtime neighbor who had "insulted" his wife, that wisp of a fig-ure he always gallantly referred to as "Miss Effie"). On one occasion (actually, more than one), he tickled me with a story about a neighborhood vigilante determined to destroy Mr. Hugh's and others' bees. The cantankerous subject of that story, a longtime beekeeper, had decided that mites from other hives were infecting his own bees – and he determined to burn out the offending hives. Mr. Hugh had already heard how the fellow had burned those of another neighbor, who had yielded to the questionable logic. And one day shortly afterwards, he looked out to see this meddler striding across his field, with gas can in hand.

"Hey! Where you goin'?"

"I'm gonna burn your hives – your bees are killin' off mine with their mites!"

Those may not have been the exact words, just an approximation; the rest of the conversation I tried to fix in memory.

"Well, have you been to Columbiana [the county seat] yet?"

"Columbiana? No, what for?!"

"To pick out your pine box – 'cause if you burn my bees, you're gonna need it!"

The intruder, can in hand, retreated. And Mr. Hugh, whose voice was as rough as rusty prison bars, was clearly pleased in telling and retelling how he had defended his land and those amazing creatures of God that busied themselves so intelligently there.

Bud Oliver in Conversation

June 14, 2009, Hopewell Primitive Baptist Church

I knew and sang with J.W. "Bud" Oliver for many years, and we chatted often when we met up at singings throughout the territory. But on this day, as we sat together briefly before the afternoon session started up, Bud's conversation strayed over into an area of his early life he'd never shared with me before.

Once when he was a young man, he said, he had "been out late" the night before, drinking and carousing, maybe – and was trying to sleep-in a little that morning.

Bud Oliver: An inspiring singer, leader and lemonade-maker. (Photo by Nate and Norma Green, April 2006)

His father had already gone to work, he said. His grandfather, who was then living with them after his wife had died, was having a breakfast prepared by his daughter, Bud's mother.

Through the bedroom wall, Bud could hear his grandfather talking about him. "He'll never be worth a dime," he heard. "He'll end up being just like Clarence!" [Bud's uncle, who, he said, had been "a drunk"].

Bud chuckled about that early rendering of his career and character.

"That was a shock to me, hearing that. My grandfather saying that, telling his daughter that her son would never be worth a dime!"

And then he remembered another jolt to the ego.

"That was about as big a shock as hearing my daddy tell me I couldn't sing bass.

"I had just come home from the war, and I was at a singing. I sat down on bass between Daddy and Uncle Orphy [O.D. Oliver]. At the first recess, my daddy said, 'Son, you need to find another part to sing – you're not any good at bass.'

"That was the last bass I ever sang."

Hearing that pure tenor voice, no one who ever sat near Bud at a singing could have regretted Daddy Oliver shooing his son off the bass part for good.

A Song for Doing Battle

Hugh McGraw, with some amusement, related to me back in the early '70s a letter he had received from some young hippie rebels in Chicago who had gotten into Sacred Harp and who had ordered songbooks from him. This one of their party who wrote said that just before daylight – before they went out to do battle with the establishment – they liked to gather and sing the song MORNING! Imagine these words in such a setting, or at such a purpose: "A solemn darkness veils the skies, / A sudden trembling shakes the ground."

We don't know what happened to those young comrades; as best I can tell, there's no link between them and the singing Chicagoans we later knew. When I mentioned the story to Hugh a few years back, he could no longer retrieve it; intrigued as I was when I first heard it, I haven't been able to forget.

The Lamar and Pickens County Convention

Posted August 11, 2000

Though this singing out from Gordo, Ala. (25 miles southwest of Tuscaloosa), still keeps the name of a convention and is reported to have been sizable in its heyday, it's just a very small, one-day country singing these days.

There were about a dozen singers in the class up front, with maybe a half-dozen more sitting further back and singing on some of the better-known songs. Ten or twelve listeners completed the group. Roughly half of those singing had earlier-edition books.

At lunchtime we were considerably outnumbered by a swarm of flies, which quickly descended on the ample lunch spread along a table under a big tree (a chicken house nearby was someone's explanation). I fought my way through the pests to get two pieces of pecan pie – well worth the initiative, as it turned out.

Clarence McCool was chairman of the convention. His two sisters were there as well, Earline Ellis and Annie Price. Earline was the first woman I ever saw provide her own pitch at a singing, a good many years ago in Tuscaloosa, and she did so again today.

Toney Smith, along with his wife, Lavoy, made a surprise appearance. Lavoy had suffered a stroke within 30 minutes of Toney's return from the National Convention back in June. She is recovering well and walks with a walker, but Toney's travel to singings is now curtailed. His bass and pitching, though, made the difference today.

When I was called to lead, I scribbled my name on a small piece of paper and handed it to the secretary. I had reviewed the previous year's minutes before heading off this morning, and didn't see my name. I then saw the songs I thought I had led last year – listed with the name Mual Coble. . . .

At lunch, I spoke to Etma Barton, a slight, spirited woman who last Sunday had laid it on me heavily to join this small group again today. "You did what I told you to, didn't you?" she said, and gave me a significant look. I passed by her again down the table, just as her daughter told someone that Etma was 92, soon to be 93. "Hush!" she said. "I've told you not to tell that. I'm never gonna get a boyfriend now!" She led 300, CALVARY, in the morning session, and told the front bench to "move it along."

After lunch she led again and faltered only twice. She called for 289 and then when she got there, didn't want GREENSBOROUGH. 389? someone asked. "No, MONTGOMERY," she said. Oh, 189. When we finished that off, she said, "What number is SARDIS?" 460, several of us said and turned to it. She continued to flip pages. Exasperated, she finally said, "It's not in my book!" Lonzo Malone was Johnny-on-the-spot.

He swapped books with her, and then saw the problem: "There's two pages stuck together!" (Funny, isn't it, how at any age the simplest of things can leave us confounded and then, in quick reversal, bring us again to clarity.)

One other moment from the singing comes to me. A woman of some years led two or three songs without beating time. Instead she clasped her open book from the top with both hands. At the bass repeat on the first song, she tilted the book *slightly* in that direction. On the next song, LET US SING, she didn't turn her head toward Clarence and me on the treble entrance, but just looked toward us out of the corner of her eye. When great signs are absent, we look for little signs. And in both cases, the class acquitted itself well. Though the good woman was perhaps uncomfortable separating her hands from the book, she had nodded to tradition, and tradition led us on.

The appearance or absence of only two or three singers, in cases such as this, can determine whether to call off an annual event of 79 years' standing. When I first attended one of the sessions several years ago, it was the same: Will we have enough this time, or will we have to give in? Again this time we had just enough. The chairman asked us to come back again next year; it will be bigger and better, he said with a smile. [And for now, the singing persists.]

Human Nature? Freeman's Good Story . . .

Freeman Wootten and I sat together at many a singing and during the breaks shared many a chuckle. He was once as tickled as could be, the laughter just chugging up out of him, as he recalled a man at a country church who had gotten caught up in the spirit of the moment and started testifying, in a vision, unfortunately, collapsible under its own weight. Speaking excitedly, this fellow had asked everybody present to pray that he would live a better life in the coming year than the one he was now living – but then abruptly: "'Course, I don't have no idee that I will. . . .'"

Singing for Mamie Creel

POSTED FEBRUARY 14, 1998

On Tuesday the tenth we sang for Mamie Creel, who was born in 1901 and who died Saturday the seventh. She was the last of her generation, the surviving daughter of one of the patriarchs of Sacred Harp singing in north Alabama in the early years of the century, Singin' Jim Reid. They were from Reid's Gap in the countryside near Warrior, north of Birmingham.

Mamie and Mattie Reid, sisters seven years apart, married twin brothers, Chester and Hester Creel. These proved to be sturdy, life-long unions. One of Hester's and Mattie's daughters is Kathleen Robbins, a leader we stop to watch for the sheer beauty of the act, a fluid mastery of movement in leading a "class song."

Those who have visited Little Vine or Old County Line any of the last few years may have seen Mamie and noticed the great deference accorded her by other members of the Reid-Creel family. They tell me she suffered considerably the last few months of her life.

Mamie sang a keen tribble ("as clear as a bell" when her voice was young, Kathleen said), and Mattie sang alto; Chester, bass ("beautiful and smooth") and Hester, tenor. A ready-made quartet. I don't know if they took advantage of that fact and sang on their way to and from singings, in wagon or automobile, through those decades. What I do know is that they were stalwarts in the class – every song, every note. And they must have "carried dinner" – fried okra and turnip greens, ham and sweet potatoes – many hundreds of times over the years.

They were plainspoken people, when they spoke at all in public, and what they said counted. Chester and Hester were miners and part-time farmers. If you wanted a portrait of Sacred Harp folk in the decades preceding ours, Chester and Mamie, Hester and Mattie Creel would have been fitting subjects. They were, in all the ways I can think of, representative of the ordinary, extraordinary people who kept and guarded and loved with a full spirit the essence of the singing tradition, the thing that brings us to this site to talk and listen and wonder about, the thing that catches us, sometimes unexpectedly, in awe.

Mattie Creel I can see now as I used to see her at the Cullman courthouse singings, on the front row of the alto, her book (as often closed as open) on her lap, both hands lightly pumping time with the music, with a flared, bent-knuckle hand motion: ". . . by night or noon, by night or noon. . . ." When she was just a girl, Mattie was said to be the first "woman" to lead at the Mulberry River Convention.

Mamie, a widow for more than 20 years, was a diminutive figure with her hair always wound in a circlet of double braids. In the years when I first used to see her, she always wore a hat (and wore one when most of the other women in her company no longer did, through the '70s, maybe up into the '80s) – not always the same one, I'm sure, though in my mind's eye I see a black or navy form, simple but significant.

Mamie's great-grandson, now a preacher, opened the remarks at the funeral service, and Elder Ricky Harcrow gave a moving testimony about her life and her faith. Before the service started, we sang for an hour. Two rows of tenor sat at the front, followed by a row of treble, a row of alto, and a half-row of bass (though they were not short-handed with Charles Kitchens, Harrison Creel, Milton Oliver and Thurman Nall – along with Ricky Harcrow sitting on the front). The altos were right behind me, and it was wonderful to hear that solid sound, like a big wave pressing against my shoulders.

John Hocutt led most of the singing. I saw again that characteristic touch. At the close of many of the songs, he would cut the last note off with a quick, upward thrust of his right hand, forefinger extended, the way you might cut a taut cord with a knife.

For most of the songs we sang to start with, the half-pagers toward the front of the book, we sang notes and all or most verses, but not the repeats. A reservation, unspoken, hovered there – as if the repeat would be an indulgence or affectation. When we got to LIVERPOOL, though, the whole class pushed through to the repeat.

Together the songs were a feast of memory. JACKSON, CORINTH, WEBSTER, OGLETREE, SWEET RIVERS, THE GOLDEN HARP, STRUGGLE ON, FLEETING DAYS, GOLDEN STREETS, WEEPING SINNERS, SAINTS BOUND FOR HEAVEN (when we sang "our three-score years and ten," I thought of how far Mamie's span had eclipsed that estimate), SAINT'S DELIGHT ("This is one of them old-time songs," John said), THE GOSPEL POOL (John: "One of her fay-vo-rites"), 36b, 119, 123t, 129, 48t, 285t, 111b, 72b, 82t . . . .

It was what Mamie Creel was privileged to hear, and to join in on, for almost all of her long life – good country singing.

She was buried at Little Vine, along with Chester, Hester and Mattie.

Hopewell Hospitality

POSTED JUNE 14, 1998

The second weekend in June for a good number of us means Hopewell Primitive Baptist Church, near Oneonta, Ala. For some years, Virgil Phillips has been the chief presence at this event, and, though hooked up to oxygen almost the entire time and struggling for breath at certain points, he was again the main figure today (who seemed greatly gratified by all that transpired).

Of the two-day singing, I attended only the Sunday session. There were Iveys, Woottens, Sheppards, Ballingers, Creels and Greens, and in the afternoon the sound was such that the low-hanging ceiling seemed in danger of splitting open.

We could no doubt stir up a real commotion by trying to name the top dinner tables out on the singing circuit. But in such a ranking, Hopewell, year in and year out, would have to be among the ones vying for highest honor. A long set of tables under the awning out by the trees is each year laden with all one could wish for in a midday meal.

A fine breeze cooled us throughout the lunch hour today. I noticed that flies, a perennial presence at this table, could be downgraded, as someone has said, from scourge to mere annoyance. (I remember Jewel Wootten one year slowly waving a pine bough over her section of the table, so that visitors could select from the delectables there without so much pesky interference.) I soon knew the reason why. Elwyn Thomas (singer Linda's husband, and now leading in a run-off for his party's candidacy for state representative from Blount County) told me he had been out early to spray insect repellant – a practice, I might say, that should serve him well in the legislature, if we're fortunate enough to see him there.

But on to the food itself. You might know that I would be partial to cobbler. My favorite pie, in fact, is coconut cream – or any kind at all of cobbler. It so happens that one of the features of the extraordinary table at Hopewell each year is the sweet potato cobbler heaped up by Virgil's sister Alma.

I had probably enjoyed that cobbler – and didn't know whose it was – for a couple of years or more before I began to notice that it was there each time and always in the same place. In a large oval dish of midnight-blue-speckled crockery, it sits deeply just on the other side of the drinks and plates that you see when you start down the line of tables. Year before last, I think, as I came upon it, I eyed it but decided to start with the basics and then come back to dessert. But generously endowed as it had seemed at the time, it was all but gone when I made my way down and then back up. I was surprised, but not as surprised as I was about to be.

As I lifted the big spoon to transfer the remaining scrapings to my plate, one of Virgil's other sisters came up close by me and said, behind the back of her hand, "You know why that's so good, don't you?" No, I had to say, I didn't. "She puts five pounds of sugar in it!" she said, and laughed at the secret now spilled.

I was retelling that episode to David Ivey across the table today as he reached into the blue-speckled tub (I think I had already spooned out my portion, basic foods to be added later), and Alma, grinning, said over his shoulder – just as she had confessed before when I had asked her – "It *is* just a cup and a half shy of that." Five pounds. More or less.

Further down the tables, I was talking to Eloise Avery, who grew up in the Hopewell community. She said that Virgil and Alma's mother used to make a cobbler in a big washtub on one day of the singing and chicken-and-dumplings in it the other day. "She always had a white cloth that she would put around that tub when she put it on the table, and then she would tie it." And when the event was over, Eloise said, Mrs. Phillips would wash and dry the cloth and clean out and scald the tub. She then would fold the cloth, put it in the tub, and put the tub inside a big cloth sack. She only used the cloth and the tub for those big occasions. Is that not country cleanliness at its essence and a beautiful ritual besides?

Hospitality there is more than a ritual, though, and sometimes it beggars imagination. Eloise told me she had once asked Virgil about the largest number of guests his parents had put up at their place for a singing or church meeting. His answer was 72.

They had a big porch around the house when Virgil was growing up, Eloise said, and at times bales of cotton were stacked up on it. On the weekends of those big community events, guests slept inside on the floor, on a quilt if they were lucky enough to get one, and all around the porch on laid-up cotton, in the (cotton) seed house and in the barn loft. They laid children across a bed, one right next to the other. "Get off-a me!" she said you would sometimes hear in a child's voice well into the night.

Virgil once told her about a preacher in a blue serge suit who stayed there on one of those occasions. In those days and in those circumstances, as she said, a serge suit made a statement; it was an "I have arrived" sort of look. On this particular morning after, the preacher, who had slept out on the porch or in the seed house or loft, appeared around the corner of the house – with cotton wisps, like a fine white powder, all over that blue serge. He had indeed arrived.

Hopewell, the second weekend in June, always means good singing. But it's distinguished – for most of us in attendance, I think

– by something more: community, and the exuberant hospitality of a community.

Jessie Lee

Jessie Lee Bishop, from around Lanett, Ala., was a woman of some age that I used to see at area singings in the late 1960s-70s. She was an accomplished singer and a good-humored, if somewhat formidable, figure. I quoted her anonymously in my 1978 book, as I made the point that variances from the printed pages of the songbook were often handled with admirable simplicity by the singers in actual rendition. Jessie Lee's remark to the class after she finished leading a song on that particular occasion was: "Now I know enough about music to know that that song doesn't have a repeat sign at the end, but I *wanted* to repeat it, so I did."

She had a particular conceit that amused me. When called to lead, if she didn't already have a tune in mind, she would sometimes say that she would "let the book decide" or "let this book tell me what to sing" – and then, with but minor flourish, allow the big oblong to fall open across her hands at any random page. It would have been a slight to her pride if the book had signaled a song beyond her reckoning. I'm comfortable in thinking that never happened.

Flora Skinner

I saw Flora Skinner only twice, once when she was 88 and the second time a little over three years later. Both sightings made an impression.

The first glimpse was at the 1996 Young People's Singing, at the good little wood-framed church on the Burritt Museum grounds, out from Huntsville. The second was at the Uncle Bob Burnham Memorial singing, just off the square at Jacksonville, Ala. And a few words about those two occasions:

Huntsville was not a storied place for Sacred Harp, though it was not far from other communities that were (and though the Madison

County courthouse there had an annual singing for probably a good many years). But within the past few decades it had gained a number of representatives from strong old singing families from surrounding areas. Brothers Sam and Joe Jones were descendants of M.F. McWhorter, who in 1908 wrote the tune for JACKSON ("I am a stranger here below" – the song that Donald Smith, himself a Primitive Baptist elder, called, with a smile, "the Primitive Baptists' national anthem"). Paul Frederick was the son of Floyd Frederick, who composed AT REST and SUPPLICATION. Ballingers, originally from Fayette County, were in the community. Pam Wilkerson represented Sand Mountain's Wootten clan. A number of the Hoppers lived nearby. These and other traditional singers, to all appearances, blended beautifully with a number of newcomers to the tradition. Much of the success for that blending must to be credited to David and Karen Ivey, whose genial presences were felt throughout the singing session. Also present on that late September day were Virgil and Ruby Philips, Linda Thomas, Bud Oliver, Amanda Denson Brady and, from far-off Texas, Leon Ballinger. An outstanding singing in this one-room building that really rings with the sound, the event had a solid representation of young folks (Cassie Franklin chaired the day, with Allison Ivey as vice-chair).

A reminiscence about the Burritt singing place that I once shared with the class there occurs to me now: I was mid-morning arriving at the church on that occasion, and I heard strong surges of sound from inside as I strode hurriedly up to the steps. A handrail separated left side from right, and on the other side of it, coming down the steps, were a couple of women of a certain age who appeared to be bringing their early visit to a conclusion. One of them looked over at me, as if in explanation as she stepped down, and said, "You've got to have *good ears* to stay in there!" Throw me in that briar patch! – I thought to myself, and bounded on up the steps.

My highlight of this particular session, though, was seeing Flora Skinner, a new singer to my eyes, though she turned out not to be a new singer at all. I had noticed her on the front row of the alto that day, but she was pretty much hidden from my view during most of the session. David mentioned that she was originally from Cleburne County, a good bit to the south and east (and one county over from the one in which the Jacksonville singing was held). I assumed she had not often been able to attend singings for many years or I would have seen her before.

She led with what seemed a beatific attitude. Called to lead after lunch, she asked for REESE. She led a steady rendition through the notes, and then, requesting a quicker tempo, finished the words off in spirited fashion. MURILLO'S LESSON she called for next and dispatched it with a beaming smile. There's a whole world out there beyond the book if you can free your eyes from it while singing, and I made this visual note as Mrs. Skinner led: Rather than beating time up and down, she used lateral motions. Sweeping her hand back and forth, she seemed to be smoothing out disheveled air. On a day for pledging and celebrating the future of Sacred Harp, she seemed very happy and very much at home.

Flora Skinner leading, at 93: As if smoothing out disheveled air. (Photo by Martha Beverly, 2001)

The Jacksonville singing, too, had as usual a fine class and many high moments – and throughout the day the regal presence of Ruth Burnham Brown. Ruth had been among the company who made the historic appearance at the Waldorf Astoria in 1952, and in the intervening decades had led a number of charter-bus trips to singing events far out of region.

At 91, Mrs. Skinner, a contemporary of Ruth Brown, seemed that day not to have lost a step. She led FILLMORE before lunch and did so with characteristic style, lovely to watch. Before the afternoon session ended, she was requested to lead again – and brought up 426b, JASPER, the Tom Denson fuging tune from 1935. Watching her lead it, I thought of how that song and others of its vintage must have been for those of her generation – like A THANKFUL HEART is for many of us, a song written by one from our own time, a grand old man of the tradition (John Hocutt in our case), that blossoms before us and that, in the company of so much rich music, seems the more special to us for coming from one of our own.

During the lunch hour, I saw David Ivey and Estelle Flowers being entertained by Mrs. Skinner, and I walked over to join them. They were sitting in a cluster of chairs, and Mrs. Skinner had a plate with several desserts on it. She was telling David and Estelle how much she enjoyed her Sacred Harp recordings. Sometimes at night, she said, she would wake up and be unable to sleep. "I just get up and turn on my tapes, get in the rocker – and sometimes I don't go back to sleep till morning, just listening to those tapes."

One of the fine things about aging, for many people, is an increasingly felt freedom from convention: Who after all are we trying to impress? Or what difference would it make anyway? The concept gained concrete reality for me that day in hearing Mrs. Skinner talk about living alone. "That's the good thing about it," she said. "I can go to bed when I want to and get up when I want to. I don't have to get up when the rooster crows."

And then: "But you know what the best thing is about living alone? You know what the *best* thing is? No matter what you've been doing all day . . . you can go to bed at night without washing your feet!"

No Piano . . . ?

Carlton Wood, from Buchanan, Ga., had grown up with Sacred Harp all around. His wife, from Centre, Ala., had not. I first met Faye at a singing in Georgia in 1989, and our conversation that day led her to recount the first time she attended a Sacred Harp singing, some 42 years before. She had gone to visit Carlton, she said, and he took her to a singing at what must have been a Primitive Baptist Church.

She knew that they were going to "a singing" that day, she said, but didn't really know what to expect. Once inside the church, she looked around for the piano – and failed to see one.

"'All right,' I thought, 'I guess I'll find out when they start singing. . . .'

"And when they started, I saw why. You wouldn't have been able to hear it if they'd had one."

Marcus Cagle – Chairing a Songwriting Discussion

His temper, along with his composing and other musical gifts, was legendary. The Sacred Harp's Beethoven.

Although I knew Marcus Cagle only briefly – and then as a genial elderly gentleman – I did hear, over the years, tales of his tirades, stories about that formidable temper.

The one I heard most often, mainly from Hugh McGraw, was about a trip that Marcus, his wife Lena Drake Cagle and fellow Georgians Bill Matthews and Ted Knight had made to a singing convention in Guntersville, Ala. With Cagle at the helm, this was an estimable foursome, good singers all and notable figures in the Sacred Harp world. Knight, in particular, was a man of distinction, much respected throughout the central territory and for a time president of the publishing company. Cagle, for whatever reason, had "pitched a fit!" at the singing, as it was described to me. (I wonder if the Committee for Deportment from earlier conventions would have held him in check.) His pique then flared up again on the drive home. The tantrum evidently frightened, or at least offended, Knight so much that, at a suddenly convenient traffic light, he jumped out of the car, leaving his bags behind, and, for hours, waited in the vicinity for family to come and pick him up (his bags to be picked up later at the Cagle home).

That story is not apocryphal – David Knight, a friend from Cullman and Ted's nephew, told me that Ted's daughters had confirmed it – but the reports about it were, for me, second- or third-hand. Another such story came straight from a one-time recipient of Cagle's ire: Hugh himself.

Around 1965-66, preparations were underway for the new revision of the songbook that would come out in 1966. As the head of the revision committee, of which Marcus was also a member, Hugh paid a visit to the senior figure at his home in Villa Rica, Ga. He wanted to recommend, *ahem*, a change in one of Cagle's earlier compositions. I'LL SEEK HIS BLESSINGS had appeared on page 542 of the previous edition of 1960, and did so to the same compositional formula Cagle would use successfully in six other tunes remaining in the songbook today: an alto and bass duet opening up the chorus. To Hugh and the rest of the committee, the nearly four-measure alto entrance in this case needed to be jettisoned; it detracted from the bass entrance it was paired with, a line that made a powerful case for being allowed to run solo.

Meddling? To the hypersensitive Marcus, this must have seemed like murder-in-progress. How dare they! And that the instigator should be this relative youngster, whom he himself, the acknowledged master of "dispersed harmony," had helped to groom! I can imagine fury rising in him like a rocket in early trajectory. He shouted at Hugh to get out of his house – and never come back! He picked up a nearby chair – he would have been around 80 at the time – and, Hugh said, "he run me out of the house with it!"

The chair, I guess, returned shortly to its place on the kitchen floor; the little scrap of alto went out the window, for good – and for *the* good, it must be said. Hearing that distinctively strong bass line, who, except for the composer, could think an entrance duet had bettered the piece? The song went on to become one of the book's most popular choices. And Marcus apparently settled into an uneasy peace with the single-part intro.

At any rate, Hugh could report: "We later made up, and he asked me to sing at his funeral." At that funeral in 1968, a quartet of Hugh, Charlene Wallace, Joyce Harrison Hamrick and Raymond Hamrick sang a single Sacred Harp song: ALL IS WELL.

More on the Knight Family

The minutes of the 1944 Cullman courthouse convention show a slight additional link between Marcus Cagle and the Knight family. From the convention's Sunday session: "Memorial committee reported the passing of Sister Dicie M. Knight [Ted's mother], Linda Kyle, Grandmother Tingle and asked Bro. Marcus Cagle to sing lesson in their memory." He did so, first leading his own song, NEW HOPE, then following with ODEM and CHRISTIAN SONG.

I once shared that information with David Knight, who had been about two years old when his grandmother died. He in turn shared with me two anecdotes about his grandparents, stories poles apart in tone.

Dicie and Erasmus Taylor (E.T.) Knight raised 11 children, two girls and nine boys – but one, Alvin, only to the age of seven. In that era, there was little recourse when juvenile diabetes struck, and, without infusions of insulin, Alvin was not able to survive when the disease overcame him. David remembered his father telling him about a family event the day following Alvin's burial. Early that morning, Mr. Knight had called his other sons together, told them to help pack the wagon with building supplies and then to ride with him. He gave no explanation, and none of them asked for one. When they came to Alvin's burial spot in the cemetery at Valley Springs Church, the father, leading the effort, began the construction of "a little shed with a tin roof" over the grave. Helpless at last to do anything else for his son, he was moved to erect not a monument but a shelter there – as I can try to grasp it, to cover and somehow protect with the tangible a great intangible.

Another reminiscence passed on to David and then to me captures a scene, from singings of that time, of Dicie Lowry Knight. She was a noted treble, ever devoted to Sacred Harp, as she was to her growing brood. With two children in the toddler stage at one point, she was said at singings to put the two of them down on the floor, one on either side. With her book spread on her lap, she would side-watch both of them, letting each venture only far enough out for her to clamp her foot down on the youngster's loose garment and hold the two of them in place while she sang. Kids will be kids in any era, and parents with youngsters in arms are inevitably challenged at singing sessions. But Momma Dicie knew how to put her foot down. . . .

Densons, Densons . . .

The early vehicles of the last century – in the country, at least – often carried a good many more passengers than present-day regulations would allow. Tales of up to a dozen riders crowding in or about the car, sitting on top of each other or clinging to the car frame over bumpy country roads, bring up a picture almost cartoonish to us today. One such carful figured in a story Dick Nail, Whitt Denson's grandson, once told me. On his way to a singing, the driver in this instance had stopped first to pick up Whitt and his older brother, "Uncle Shell" (Seaborn Ivy Denson). An additional stop or two added more to the mix. Introductions as they rode must have been dispensed with; I somehow see dust flying, chickens squawking. . . . At any rate, something was said in the front seat about some of the Densons being expected at the singing. "Densons, Densons . . . ," one of the others shot back, "there's a lot more folks that can sing better than the Densons!" Uncle Shell's baritone boomed from the back: "That may be – but not in *this* car!"

The Worst Whippin'

The Laminacks were one of the great singing families of the first half of the 20th century. Originally from Georgia, a number of them settled in Cleburne County, Ala., near Fruithurst; others moved on across to the Cullman area. J.D., the oldest of that generation, was pictured in the 1911 James book as one of the members of the Music Revision Committee. J.W. ("Uncle Will") was a well-known member of the revision committee for the '36 Denson book.

The only member of the clan I would have the opportunity to know was Glenn Laminack, who, grandson of Gene and great-nephew of J.D. and J.W, died in 2013 at the age of 96. We first met, and in most years renewed acquaintance, at the National Convention. From Gardendale, just north of Birmingham, Glenn was a guitarist who played publicly for more than 60 years – in the early years accompanying two gospel groups, the Evangeliers and the Triumphants, and playing in a five-piece country-western-gospel band until he was 94. (At about 92, he had traded in one of his instruments for a pricey Super Jumbo Gibson.)

At the 2004 convention he first shared with me a story about how he'd had a reverence for Sacred Harp singing beaten into him, as it were. It was Sacred Harp, he explained, that was responsible for "the worst whippin' I ever got."

As a boy, he was at a singing with his family in the Cullman area. As the long morning session wore on, he found himself increasingly weary of this tedious exercise that, inexplicably, so engaged his elders.

"It was right about dinner time," he remembered. Some of the non-singers from the back of the church had already slipped away and "were done out spreadin' dinner on their wagons – and I had to sit right in there when I's hungry."

At a momentary break between songs, he leaned over to a buddy next to him and said, "I wish they'd tree this thing!" – using an end-of-the-chase, coon-hunting metaphor that any country boy would understand and appreciate. His father, though, overheard, understood and did *not* appreciate. Glancing up, young Laminack caught a withering look.

At home that afternoon, he prepared for his whipping. His father, true to expectations, produced "a brush-broom."

There was a last-second matter of protocol: "Daddy told me, '. . . and don't you move, neither.'

"And I mean he wore it out on me – just wore it *out* on me! I had stripes from one end to the other. . . .

"And I've loved this book ever since," he said, laughing. "I've loved this old book ever since!"

On a Matter of Etiquette . . .

This final item in the chapter is different from the rest. It's a little piece I ghost-wrote for the old Chicago Sacred Harp Newsletter back in the 1980s, when that publication ran a series of "Miss Grace Notes" Q&A's, in parody of the popular "Miss Manners" newspaper columns.

I include it because I'm fond of it – and because, when I've used it in workshops, it's been well-received by participants. I'm fond of it in part because, while I'm normally more of a describer, I in this case get to be a bit of a prescriber. And while I stand by the points made in the column, I found it fun, while dispensing them, to assume the persona of being, well, wickedly correct. . . .

Dear Miss Grace Notes: My favorite song has several verses and when I lead it, I hate to leave any of them out. Lately at conventions I have noticed that some people seem to be irritated when others sing all the verses to a song or take all re-peats. I thought everyone was supposed to respect the leader's right to sing whatever and however he or she wants?

Gentle Singer: Miss Grace Notes sympathizes with your feelings. While going about her chores, she often adds multiple repeats to her favorite songs. She nevertheless recognizes that such indulgences on her own time might be inappropriate in group or convention situations.

If you are talking about three verses to a short song, a repeat on the last, why then we have no issue here. But Miss Grace Notes guesses that you have something more in mind. Sacred Harp singing, as your question suggests, is a democratic institution. The leader's space, however, should not be equated with the Senate floor in filibuster.

Miss Grace Notes agrees that as the leader you have the right to set the way the song is to proceed. But she will not tell you that you can make everyone like it. Just as the class has a responsibility to follow the leader's choice and direction, the leader has a responsibility not to induce tedium.

Convention etiquette is based on practical considerations and simple courtesy. If all verses are sung to every song, each with repeats, we will be singing until midnight, and by then everyone will be singing bass. Similarly, there is a place for a six-page anthem sung with both notes and words ~ your shower stall, perhaps, on a Friday evening, or in the car on your way to an out-of-town session. If you launch into such at a large all-day singing, you should do so with the realization that you will have displaced two or three other leaders and exhausted the charity of your acquaintances.

Miss Grace Notes has always believed that one of the characteristics of a good leader ~ along with sureness, presence, timing and such ~ is a sense of what the class of singers wants, and to what it will cheerfully give its assent. Sometimes that may mean singing an extra verse or, in rare instances, taking another repeat. Seasoning ~ in both the leader's space and the singer's chair ~ will lead to a sense of when to take such a liberty. In the meantime, you are encouraged to follow the pattern of experienced leaders you admire. See what boundaries they observe, and stay well within their good example.

A final distinction, then: someone set for the gallows the following day will no doubt be indulged by the group in a request to have all five verses to his favorite song sung with repeats on each verse. Anyone else making such a stand at a crowded convention should not be surprised to see a noose materialize midway through the lesson.

25

The Auburn Quartet

When I came to Auburn in the fall of '66, I was still in that smitten stage that new Sacred Harp singers anywhere would recognize. I had found the music, the ongoing tradition. I needed now to share it, to find others to join me (in boundless enthusiasm), and especially to find others to sing with. Over the next year, I was fortunate to come upon another graduate student in English, Linda Lee Bolen, who had a high singing voice, clear as a bell. A perfect treble. She turned out to know Tom Richardson, a young instructor in the department who carried a fine bass voice and who had some Sacred Harp family history. And Tom or one or the other of us knew Judy Caruthers, another English grad student with extraordinary musical ability, a mellow contralto voice and some family Sacred Harp connections as well.

I don't recall the particulars of how we got together as a group, but what we needed was at least one person per part, and, with me on tenor, we had that. Whatever about the music's format seemed strange or initially intimidating to the others was offset by the charm of the idea itself: taking up an antique but surviving Southern tradition and body of song – and then ultimately by the sheer appeal of this lively music with its engaging harmonic parts. Each of the others could read music, so all we had to do was to skim the book for some likely targets.

The Auburn quartet (from left, Buell, Linda Lee Bolen, Judy Caruthers, Tom Richardson): just before one of several performances elsewhere – though never again on live TV.

We got on well together, and the music quickly claimed each of the group, if no one of the others was as obviously fanatical as I. We met periodically and in short order learned a good number of tunes. We mastered THE GOLDEN HARP, THE LAST WORDS OF COPERNICUS, GREENWICH, CALVARY, HIGHLANDS OF HEAVEN, EVENING SHADE, LOGAN and at least a couple of dozen more. (If any of us had been true shape-note readers, we might not have savored so the final chord in SARDINIA – a misprint in that edition of the book, a *La* shape in the treble that was misplaced to the C line instead of the B – which, as we sang it, brought the song to an uncharacteristically jarring close.)

I have to say that we managed an impressive facility with our singing, though when I later played a sample tape for Hugh McGraw and a few others, I was almost as shocked as they to hear how fast our group had sung. In our quartet format and absent the presence of a real class of singers, we had fallen into a galloping pace.

On a few occasions one or more of the group traveled with me to experience, in country churches, the real thing. And the entire group of us attended – and loved – a session of the Cullman County Convention.

At some point I had shared my interest in Sacred Harp with Dr. Ward Allen, whom I came to know through classes he taught in Renaissance Poetry and the works of John Milton. Professor Allen was a revered figure, the quintessential Southern gentleman as well as a great scholar. He was a graduate of Vanderbilt, and it turned out that he had been a friend of Donald Davidson, the leader in the 1930s of the group of writers and poets known as the Southern Agrarians. Davidson, author of the libretto for *Singin' Billy*, a folk opera about the life of shape-noter William Walker, had written appealingly of the Sacred Harp. (From Ward Allen, I learned that Davidson had arranged for the tune EVENING SHADE from the *Southern Harmony* and *Sacred Harp* to be played on the organ at his funeral.)

When he heard about our little singing group, Dr. Allen and his wife, Peggy, invited us to come to their home to sing for them, and so we did. Complimentary about our singing, Dr. Allen then arranged for us to perform at a monthly campus program of readings called The English Hour. As our performance there was deemed a real success, we were invited to repeat it a few months later – to considerably more fanfare. The managers of the event saw a representation of Southern culture with much broader appeal than the traditional scholarly paper offered.

This time when the event neared, the English department distributed a campus-wide flyer announcement. A typo in the headline – referring to us as "Scared Harp singers" – probably didn't discourage attendance and, in a way, may have turned out to be weirdly prophetic.

At any rate, a relatively large crowd did gather for the event. Word of mouth had brought out a number of people in the broader community. A sense of excitement hovered in the air. Following the format of the previous program, the four of us sat on barstools in a semicircle facing the audience spread out before us in a wide swath. And having honed the execution in the earlier event, we came through the program swimmingly.

A clipping of the quartet in the afternoon performance, May 7, 1968. From the Auburn University alumni news publication. (Photo by Kay Lovvorn)

As previously, I did the commentary: group introductions, a brief description of Sacred Harp history and practice, and a short intro to most of the songs. On our first fuging song, for example, I noted, to a few appreciative chuckles, that a fugue has been described as a piece of music in which the parts come in one after the other "and the listeners go out the door one after the other." Where they might have carried special interest, I quoted from the footnotes at the bottom of the songbook's pages in that edition: for example, that the composer of PLEYEL'S HYMN was the 24th child of a village schoolmaster, that the composer of ANTIOCH had been killed "by a falling tree or limb."

Our enunciation seemed crisp enough for general understanding. When we sang THE CHURCH'S DESOLATION and came to the line "And has religion left the church / Without a trace behind her?" I could see one of my professors, sitting close to the front, punch a colleague next to him and whisper-shout, "It has! It has!"

The event seemed a hit – and the four of us rather enjoyed it, too. We not only survived this big test, we did so with some aplomb. A good group of people (including, from the Auburn area, one of the daughters of Sacred Harp composer O.A. Parris) came up to con-gratulate us at the end, some excitedly so, or to ask questions or make connections. (Some days after the event, we were invited by one of the listeners to provide the entertainment at a banquet in town.)

And Then . . .

And then Ed Wegener, a little out of breath that late afternoon, fairly rushed in to speak to us. The date was May 7, 1968, and, as we all had heard, then-governor Lurleen Wallace, wife of former and future Alabama governor George C. Wallace, had died earlier in the day. Could our little quartet – he asked – fresh off a milestone perfor-mance, with the crowd just now trailing away, come on TV, live, *this very evening* and share our music with a statewide audience?

Ed was director of the public television station on the Auburn University campus, a link in what was, from the 1950s, the nation's first statewide educational television network and the model for later ETV networks around the country (it would later become Alabama Public Television). He had called me once before, following a men-tion by Ward Allen, to discuss our doing a little segment for TV. On this occasion, though, he had an urgent need: an appropriate and distinctive way to pay tribute to Governor Wallace on his evening program. The fact that Sacred Harp represented native music and tradition from the rural South, and rural Alabama in particular, that it dealt with themes of death as well – all of this seemed to him to fit the bill.

Having just finished our version of a marathon, then, we were now being asked to race again – and at a suddenly high altitude. So this most flattering request gave the four of us pause. Could we, should we do it? We would not have had a chance to rehearse, to adjust to a different format. I don't believe any of us had ever been to the studio before. And the program was to begin in only about two hours. Leaving The English Hour setting, we would be going our separate ways, maybe having a bite of supper, and then gathering at the last minute to "go live." But we were on a roll, and Ed was encouraging. We agreed to do it – and got quick directions to the studio.

Over the next hour or so, I took the luxury of relaxing a bit – each of us had been so geared up for the day – and somehow let the time get away from me. After making a few wrong turns in the dark and then having to reverse my way, I arrived at the studio dangerously late toward the hour the lights were to go on for us. The others, rightly nervous, were all there waiting. We had only minutes, seconds it seemed, to take in the studio configuration and get the order of the evening.

There would be an introduction placing our part on the program thematically close to the intended tribute. After that, we were to sing a couple of songs from, once again, four barstools stationed at the back of the studio, and then I was to join Ed, the host, behind a desk at the front, where he would chat with me about Sacred Harp and our involvement in it.

We were hurriedly shown the layout, including the platform on which sat the long desk, maybe a couple of feet out from the edge. Late as we were, I took all of this in with but a glance – a fact that would shortly turn out to be costly.

Lights and camera. And suddenly it was our turn to sing. I sounded a pitch from a pitch-pipe, and we launched into our first song. WONDROUS LOVE would have been an obvious choice, and it's my guess for what we opened with. We then sang a second song, maybe EVENING SHADE or THE MORNING TRUMPET.

Following that, I walked around to the back of the platform, crossing through what must have been three cameras stationed in a semicircle facing it (this would not have been how a stage manager would have marked it off, but too late now . . .).

Ed greeted me there, and we sat down and had a brief, I hoped not too strained, conversation about the history and practice of Sacred Harp singing – not a detail of which I recall, except for the tail end of the interview. When he thought it time to bring the chat to a close, Ed said something like, "Well, could we get you to sing another song for us?" Feeling fairly savvy now about television and the format, I looked out at the camera, smiled, and said, "We'd be happy to."

With that, I pushed myself back in my rolling chair, pushing a bit farther than was necessary to clear the top and the legs of the desk. As they rolled, the back wheels of the chair dropped just off the edge of the platform. With not a second's hesitation, the chair and I together plunged backward, down and out of sight.

If I try now to think of which set of words in the repertoire seems most apt for that moment, the song OCEAN comes to mind:

The men astonished mount the skies
And sink in gaping graves.

The floor – only about three feet from my chair seat when I started falling – wasn't gaping, of course; it was flat and hard. But my astonishment was real – and speaks to me still across the years.

I was astonished first of all by the thing itself: the treachery of the chair wheels, the cruelty of a too-narrow back apron of platform. Astonished that such a thing could be happening on live TV – and in such a professional setting. Astonished at the quick reversal from moment of triumph personally – and for the cause! – to a now public humiliation. And surprised, even then, at the length of my frantic, ricocheting internal monologue.

Anyone who's ever had a great fall or harrowing escape knows the sensation of time slowing down as the seasons of one's life seem to pass before, or a maddening train of thought unfurls in frames almost. Now, it's possible that Reconstructive Memory has slipped in over time and rearranged or fluffed up my recollection of my thought process at the time. But I seem to remember well the following thoughts crowding across my consciousness in that blurred second or so of time: "This *can't* be happening! This is *live television!* This doesn't *happen!*" As I was reeling backwards, I almost expected that professional hands would reach out and grab me, save me from the fall, or that the camera would cut away. . . . Even in that brief moment, I felt a latent sense of my own lack of physical grace, a tendency to klutziness over the years that had chosen this of *all* occasions to manifest itself once more. *No! It can't be!*

I simultaneously felt astonishment, horror, outrage (yes!), self-pity and great need. *Help!* And yet I also knew that I and the situation both were doomed, that no help would come. And that I now must rise and face the music.

I have to give Ed Wegener credit: he was a pro. With but a quick look at the camera and with a smile in his voice at least – "Well, we seem to have lost our tenor! . . ." – he reached down to lend a hand and rescue some sense of order out of that unbelievable moment. Extricating myself from the chair now flat on its back – I picture a back-flipped cockroach, legs flailing – I next had to reach up, take hold of the desk and pull myself up. (That image actually fit with my colleagues' visualization: Tom, recalling the episode years later, told me that, with their view shielded by the cameras, the three of them had watched the fall on a nearby monitor and next saw my feet slightly waving above the desktop "like an insect's antennae.")

Nothing is more intolerable in live television than dead time. Seconds are precious; any vacuum must be quickly filled. And even in my despair, this deepest of funks, I knew that. In the few seconds I remained out of sight from the camera – oh, how I wished I could remain there! – I was swamped by dread. But it was useless to think I could remain out of sight, or now out of mind for all who might be watching. Fastening my hands on the desktop above me, I pulled myself up to face the central camera, which loomed before me like some great alien eye. It seemed to leer – hungry for footage, for the satisfaction of its now heightened, autopsy-driven curiosity. (The lead cameraman later said that ordinarily he could have cut away as he saw me start to fall, but that at that moment he had zoomed in for a close-up. . . .)

I don't recall the next frame of action. There must have been a moment equivalent to dusting myself off, or being dusted off. If I managed to bring up a smile, it could only have been through contortion. This was black-and-white television: I wonder if I was flush or if all color had drained from my face. . . .

In any case, what happened next was a study in crisis behavior. Adrenalin had kicked in for all of us. I walked briskly back to join my companions at the four stools, each of us concentrating mightily. As the cameras swung around and watched, we took a pitch and started singing – not cheerily, to be sure, but more like soldiers on a fast march.

When at last it was over and the final notes had fallen, it was as if a gigantic balloon, full of compressed air, suddenly and fully exhaled. The cameramen turned the cameras off and fell on each other with laughter. The studio erupted. All, save one, laughed uncontrollably.

Across the airwaves in Alabama (and bleeding over, I think, into a couple of neighboring states), a "you'll never believe this!" event had happened. Friends who had watched now called each other and exchanged shouts of disbelief with peals of laughter. My future mother-in-law had viewed the program while knitting an afghan. She said afterwards that she had looked down for a moment, concentrating on a purl stitch perhaps, and looked back up to see that I had simply disappeared. . . .

Amid the laughter and, still, the disbelief in the studio, I think we did the briefest of post-mortems. There must have been apologies. And apologies for laughing. And then more manic, cascading laughter. It seems to me now that the "How could it have happened?" question was quickly broached and then thrown aside. My memory on these particulars is hazy, for I was preoccupied with my grief.

I should add that the singing segments, as planned, had been recorded as they happened; the interview – and my fall – had not. Tape after all was expensive. So this event of singular awkwardness was but a moment in time and in memory.

Over the years, I met a surprising number of people who had seen the fall ("Oh no, that was *you?!* I *saw* that!"). Besides those who had already been watching, others had simply been changing channels (from the few available in that simpler era) and had paused momentarily on Public TV and caught the action.

I later read that the famous space scientist Wernher von Braun had fallen off a platform at some official ceremony in Huntsville, where he lived and worked. And of course there have been famous stumbles by presidents and celebrities in front of the camera. That shared distinction helped a small amount. But did any of them, or anyone at all, have a more spectacularly abrupt disappearance from the TV camera's dead-on view? Was there a more earnest victim than this thin, callow 23-year-old, who then had to try to walk over and sing it off? And who, watching, could have kept from hard-laughing, if not from running out to tell the neighbors next door?

In time, of course, the landing, played over in my mind so many times, has softened, and I have since been seasoned with other little shocks and reversals (material for another memoir perhaps?). The story at last became one I could tell, and appreciate, with some humor. And at least, I can now remind myself, it wasn't a tumble off the Oscars stage. . . .

I leave the episode with one question more.
Did I as a young man fall hard for Sacred Harp?
Oh, more than I can say. . . .

Acknowledgments

Writing, as it's often said, is a lonely business. On a project such as this, one is always alone with one's memories and with the task of readying them for going out in public. Early on, Mary and Tad joined me in the effort by reading portions of the draft and trying to nudge me toward clarity. As well as catching narrative lapses and so forth, they made my job less lonely. I owe them gratitude as well as great love, as I do Will, who escaped reading duties but who, equally with other family members, lovingly wished me success in bringing to a close a project he and they all knew I had much at heart.

Collaboration, then – at points all along the way – not only rescued me from the vault of solitude but greatly improved the final book. Jim Carnes, without family obligation, undertook a close reading of the manuscript, made judicious, even crucial, suggestions throughout and prevented many embarrassing false steps. I am tremendously grateful to him for taking on that labor so cheerfully and for, among other contributions, attempting, as I requested, to "save me from myself." That his efforts in that regard could not be entirely successful owes nothing to any lack of seasoned counsel from him but finally, on my part, to a stubborn streak I can claim to have inherited from Granny Cobb, Great-uncle Virgel or more distant stiff-necked members of my clan.

Martha Patton Jax, a friend from our college days, also provided most helpful suggestions for many of the chapters here when they were in rawest condition and deserves credit for courage as well as for a fine editing eye. Richard Schmeidler volunteered for proofreading and copyediting duty and did a superb job in that effort. I'm much indebted to him for a careful scrutiny and cleaning of the whole. In addition, Richard pressed me to include an index of names – and then generously provided me with a draft of one. Anyone who uses the index here and finds it helpful should know that he is to be credited with its inclusion. I'm also most grateful to Keith Willard, who, as mentioned in the Introduction, has for decades now hosted an online discussion group for Sacred Harp and other shape-note singers. This service, so valuable to our broadening community, provided an incubation spot for postings I would make in the 1990s and early 2000s that, as I gathered my reminiscences years later, brought fresh detail to the final product.

In 1996 Melissa Allured presented me with a copy of the taped interview with George M. Mattox, which opened up that whole chapter for me. Even if it had never made its way into this book, I would be grateful for that expressive gift from the past. Members of Mr. George M.'s family – daughter Jeanette Dewberry and grandchildren Carolyn Brewer and Jerry Dewberry – later furnished me with additional information and resource materials about George M. (and about Lon Odem), including that charming early photo of George M. and his Emma, to help round out a colorful picture.

I am doubly indebted to Ted Mercer, first for his wonderful, open-ended interview with Dewey Williams and then for generously allowing me to quote from it in depth. I first received a copy of that interview many years back from, and thus am also grateful to the memory of, Jerry Enright, whose death in 2010 so saddened our Sacred Harp community. Bernice Williams Harvey provided me additional information, as well as a photo of her father in full singing mode. Family of other figures portrayed here were similarly helpful when I undertook the project: Lonnie Rogers' daughter Karen

Rollins and sister Opal Cannon; Jan Nesbitt, daughter of Willie Mae Latham Moon and granddaughter of Ed Thomas; Nell Estes, daughter of Elder Roy Avery; Janice Jackson, daughter of Japheth Jackson; and, unforgettably, each of Amanda's children: Jim, Mandy, Tim and Howard Brady.

Many others, some of them now gone from us, provided help in various ways: Hugh McGraw, Richard Mauldin, David and Johnny Lee, Myrl Jones, Jeff and Shelbie Sheppard, Daphene Causey, Bud Oliver, Dick Nail, John Ramsey, Phillip Denson Aaron, Rebecca Over, Carol Hand Selleck, Linton Ballinger, Elder J.L. Hopper, Jewel Wootten, Matt Hinton, Hunter and Suzanne Hale, Frances Robb, Jesse Pearlman Karlsberg, Nathan Rees, Tim Eriksen, Charlotte Romine Slatton, David Ivey, Doug Rodgers, Dan Brittain, Toney Smith, Charlene Wallace, Aubrey Barfield, Margaret Keeton, Lorene Bailey, Larry Brasher, Dave Richardson, David Paul Boyle, and members of the Calvary Convention, especially Alfred Jennings. I am grateful to them all.

My reader might join me in thinking how much poorer this account would be without photographs that captured the subjects here in the midst of life: Aunt Jewel striding into her lesson, Dewey with hat and wide-brimmed smile, the young Amanda convention-singing with Aunt Ruthy. For use of those and dozens of other photos here, I'm extremely grateful to the following individuals and institutions: Joe Dan Boyd, Joel Cohen, Steve Grauberger, Joey Brackner, Martha Beverly, Ginnie Ely, Betty Oliver, Laura Densmore, Kim McRae, Melissa Springer, Cary Estes, Charles Franklin, Susan Lovvorn Rice, Larry Brasher, Tat Bailey, David Paden, Nate and Norma Green, Linda Thomas, James Robert Chambless, Mary Kitchens Gardner, Pamela Helms and the other grandchildren of George Pullen Jackson, the grandchildren of "Uncle Tom" and Lola Akers Denson, the Cullman County Museum, the Auburn Alumni Association and the Alabama Center for Traditional Culture.

In addition to those mentioned above, so many people provided encouragement along the way, including, unfailingly, Charles

McNair, Dianne and Wes Foster, Judy Hauff and Helen and Ted Brown. Participants at Camp Fasola, where I read sections of the work-in-progress, gave hearty responses that reinvigorated my efforts. I should mention especially Dave Lapham, whose suggestions and encouragement, at a few points when my spirits sagged, had such a bolstering effect.

I am fortunate to have known an amazing host of people who preceded or joined me in loving Sacred Harp – the central figures featured here certainly, but many more besides. Their friendship and forbearance have been gifts in my life. Of that host, I should single out Ruth Denson Edwards, who so generously guided me through my early years of Sacred Harp involvement and who even bought for me my share of stock in the Sacred Harp Publishing Company. I must somehow mention, too, the sudden loss, over a good many years, of four singing friends whose departure in the prime of their lives grieves me still: Karen House, Kenneth DeLong, Anthony Prichard and Ginny Easter. To them and all the rest now gone, I dedicate this book. My memories of them do indeed draw like cords around my heart. I could be despondent about such a great and widening loss were it not for fresh infusions of so many new and worthy members into our community.

A last but significant name to mention: If anyone else should be given credit for my Sacred Harp story, it is Mike Hinton, who launched me on my journey all those years ago. As well as offering his great friendship, Mike, along with his cousins Amanda and Richard, provided a wealth of information over the years, particularly about the Denson family, as well as the many old family photographs. His sterling leadership with the Sacred Harp Publishing Company has only increased my admiration and gratitude.

Finally, one thing more to acknowledge: As this book is a memoir, I'm inclined to regard some asymmetry and inconsistency throughout as just the fleas on the dog. And to that point, one of my early readers asked a question that might occur to others: Weren't there other notable individuals or families I could or should have included? My answer was that I focused on those I had good stories about or had information or perspective I thought would interest the reader. I could have attempted a portrayal of any number of other figures, including some I knew as well as several depicted here. But about those individuals, I felt I wouldn't have been able to give the reader something significant or savory, as I hoped I could do with much of what I did include. Similarly, when I had access to good or at least pertinent photos, I used them. (The images of Odem's Chapel, for example: Where else would those records of singing life from the 1940s have had a reasonable chance to be discovered and appreciated?) Where I had none, my text went unaccompanied.

Finally then, in all humility, I think of a line by lexicographer Eric Partridge: "Every worthwhile book contains many faults, and every worthwhile writer commits them." Faults known and unknown to me may overrun this work. Still I hope that I and my failings here qualify to fit somewhere within the bounds of that generous dictum.

> And [let] all my conversation prove
> My heart to be sincere.
>
> ~ PLEASANT HILL, page 205
> *The Sacred Harp*

Endnotes

1   The University of Georgia Press, 1978, 1989.

2   The writer knows, but probably shouldn't disclose, the name of the person, a member of one of the old singing families, who, as the second leader of the day, won the distinction of being maybe the first in history to receive so early, amid general chuckles, the word that her chosen song had already "been used."

3   See *The Chattahoochee Musical Convention, 1852-2002: A Sacred Harp Historical Sourcebook*, edited by Kiri Miller (The Sacred Harp Museum, Carrollton, Ga., 2002), 112-113.

4   *The Story of the Sacred Harp, 1844-1944* (Nashville: Vanderbilt University Press, 1944), 37.

5   "The Folk Celebrates a Centennial," *Bulletin of the Tennessee Folklore Society*, 10 (1944), 7.

6   Courtney Haden, "Heavy Metal Gospel," http://www.bham-weekly.com/2010/06/16/heavy-metal-gospel/

7   Simon Jones, "Music takes a sacred shape," *Church Times*, December 7, 2012.

8   Though well afield from those examples, another gem from those years I have shared as often, and as proudly, with friends: For some time I received copies of a little publication from the parishes of southern Louisiana called *The News of News*, which at one point contained a photo of a recent ministerial appointment and a short article about him evidently written by the language-intoxicated reverend himself. It opened as follows: "John E. Doe, Jr., the second of four sons born to the marriage union of John E. Doe, Sr., and Jane A. Doe of which the latter is late."

9   The only Sacred Harp interlude during my time along the coast came in the form of my preparation of liner notes for The Word of Mouth Chorus's album *Rivers of Delight* (Nonesuch Records). Every morning, before or after breakfast, I still wouldn't mind listening to the Chorus's version (in women's voices only) of the beautiful hymn SWEET PROSPECT.

10   The personality Tat brought to such reminiscences can be more fully glimpsed in Chapter 23. But as additional information: "Coy's daddy," Sam, Tat said, was "a big-time singer." He and Tat's granddaddy, Ben Berry, "used to hook up to go to singings." Coy, a school teacher, also had a younger brother who was, Tat said, "a better singer than him – two to one." But he had left the area, and Tat had never heard whether he had continued to sing. "Coy had a song in the book," Tat mentioned, "but I don't think it had much tune to it." The revision committee for the 1966 edition evidently agreed; they removed the two songs by Putnam that had been included in the 1960 edition.

11   *Judge Jackson and* The Colored Sacred Harp (Montgomery, Ala., 2002), 97.

12 *Judge Jackson*, 101-102.

13 Denson may have taken another teaching tour in Texas in 1934, as has been previously reported, but it seems likely that his second, and probably only other, teaching stint in the state was in 1933. The *Mineral Wells Index* announced his two schools that summer in Fort Worth and Garden Valley, and Mike Hinton has found a letter from his grandfather, from Garden Valley, to Mike's mother in July of 1933 in which the professor says, "I sure have a good school. They sure are learning fast."

14 The two Smith sisters, Myrl and Myra, to me, represented the apex of that Denson leading style. Some of the men of my early acquaintance showed glimpses of it: Uncle Bob Denson, Leonard Lacy, Tom Harper, Barrett Ashley, Ed Thomas, Lawrence Underwood, Jeff and Jerry Sheppard . . . . But it was usually the women who won the day and showed the style in purest form: along with the Smith sisters, Marie Creel Aldridge and her daughter Lucy Marie Heidorn, Mary Kitchens Gardner, Velma Richardson, Willodean Butler, Amanda Denson Brady . . . . Other marvelous leaders, just a shade off from that strictest style (and often with a book in hand): Kathleen Creel Robbins, Shelbie Sheppard, Maude Doss Quinn, Kathleen Doss Traywick, Reba Dell Windom, Elene Stovall, Joyce Walton, Rosa Hughes. (I hope I can be forgiven for forgetting any other obvious member of that highly skilled group, every one of which, in their prime, it was a privilege to simply stop and watch as, with flowing ease, they mastered anew the variably sized square and the newly inspired class before them.)

As I told workshop participants over several years, Myrl Jones' leading of the song ARBACOOCHEE that Friday at the 1998 National was the most beautiful thing I ever saw out on the floor at a singing – or just about anywhere else. When we were fortunate enough to have Myrl (at 81) and Myra (three years older), attend the 2001 session, I called them up at the end of the singing to lead a song for us together. When they gave me their permission to do so just before, they told me they had never led together in all their lives! I, and others who heard, found that an astonishing fact. When I tested my memory on this with Myrl in mid-summer of 2013, she said, "That's right, we'd never before been out on the floor together. I told you at the time we were always afraid we'd run over each other!" The sisters each had their standard numbers: Myrl, usually from the minor tunes; Myra, the major ones ~ and "We never led each other's songs." In this case, Myrl yielded to Myra's choice of 299, NEW JERUSALEM. "I'd never led that song before," Myrl told me; you wouldn't have known it.

That day of singing was, to me, easily the best ever at the National. We were, for that session only, in a large room with wooden floor and near-perfect Sacred Harp acoustics. One of the singers, after we closed, came up to express her amazement: "I've never before felt as if I were sitting at the very throne of God!" And unquestionably the highlight of the day was the sight and sound of the two octogenarian sisters from Texas leading us, with synchronized beauty, in that grand old style.

15 Coston's support, and especially financial support, of Sacred Harp throughout the region was well known at the time. According to Myrl Jones, who with her family attended the 1931 Texas Interstate Convention, Coston had rented the bottom three floors of a Mineral Wells hotel to put up visiting singers, especially the youth, with adults on the first floor, girls on the second and boys on the third.

16 Further details from *The Daily Mountain Eagle*: Thomas Jackson Denson, it said, "passed away suddenly and unexpectedly at his home in Manchester [in Walker County, a few miles north of

Jasper]. Mr. Denson had planned to attend a singing at Winfield Saturday, but shortly after he had arisen from his bed he fell into his wife's arms and expired without speaking. Short funeral services were conducted at the residence of Howard Denson, son of the deceased, in Jasper Sunday, and the remains were carried to Double Springs, where services . . . were concluded, and interment took place at Fairview cemetery, three miles out from Double Springs . . . ." Pallbearers listed were L.P. Odem, H.M. Blackmon, the brothers Fred and Otis Drake (brothers of the great treble singer Lena Drake, who in time would become the second wife of Marcus Cagle) and brothers Tom and H.N. McGraw.

17 Born April 16, 1882, at Chulafinnee, Ala., Mitchell is said to have died in Lakeland, Fla., in March of 1950. He would contribute to the 1936 Denson Revision the song LAKELAND, which remained in subsequent editions until the 1991 revision. His brother Edwin, around the age of six at their parents' death, was raised by uncle and aunt James A. and Annie Burdette.

18 The funeral services for her did begin, and continue at the grave site, with Sacred Harp singing. During the main service, Hugh McGraw sang a Sacred Harp song (he can now no longer recall which one) as a solo.

19 *Judge Jackson*, 79.

20 An offshoot of the South Alabama singings for some time existed in and around Union County, New Jersey, where blacks from the South had traveled northward for work and had taken the singing and songbooks with them.

21 Bruce Ingram, "Singers get into shape," *Evanston Review*, May 28, 1992.

22 Kathy Kemp, "Sweet soul man," *Birmingham Post-Herald*, October 2, 1995.

23 Mr. Mann, then of Alexander City, Ala., was one of the "men over eighty years old" individually recognized by leading a special lesson at the Centennial Sacred Harp Singing Convention held in Ashland, Ala., July 6-9, 1944.

24 Hardshell is lingo, usually affectionately sounded, for Primitive Baptist (contrasting, by the way, with the more pejorative term "streaked-head," used to refer to those Baptist bodies loosely situated between Primitive and Missionary branches). By extension, Hardshell coffee can be thought of as especially strong or "primitive" brew.

25 Sarah Rice, "Made A Good Crop, Paid Every Dollar They Owed," *Lawrence County Advocate* (May 1, 1985).

26 Runie and her sister, Ann Heath Johnson, formed a forward wall of the most powerful alto section I ever heard. Truth to tell, Ann was an alto section by herself. I remember seeing her sitting, in a flowing dress, on the second bench of the bass section at her home church of Mabson Methodist – with one leg stretched out across the bench. When I once mentioned Ann to Hugh McGraw, he responded: "Ann had a voice like a *lion* – the first time I heard her, it scared me!"

27 Minutes from the Cullman courthouse singing – included, along with other conventions' proceedings, in the published minutes of the Alabama State Sacred Harp Musical Association – call the 1930 session its 33rd, indicating a start-up date of 1898. Reinforcing that: the 1933 minutes printed in the Cullman *Tribune* list that year's session as the 36th. On p. 132 of his history of the Chattahoochee Convention, Earl Thurman had written

that the Cullman courthouse convention was organized "about 1891."

28 Irving Lowens, *Music and Musicians in Early America* (New York, 1964), 282.

Index of Names

Aaron, Annie Denson (see also Denson) and Newton, 79, 81, 85, 86, 89, 93-94, 274, 281 (photo, 83)

Aaron, Phillip Denson, 86-87

Abercrombie, Mae, 324-25

Acuff, Roy, 57

Adams family (Azilee, Kermit, Ralph, etc.), 327-28

Adams, Syble Wootten (see also Wootten), 60

Adkins, Tressie, 325

Akers, Joe, 73

Akin, E.G. and Florice, 33-34 (photo, 33)

Aldridge, Marie Creel (see also Creel), 229, 231-32, 267-68, 379 (photo, 40)

Alexander family, 255-56

Allen, LaRue, 128

Allen, Ward and Peggy, 363, 365

Aplin, Bill, 166

Ashley, Barrett, 379

Avery family (Roy, Elma, Marshall, etc.), 123-37 (photos, 124, 127, 131)

Avery, Eloise, 348

Ayers, Jim, 32

Bailey, Tyrus Cobb "Tat" and family, 46, 306-23, 378 (photos, 311, 313, 319)

Baker, Kathy, 49

Ballinger: Hamilton, 257, 325; Larry, 326; Leon, 350; Linton, 256-57; family, 256, 325, 346, 350

Barrand, Tony, 61-62

Barton, Etma, 342-43

Barton, Willodean, 191-92, 264

Bass, Tommie, 43

Beasley, Sarah, 327

Becker, Earl and family, 336-37

Bejnar, Alice, 164, 166

Bell, Hobart M., 256

Berry, Ben and family, 306-07, 309-10, 312, 313, 315-17, 322, 378

Billings, William, vi, 258

Bishop, Jessie Lee, 349

Black, Edward, 257

Black, Gene, 41

Blackmon, H.M., 381

Bolen, Linda Lee, 361-69 (photos, 362, 364)

Boyd, Annie Jewel Casey, 200-10 (photos, 200, 203, 205)

Boyd, Joe Dan, 51, 53, 58, 106, 112

Brady, Amanda Denson and family (see also Denson), 69, 98, 272-99, 350, 379 (photos, 273, 275-77, 296)

Brasher, Larry, 99

Breedlove, L.P., 265

Brittain, Dan, 34, 56, 57

Brittain, Ellis and Ima, 32

Brown, Jim, 43

Brown, Leman and Ruth Burnham, 35, 352 (photo, 40)

Bucke, Emory S., 196

Burdette, James A. and Annie, 381

Burdette, William Howard, 79

Burnett, T Bone, 47-50

Bush, George H.W., 292

Butler, Willodean, 379

Cagle: A.M. (Marcus), 45, 46, 79, 87, 229, 246-48, 254, 332, 353-55, 381 (photos, 45, 248, 250); Lena Drake, 353, 381; family, 93

Cagle, Hoyt and Mary Lou, 32

Carlisle, Fatha Mae, 172

Carnes, Jim, 168, 285, 298, 301, 304

Caruthers, Judy, 361-69 (photos, 362, 364)

Casey, Nancy, 207

Causey, Daphene, 128, 257-58

Cauthen, Joyce, 168

Chafin, Ozella, 325

Chafin, Velton, 244, 333, 334

Chandler, Arrie and Walter, 263

Cherry, Ken, 37

Childers, Pauline Creel (see also Creel), 232, 234-35, 267

Clark, Don, 166

Cleghorn, Iva Denson and husband (see also Denson), 264-66

Cleland family, 14

Cobb family (Belle, Buell Sr., Joe, etc.), 4-11, 13, 179-81, 272, 315, 326 (photos, 9, 10)

Cobb, Clelon and Forney, 35

Cobb, Ty, 308

Coble, Mual, 342

Cohen, Joel, 205

Cole, Nat King, 49

Conwill, Elmer, 259, 334

Cooper, Wilson Marion, x, 112

Costello, Elvis, 49, 50

Coston, W.T. and wife, 74, 380

Creel (see also Reid, Jim and family): Annie Reid, 230; Charles Emory, 227-32, 235-238; Charlie, 230, 329; Chester and Hester, 230, 233, 344, 346; Edith Creel Tate, 231-35 (photo, 40); Flarce, 231, 234; Harrison, 231, 232, 236, 265, 345; Haydn, 232; Irvin, 329-30; Kathleen Creel Robbins, 344, 379; Lucille Creel Tolbert, 232; Mamie Reid, 230, 233, 344-46; Marie Creel Aldridge, 229, 231-32, 267-68, 379 (photo, 40); Mattie Reid, 230, 233, 344-46; Pauline Creel Childers, 232, 234-35, 267; family, 229-238, 329, 344-46

Crider, Preston, 228

Cullmann, Col. John G., 268

Cumming, Joe, 30

Cunningham, Benjamin, 257

Daniel family, 181, 191

Davidson, Donald, 363

Davis, Mark, 266

Davis, Robert M., 112-13

Dean, Louise, 128

del Re, John, iii

DeLong, Doris and Horace, 32

Denney: Charlie, 217-18; Newman, 32, 216, 226; Vivian Denney Rogers (see also Rogers), 216, 217, 219, 223-26 (photo, 221); Willie Myrt Shadinger, 216; family, 216, 225

Denson: Amanda Denson Brady and family, 69, 98, 272-99, 350, 379 (photos, 273, 275-77, 296); Amanda Burdette, 78-81, 86, 282; Annie Denson Aaron, 79, 81, 85, 86, 89, 93, 274, 281 (photo, 83); Belle, 101, 281; Evan, 264, 266; Howard, 79, 82, 274, 282, 381 (photo, 277); Irene Kitchens Parker, 102; Iva Denson Cleghorn, 264-66; James, 278; Lola Akers, 76, 79, 381; Maggie, 79, 85, 93 (photo, 83); Paine, x, 79, 82, 85, 87, 95, 229, 253, 274, 282, 287, 312-13 (photo, 94); Reedie Denson Powell Evans, 263-64, 266; Robert E., 99-102, 280, 287, 379 (photo, 100); Ruth Denson Edwards (see Edwards); Seaborn Ivey (Shell), 356-57; Seaborn McDaniel, x, 78, 100, 240, 245-46, 254, 264, 266; Sidney Burdette, 78, 100; Thomas Jackson, x, xiv, 12, 19, 21, 48, 70-83, 85, 86, 215-16, 223, 238, 245-47, 249, 253, 254, 260, 265, 266, 336, 352, 379-81 (photos, 71, 72); Tommye Denson Mauldin, 79; Vera Denson Nunn, 79; Violet Denson Hinton, 79, 379; Whitt, 229, 240, 264, 282, 356; William, 82; family, 78-79, 84-85, 87, 90, 93, 95, 99, 253, 278-83, 287, 290, 291, 335, 356-57

Drake, Fred and Otis, 381

Draper, William H., 46

Dumas, Edmund, 264, 265

Dunnegan, Grandma, 83

Eastburn, Kathryn, 281

Edge, J.L., 237

Edwards, Ruth Denson (see also Denson), ii, 21, 51, 52, 54, 65-70, 78-103, 249-53, 265, 272, 274, 279-82, 287, 299, 313, 381 (photos, 52, 55, 64, 83, 84, 94, 97, 100, 103, 248, 250, 251, 275)

Ellis, Earline, 242

Enochs, Aubrey and Elmer, 43

Eriksen, Tim, 47, 49 (photo, 35)

Evans, Reedie Denson Powell (see also Denson), 263-64, 266

Fannin, Ora Lee, 51, 327 (photo, 52)

Flowers, Estelle, 352

Fisher, Myrtie, 67, 68, 91

Folsom, "Big Jim," 260-61

Frazier, Charles, 47

Franklin, Cassie, 350

(Floyd) Frederick family, 350

Frederick, Maudie, 102

Freeman, Dr., 82

Fuller, Buckminster, 57

Gardner, Mary Kitchens, 379 (photo, 242)

Gilliland family (Ozetta, C.H., Cecil), 332-33

Gilmore, Joe, 334
Gleeson, Brendan, 48
Glover, Runie Heath, 257, 382
Godsey, Hollis, 259
Godsey, Palmer, 51, 52 (photo, 52)
Graham, Billy, 56
Grauberger, Steve, 174, 175, 177
Green family, 346
Griggs, Pauline Jackson (see also Jackson), 143, 152, 153, 155 (photos, 152, 155)
Grimmett, Mr., 302
Gulledge, Otis, 267
Guthery, Henry, 263, 265 (photo, 40)

Hale, Hunter and Suzanne, 287-89
Hallmark, Henry, 138
Hamrick, Joyce Harrison, 355
Hamrick, Raymond, 32, 33, 51, 355 (photo, 53)
Hand, Gerald, 260
Harcrow, Ricky, 334, 336, 345
Hardin, Louis, 32
Harper, Tom, 334-36, 337, 379 (photos, 252, 335)
Harvey, Bernice Williams (see also Williams), 56-58, 112-14, 121, 122
Hauff, Judy, 3, 71
Hawkins, Lydia Avery (see also Avery), 130
Hearne, Jim and wife, 38
Heidorn, Lucy Marie, 379
Hendrix, Ivy, 88, 95
Hinton, Erica and Matt, 50
Hinton, Mike, 19, 21, 61, 70, 79, 81, 87, 89, 96, 101, 102, 216, 379
Hinton, Violet Denson (see also Denson), 79, 379
Hocutt, John, 95, 330-32, 334, 345-46, 352 (photo, 331); family, 331-32

Holloway, Samuel, 169-70, 173, 175
Holsomback family, 14
Holmes, Wilda, 334
Hooker, John Lee, 117
Hopper: Dan, 329; J.L., 254-55; family, 350
Howton, Bickett, 198
Hughes, Carl, 32, 300-01
Hughes, Rosa, 379

Ingle, Ila, 336
Irvine, Peter, photo, 40
Ivey: Allison, 350; David, 301, 347, 350-52 (photo, 40); Karen, 350 (photo, 40); Rodney, 285, 315 (photo, 40); family, 346

Jackson, Bobby, 177
Jackson: Dovie Jackson Reese, 56-58, 152 (photo, 155); Emma, 146; Gussie Matthews, 150-52 (photo, 143); Henry Japheth, 42, 56, 57, 114, 142-53, 155, 202, 204, 208-09 (photos, 143, 145, 147, 148, 155); Janice, 149; J.C. (John), 152, 156 (photo, 155); Judge, x, 112, 114, 142-44, 150, 153-55; Judge Ham, 143; Pauline Jackson Griggs, 143, 152, 153, 155 (photos, 152, 155); Ruth Jackson Johnson, 152-55 (photo, 154); Shem Campbell, 143, 151-53 (photo, 155); family, 142-44, 149-53, 155
Jackson, Estes, 257, 259-60
Jackson, George Pullen, xiv, xv, 36, 46, 93
James, Joe S., ii, x
Jennings, Alfred, 178
Johnson, Ann Heath, 382
Johnson, Bruce, 258

Johnson, Ruth Jackson (see also Jackson), 152-55 (photo, 154)

Johnson, Ted, 3

Jolly, Gordon, 121-22

Jones, Emily, 327

Jones, Joe and Sam, 350

Jones, Myrl Smith and family, 71-74, 379-80 (photos, 72, 73)

Keeton, Glenn, 334

Keeton, Mr., 325

Kellen, Erin, 304

Kennerly, Gilbert, 90

Kerr, Henry and John, 35

Kidman, Nicole, 49

King, Elisha James, ii, vi

Kipling, Rudyard, 228

Kitchens, Charles, xv, 345

Kitchens, Elmer, 51, 54, 265 (photo, 52)

Kilgo, E.E., 267

Knight, Ted and family, 353-56

Krauss, Alison, 49, 50

Kyle, Linda, 355

Kyles, Lee and Margaret, 176 (photo, 176)

Lacy, Leonard, 379

Lambert, Ludie McWhorter, 32

Laminack, Glenn and family, 357-58

Law, Jude, 49

Lawrence, Thomas Y., 112

Lee: Clarke, 165-66, 169; David, 164-69; Delorese, 165; Johnny, 165, 168; Julie, 165-66; Kathy, 164-165; Silas, 165-66; Tollie, 165-66 (photo, 167); family, 58, 164-68

Lomax, Alan, 2, 59

Love, Davis, 294-95

Lowe, Vera Alexander, 302

Lowens, Irving, 333

Louis, Joe, 114

Lytle, Andrew, 24

Macklin, Kelly, iii

Malone, A.A. ('Lonzo), 326, 327, 342-43

Mann: Erma Mann Jones, 128, 134, 135; Ila Mann McGhee, 128, 132; J.B. (Tobe), 128, 382; Moses Lee, 128, 132-35

Matthews, Bill, 353

Mattox, George M. and family (see also Daniel), 179-93 (photos, 180, 184, 251, 252)

Mauldin, Richard, 76, 81, 87, 249

Mauldin, Tommye Denson (see also Denson), 79

McCool, Clarence, 326-27, 342, 343

McDaniel family, 13-15, 315

McGough, Jimmie Lou, photo, 252

McGraw: Buford, 157-62, 262, 337-38 (photos, 158); Gladys Wallace, 157; H.N. (Bud), 32, 157, 159, 262, 381; Hugh, ii, 24, 30-32, 37, 41, 51, 52, 54, 56-59, 62, 68, 69, 88, 96, 101, 136-37, 159-61, 177, 262, 280, 300, 334, 336, 341, 353-55, 362, 381, 382 (photos, 52, 53); Tom, 32, 101, 159, 262, 381; family, 93, 157

McGuire, E.I., 32

McKenzie, Hattie Mae, 156

(M. F.) McWhorter family, 350

McWhorter, Millard, 35

Mencken, H.L., 2

Mercer, Ted, 109, 113, 115, 116, 122

Merritt, John, 260-61

Miller, Ben, 240-41

Miller, Frank, 240-41

Minghella, Anthony, 47-49, 239

Mitchell, Edwin, 381
Mitchell, William Thomas ("Pansy"), 79, 82, 381
Moon, Arnold, 326
Moon, Willie Mae Thomas Latham, 197-99 (photo, 197)
Morgan, Justin, vi
Morgan, Wilber E., 76
Morrison, Willie Bob, 35
Mosely, William Jefferson, 239-40
Motte, Minnie, 330
Moyers, Bill, 116
Murry, Jackie (Ruth Jackson Johnson's daughter), 154
Myers, Joe, 334

Nall, Thurman, 345
Nail, Dick, 240-41, 356
Nin, Anaïs, 237
Nolen, Wyatt, 307-08
Nunn, Vera Denson (see also Denson), 79

Odem, Lonnie P. and Comella, 247-254, 381 (photos, 248, 251, 252)
Oliver, Bud and family, 138, 258-59, 339-41, 350 (photo, 340)
Oliver, Milton, 345
Owens, Dock, 313

Padgett, Ben, 90-91
Paley, William, 46
Palmer, Myra Smith, 74, 379-80
Parris, O.A. and family, 191-92, 365
Parker, Irene Kitchens (see also Denson), 102
Parker, Mr., 265
Parker, Nora and Walter, 51, 52 (photo, 52)
Pate, Ellen Huggins, 32

Patterson, Mac, 337
Pelfrey, Pernie, 51, 327 (photo, 52)
Phillips, Virgil and family, 346-48, 350
Poyner, Pat, 112
Price, Annie, 242
Putnam, Coy and family, 46, 378

Quinn, Maude Doss, 379

Rains family, 14-15
Ramsey, John, 136
Read, Daniel, vi
Reagan, Ronald, 117
Redding, Loyd, 33 (photo, 33)
Reese, Dovie Jackson, 56-58, 152 (photo, 155)
Reese, H.S., xii
Reese, J.P., 264
Reid, Jim and family (see also Creel), 229-30, 236, 238, 344-46
Reynolds, William J., 41, 196
Rhea, Claude, 41
Richardson, Dave, 278
Richardson, Tom, 361-69 (photos, 362, 364)
Richardson, Velma, 379
Richter, Al, 308
Riddle, Almeda, 117
Rinzler, Ralph, 47, 51
Robbins, Kathleen Creel (see also Creel), 344, 379
Roberson, Barney, 175, 206 (photo, 40)
Rodgers, Douglas, 240
Rogers, Lonnie Lee and family, 211-26 (photos, 33, 212, 214, 217, 221, 222, 224, 225)
Roth, Joe, 50
Ryan, J.T., 77

Sabol, Steven, 298-99

Sawyer, Forrest, 51

Selleck, Carol Hand, 260

Seymour, Mae Howton, 198

Sharpton, Geraldine, 315

Sheppard, Jeff and Shelbie and family, 35-36, 260, 346, 379 (photo, 35)

Sinatra, Frank, 49

Sistrunk, Columbus, 112

Skinner, Flora, 349-53 (photo, 351)

Smith, Donald, 350

Smith, Helen "Sunbeam," photo, 72

Smith, Stanley, 146, 166

Smith, Toney and Lavoy, 51, 56, 274, 280, 342 (photo, 52)

Snell, Edd, 333

Snell, Estelle, 206

Spurlock, Tommie, 166

Steel, Warren, 327

Stewart, Robert Archie and wife, 24

Sting (Gordon Sumner), 49

Stovall, Elene, 48, 379

Tate, Edith Creel (see also Creel), 231-35 (photo, 40)

Thomas, Ed, 195-98, 379 (photo, 194)

Thomas, Elwyn and Linda, 347, 350

Tingle, Grandmother, 355

Tolbert, Lucille Creel (see also Creel), 232

Thro, Kathleen, 301

Thurman, Earl, xii, 70, 213, 382-83

Traywick, Kathleen Doss, 379

Underwood, Lawrence (Larnce) and Lula, 138-41, 379 (photo, 139)

Vaughan (or Vaughn), James D., 190-93

Vogel family, 314

von Braun, Wernher, 370

Walker, Michael, 3

Walker, J.D., 144

Walker, Velma, photo, 176

Walker, William, 363

Wallace, Charlene, 32, 51, 56, 58, 68, 355 (photos, 34, 52)

Wallace, George C. and Lurleen, 365

Waller, Helen Hiett, 46, 47

Walton, Joyce, 379

Warren, Preston, 35

Waterson family, 60-62

Weaver, Wallie, 8

Wegener, Ed, 365-68

Welty, Eudora, 24

White, Benjamin Franklin (B. F.), vi, x, xi, 70, 189, 228, 233, 247

White, D.T., 99, 280, 325

White, J.L., x

Wilkerson, Pam (see also Wootten), 350

Willard, Jenny and Keith, iv, 38

Williams, Billy, 232, 263, 268

Williams, Carlos, 259, 260

Williams: Dewey and family, 42, 52-54, 56-58, 105-22, 147, 149, 152, 202 (photos, 53, 104, 110, 120); Alice Casey, 107, 121, 207 (photo, 53); Bernice Williams Harvey, 56-58, 112-14, 121, 122

Windom, Reba Dell, 379

Woerner, Julie, 310

Wood, Carlton and Faye, 353

Wootten: Beulah Haynes, 304-05; Carnice, 59; Chester ("Check"), 59, 60; Freeman, 59, 60, 305, 343 (photo, 40); Gertha, 59; Jeffrey, 320 (photo, 302); Jewel Alexander, 255-56, 302, 347 (photo 40); Mack, 59, 301; Marlon, 305; Marty, photo, 302; Olivia, 59, 305; Phillip, photo, 302; Postell, 59, 305; Shane, photo, 302; Syble Wootten Adams, 60; Terry, 303, 329 (photo, 302); family, 58, 99, 300-305, 346, 350 (photos, 302, 303)

Yared, Gabriel, 48
Yates family, 128

CPSIA information can be obtained at www.ICGtesting.com
Printed in the USA
LVOW05s0931011014

406741LV00004B/477/P